Telling Stories

Telling Stories

Indigenous history and memory in Australia and New Zealand

edited by
Bain Attwood and Fiona Magowan

First published in New Zealand in 2001 by Bridget Williams Books Limited
PO Box 5482, Wellington, New Zealand
Co-published with Allen & Unwin
83 Alexander Street Crows Nest NSW 2065 Australia

ISBN 1 877242 23 3.

Typeset in 12 /14.5 pt Adobe Garamond by Midland Typesetters, Maryborough
Printed by McPherson's Printing Group

10 9 8 7 6 5 4 3 2 1

Contents

Acknowledgments

We wish to acknowledge: the Faculty of Arts, Monash University for a visiting scholars' grant which enabled us to do the work of editing this volume; Barbara Caine, Esther Faye, Mark Peel and John Rickard, who organised a conference at Monash University in 1997 that first planted the seed for this volume and where three of our contributors offered versions of the essays which appear here; our able editors Jo Jarrah and Simone Ford; publishers John Iremonger and Bridget Williams, whose commitment over the last two decades to doing books on indigenous history in Australia and New Zealand, respectively, is unrivalled; and, finally, Monash University Publications Committee and the Australian Academy of the Humanities, whose generous subsidies assisted the publication of this book.

Glossary of Maori terms

hapū	sub-tribe
iwi	tribe
kāinga	settlement
kaiwhakahaere	conductor
kaumātua	elders
mana	authority
marae	community space
mātua	elder relatives
pā	fortified village
rohe	boundary
take	basis of claims
tangata whenua	the people of the land
teina	junior-line relative
tīpuna/tūpuna	ancestors
tohu	landmarks
tongi	sayings
tuakana	elder male relative
urupā	burial grounds
utu	compensation or satisfaction
waiata	songs
waka	canoe
whakapapa	genealogies
whānau	extended family

Contributors

Bain Attwood is a Senior Lecturer in History at Monash University, and the author of *The Making of the Aborigines* (1989), and *A Life Together, a Life Apart* (1994) and editor of *In the Age of Mabo: History, Aborigines and Australia* (1996).

Jeremy Beckett is Emeritus Associate Professor of Anthropology at the University of Sydney, and the author of *Torres Strait Islanders: Custom and Colonialism* (1987) and the editor of *Past and Present: The Construction of Aboriginality* (1988). His *Wherever I Go: Myles Lalor's Oral History*, which he discusses in his chapter, was published in 2000.

Judith Binney is Professor of History at the University of Auckland, and the author of several books, including *Mihaia* (1979), *Ngā Mōrehu* (1986), and *Redemption Songs* (1995), the 'trilogy' she discusses in her chapter. She has recently written an overview report on the early history of the Urewera, c. 1840–75, for the Treaty of Waitangi Tribunal.

Andrew Erueti (Nga Ruahine, Ngati Hau, Araukuku) is a Lecturer in Law at Victoria University, Wellington. He teaches Maori customary law and Maori land law, and is co-author of *Maori Land Law* (1999).

Fiona Magowan is Lecturer in Anthropology at the University of Adelaide and has published widely on Yolngu performance in northeast Arnhem Land. She is co-editor of a special issue of *The Australian Journal of Anthropology* on 'The Politics of Dance' (2000), and has worked as an anthropological consultant in Arnhem Land and North Queensland.

W.H. Oliver is Emeritus Professor of History at Massey University and a consulting editor for the Dictionary of New Zealand Biography, for which he was the General Editor 1983–90. His books include *The Oxford History of New Zealand* (1981), which he co-edited with Bridget Williams, and *The Social and Economic Situation of Hauraki Maori After Colonisation* (1997).

Ann Parsonson is a Senior Lecturer in History at the University of Canterbury, and Senior Fellow at the new Waikato University College. She has published several articles in the *New Zealand Journal of History*. Over the past twelve years she has worked with iwi, assisting in the preparation of research and writing a number of major reports for their Treaty claims before the Waitangi Tribunal and Treaty settlements with the Crown.

Deborah Bird Rose is a Senior Research Fellow at the Australian National University, and the author of *Dingo Makes Us Human* (1991), *Hidden Histories* (1991), and *Nourishing Terrains: Australian Aboriginal Views of Landscape and Wilderness* (1996). She has worked with Aboriginal claimants on land claims and in land disputes, and with the Northern Territory Aboriginal Land Commissioner as his consulting anthropologist.

Basil Sansom is Emeritus Professor of Anthropology at the University of Western Australia, and the author of *Camp at Wallaby Cross: Aboriginal Fringe Dwellers in Darwin* (1980). He has worked as a consultant anthropologist on Aboriginal land claims in Western Australia and the Northern Territory.

Penny van Toorn is an Associate Lecturer in the Department of English at the University of Sydney, where she is presently research-ing pre-1900 Aboriginal writing. She is the author of *Ruby Wiebe and the Historicity of the Word* (1995) and co-editor of *Speaking Positions: Aboriginality, Gender & Ethnicity in Australian Cultural Studies* (1995). From 1995 to 1997, she worked as an editorial assistant to Ruby Langford Ginibi on *Haunted by the Past* (1999).

Alan Ward is Emeritus Professor of History at the University of Newcastle, New South Wales, and his major books include *A Show of Justice: Racial 'Amalgamation' in Nineteenth Century New Zealand* (1974), and *An Unsettled History: Treaty Claims in New Zealand Today* (1999). He has been a contract historian for the Waitangi Tribunal since 1987.

Introduction

Bain Attwood and Fiona Magowan

Recent decades have seen a remarkable upsurge of interest in indigenous history among both indigenous and settler peoples in Australia
and New Zealand. Among the former, this has taken various forms:
communities pressing claims for their traditional lands; elderly men
and women recording their community histories and/or life stories;
a younger generation writing, telling and singing their people's
stories; young and old compiling or reconstructing family histories
and genealogies; and radical spokespersons proclaiming rights of
ownership to the past.[1] Among the latter, anthropologists, historians
and lawyers, in particular, have conducted research and/or represented Maori and Aborigines, advocated indigenous rights and
challenged established understandings of the colonial past; editors
and publishers have promoted indigenous work; museums and
galleries have mounted exhibitions; and artists and designers have
drawn upon indigenous art.[2]

At the same time, in the context of globalisation and the rise of
identity politics, indigenous matters have assumed enormous significance, and consequently indigeneity has been accorded a critical
place in Australian and New Zealand nationalism. For example, in
recent commemorations—most obviously the Australian bicentenary
of 1988, the New Zealand sesquicentenary of 1990, the Auckland
Commonwealth Games of the same year, and the Sydney Olympics
in 2000—it took centre stage in the pageants that were performed on
these occasions.[3]

As a result of these factors, what can be called postcolonial stories
about history—about the relationship between past and present—
have become increasingly telling. Indeed, they have become a form of
cultural and political capital, and control over the knowledge they
represent has been fiercely contested as indigenous and settler alike
seek to appropriate their power. This has been strikingly evident in a
number of (in)famous cases in New Zealand and Australia in recent
years: for example, the theft of *Urewera Mural*, a painting by a
leading Pakeha artist, Colin McCahon, by two Tuhoe men in 1997,

xi

and a legal challenge by the Tasmanian Aboriginal Land Council to stop archaeological research in 1995.

There is, we hasten to add, nothing new about indigenous story-telling or history-making. Maori and Aborigines have long been telling histories in which, for example, they have created a sense of landscape, community and place. This has continued in the wake of colonisation: the colonial state has demanded that they do so, and indigenous peoples have often sought to show and explain their cultures and historical experience to settlers in the hope that they and their worlds will be understood and recognised. Stories for land have been among the most important in these cross-cultural contexts. Maori and Aborigines alike have strategically deployed indigenous forms of history and adopted various forms of colonial narrative in the process of trying to persuade tribunals (such as the Treaty of Waitangi Tribunal and the Northern Territory Land Rights Commission) of their rights of ownership.

Most importantly, perhaps, indigenous people in Australia and New Zealand have told histories of their experiences of colonialism. The purpose of these narratives has been twofold. Colonised peoples not only have had to 'endure their situation', it has been remarked; they have also had 'to make sense of it'.[4] And one of the most important means of their doing so, as for all peoples, has been by telling stories. This is because narrative is 'a cognitive instrument'—a primary means of understanding or making sense of the world—and by comprehending or making the world interpretable, it can become bearable.[5] Indigenous people have often worked up histories—historical interpretations—in order to explain their plight to themselves, and so helped themselves to survive.[6]

Stories are not only vehicles for understanding, however; they are also a means of remembrance. Narrative, it has been said, is the most fundamental mnemonic act: we mainly remember the past by telling stories.[7] But to remember the past is also to reform the present or to change the future. By recounting histories of colonialism, indigenous peoples have not only created an understanding but also a critique of it, and in constructing stories of freedom they have been able to challenge their oppression.

So many of these accounts, however, have been 'hidden from history': they have not formed a part of colonial memory but instead have been either unknown or have gone unacknowledged in the settler domain. Many of these indigenous narratives present interpretations that are very different from the dominant ones. For example, whereas Te Kooti has been most often remembered in Pakeha history as a warrior, Tuhoe accounts tell of a man of peace. Likewise, Captain Cook stories told by Aboriginal people are histories that counter the understanding of this mythic figure as the noble founding father of Australia; Cook is represented as the source of an unjust law that has denied Aboriginal people human rights.

Much of the historical work that has been done in Maori and Aboriginal communities in recent years has been primarily concerned with preparing land claims. This has entailed the collecting of oral histories and the scouring of the colonial record by both indigenous and non-indigenous researchers, and in many instances has involved collaboration between indigenous communities on the one hand and academic historians and anthropologists on the other (more of the former in New Zealand, more of the latter in Australia).[8]

In some cases this indigenous history-making has taken the form of community oral history and life stories, and this too has seen collaboration of various kinds. For example, indigenous peoples who have wanted to ensure their stories are handed down within their own communities or passed on to a non-indigenous audience have sought scholars' help to do so; and historians and others have played a role in both prompting old and/or bringing new historical sources of knowledge to indigenous communities. In this collaborative work, there are very important matters of debate and negotiation concerning the production and presentation of indigenous texts, and this has increasingly become the case as anthropologists and historians have come to regard these works as sources *of* rather than merely sources *for* history or anthropology. One issue is simply that of control, often posed in terms of the question: whose text or work is it? But this raises in turn a much more complex one: who *is* the author? Both entail serious ethical considerations given the fact that a person or community entrusts researchers with their precious stories and the latter incurs enormous obligations in the course of receiving this gift. Considerations of this kind lead to what are probably the most difficult conceptual and practical questions: how is a text produced and how should it be presented? Scholarly and editorial practices have changed considerably in recent years, but questions such as how one transcribes or translates a text in order to capture as much of the spirit and meanings of the original idiom as possible, and whether one should alter any text so that it can be comprehended by a particular audience, remain difficult to resolve and always will be.

Having noted the ways in which much indigenous storytelling has involved non-indigenous scholars, it must be observed that indigenous history-making has forced both anthropologists and historians to reconsider the nature of their disciplinary knowledge and practice; indeed, this has been the context in which collaboration has occurred in recent years. This challenge has taken various guises. Given that a good deal of indigenous history, at least in Australia, has taken the form of life stories, it has drawn into question the subject or subjectivity that modern European textual forms—particularly that of (auto)biography—has taken for granted. The notion of a singular, bounded individual, who has a unique self marked by particular motives, aspirations, attitudes, conscience and so forth, and who recounts a life in terms of a mythic journey by which s/he purposefully moves in a more or less linear and irreversible fashion towards knowledge, fulfilment and mastery of the world,[9] has rarely squared with Aboriginal conceptions of self. In their life stories, indigenous narrators seldom represent their lives in terms of an 'I' but rather of 'we', and emphasise relationships with family, kin and others; their accounts often seem fragmented and discontinuous; and they only infrequently reveal any sense of agency and self-reflection.

Indigenous history-making has also challenged the discipline of history because much of it takes the form of oral narrative. There has been considerable debate about the similarities of and differences between indigenous, oral tradition and European, written history.[10] Much of this discussion has focused upon the nature of memory and the question of how historians might treat such sources: are they to be used in a relatively conventional manner in order to learn of the past being remembered; or will they be used for what they reveal about relationships between past and present or present and past, and of the times of remembering; or should they be approached in some other way again? More generally, this debate has raised questions about the different purposes and roles of indigenous oral memory and written academic history in contemporary culture and society, and provoked consideration of whether or how one can work with both without undermining the integrity of either tradition.

There are also other important differences between indigenous and colonial histories and the cultures of which they are such an important part. Most fundamentally, perhaps, indigenous accounts, especially 'myth-narratives', are often framed by a radically different sense of reality, causation and time. Events can be sequenced in ways other than those usually demanded by history—for instance by reference to place rather than time—while chronologies are either absent or follow a different logic (for example, in one Captain Cook story Ned Kelly precedes Cook).[11]

The most basic challenge indigenous narratives have posed to academic scholarship, however, has been political. In one mode this has been framed in terms of 'who owns the past': whose history is it, who has the right to tell it, and on what terms can and should it be told? These have always been matters of the greatest import for indigenous peoples, because precolonial and colonial communities always had strict rules that determined who could tell and hear which stories. More recently, though, they have also assumed another, somewhat different cast. In a postcolonial context, in which history is necessarily central to the demand for indigenous rights (rather than equal rights) and the articulation of indigenous identity, Maori and Aborigines have tried to wrestle control of indigenous history from those they have seen as colonialist gate-keepers, claiming that it is *their* history.[12] In one sense they might seem to have succeeded: in recent years much of the indigenous history-making has been done by Maori and Aborigines. Yet, as the make-up of this volume testifies, the work of *analysing* such historical narratives—of considering how and why histories are told and are telling—still seems to be predominantly the province of the non-indigenous scholar.[13]

The most notable public challenge posed by indigenous history and memory has been the histories, produced by both indigenous and non-indigenous authors, that have drawn into question the commonly held historical accounts of the 'settlement' of Australia and New Zealand.[14] During the last three decades, historical narratives in Australia have struck at the heart of its national story. These have been deployed to expose a yawning chasm between morality and justice on the one hand and the law on the other, and both governments and the courts have had to respond to the resulting crisis of legitimacy. Over more or less the same period of time in New Zealand, further history-making has questioned the justice of Pakeha law in even more fundamental ways than had hitherto been the case.

In these circumstances anthropology and history have assumed even greater significance, as they have been called upon to help indigenous peoples seek redress for the wrongs of the past, assist in the adjudication of competing claims, and facilitate reconciliation between the colonisers and the colonised. There has been, consequently, an enormous growth in anthropological consultancy and what has been called 'public history': the work of academic anthropologists and historians has, along with indigenous histories, been applied to a range of contemporary political and legal matters that are inherently colonial.

In considering the nature of indigenous history and memory, this volume has not sought to compare Australia and New Zealand, though the similarities and differences are revealed by many of its contributors. Similarly, while this collection of essays obviously has a common focus, the authors do not have a common stance but represent instead a range of disciplinary approaches, theoretical perspectives and political positions. Yet it does seek to cast some light upon the ongoing dialogue between history and anthropology. Twenty years ago, a merging of historical and anthropological accounts of indigenous stories would probably have been inconceivable, at least in the Australasian context, and the fact that such a confluence is possible today tells us much about the changes that have occurred in both disciplines. A series of shifts have taken place in both anthropology and history, part of the broader postmodern and postcolonial revolution in the study of culture and society.

In the late nineteenth century, anthropology began from the premise that it was a study of primitive societies as distinct from modern society, which distanced 'them' from 'us' and masked other equally problematic concepts. In this approach the properties of the past were deemed to lie in those things that apparently belonged to antiquity and were resistant to change, and so the study of 'primitive' peoples focused upon documenting traditional forms of cultural beliefs and practices. For its part, history had more or less the same premise, conceiving its task as that of recording the evolution of 'new' European, literate nations. In this grand narrative of progress, 'primitive', oral societies such as Aboriginal ones tended to be precluded since it was held that they were neither capable of change nor compatible with modernity and therefore irrelevant to a study that traced the past becoming the present.

As anthropology has abandoned its conceptions of indigenous cultures as static and bounded cultural traditions, and adopted instead a reading of the present as emergent from the precolonial and colonial past, it has undergone a radical shift, moving from a distancing of the 'primitive' other to an understanding of the contemporaneous and intersubjective relationships between structure, agency and event. Likewise, as history has forsaken its preoccupation with documenting the rise of the nation-state and its political formations, its subject matter has broadened to include those oppressed by modernity, who had previously been excluded from its purview, and its sources and methods have widened to include oral memory and fieldwork. As a result of this refocusing of the anthropological and historical lenses, each discipline has been able to consider indigenous subjects anew, conceding them agency and perspectives that can be considered and acknowledged in highly complex ways.

Some of the essays here grow out of a synthesis of the methodological and theoretical approaches used by the two disciplines—for example, the making of history in ethnographic inquiry and the use of ethnography as a tool for historical study. There is also a growing convergence in the philosophical approaches used by anthropology and history which, in turn, has ongoing epistemological ramifications for historiographic and ethnographic ways of telling. Yet, notwithstanding this, each discipline offers its own particular approaches to intersubjectivity and the making of selves past and present through telling stories. It is at these differing points of convergence that the two divergent disciplines have most to offer one another.

Note
In Chapters 2, 5, 8 and 9 macrons (used to indicate long vowels) are included for passages in te reo Māori, and also in quoted passages of English said or written by Maori people which include Maori terms and concepts. Macrons are not used for Maori words within the English-language text.

1

Indigenous Australian life writing
Tactics and transformations

Penny van Toorn

Indigenous Australian life writing is often viewed as a recent phenomenon, a new literary and historiographical form that emerged initially in the mid twentieth century, expanded gradually through the 1960s and 1970s, and eventually proliferated spectacularly in the 1980s and 1990s.[1] However, today's indigenous life writings are part of an older discursive formation that dates back to early colonial times, and incorporates traditional indigenous paradigms and protocols of oral communication. In the discipline of literary studies, this older, intercultural body of life writing has remained largely invisible because literary criticism and scholarship have focused exclusively on long narratives published in book form. In the name of interdisciplinarity, however, it is now possible to ask what the history of Aboriginal life writing looks like if we cease to focus exclusively on books and comprehensive 'childhood to maturity' stories, and take account of the full range of written textual forms Aboriginal people have used to record and transmit stories about even very brief portions of their lives. From as far back as 1796, Aboriginal people were recounting small segments of their lives in piecemeal, fragmentary written forms, in hundreds of handwritten letters, petitions, submissions to official inquiries and court testimonies. This fragile, multifarious archive offers brief glimpses into a multitude of individual lives. These documents have usually served as raw materials or sources *for* history, but they also represent a genre *of* history in their own right. Together they may be viewed as a fragmented, collectively produced autobiography of a people.

This collective autobiography is a product of various forms of negotiation and collaboration with non-indigenous individuals and institutions. It is this intercultural political aspect that produces what might be called a family resemblance between the fragile, fragmentary life writings presently housed in archival institutions, and the ranks of comprehensive 'lives' that line the booksellers' shelves today. Despite their manifest differences, early and recent indigenous life writings share a fundamental condition of existence: they are products of colonial power relations, and have been authorised, produced, transmitted, interpreted and put to work (or consigned to oblivion) in institutional settings designed primarily to serve non-indigenous purposes. Indigenous life writing as we know it today begins not with the first book-length publication of a life story, but at the moment when Aboriginal people began to verbalise their life experiences in ways that were structured by colonial power relations.

During the nineteenth century, Aboriginal people engaged in various kinds of formalised dialogue with members of the settler society. They were encouraged to confess their sins to missionaries, describe their needs to local Guardians of Aborigines, testify at official inquiries and tell their stories to ethnographers and anthropologists. Those who lived on missions and reserves in the second half of the nineteenth century were acutely aware that, if they wanted their complaints to be heard, they had to provide government and mission authorities with written accounts of 'what really happened'.

These early, dialogically produced narratives are precursors of today's book-length life writings that seek to educate broad national and international readerships about Aboriginal historical experience. Whether called forth in colonial institutions such as missions, reserves, courtrooms and prisons, or edited, mass produced and packaged by today's commercial publishers, indigenous testimonies remain for the most part 'tactical' in Michel de Certeau's sense of being made and deployed in cultural territories predominantly or

2

officially under someone else's control. What today's stories and yesterday's narratives have in common is that they 'must play on a terrain imposed . . . and organised by the law of a foreign power'.[2] As indigenous life histories are produced and disseminated through non-indigenous institutions, old and new life narratives alike 'continually turn to their own ends forces alien to them'.[3] Making use of the blindspots, interstices and fleeting, opportune moments, they take advantage of the play within and between the institutions through which the dominant group routinely asserts and perpetuates its power.

In emphasising the shaping influence of non-Aboriginal institutions, one should not underestimate Aboriginal agency in the making and deployment of life narratives. For one thing, many narratives are produced entirely for family and friends. Because such stories are by, about, and for particular local communities, they are created, circulated and utilised 'strategically' (rather than 'tactically' in de Certeau's terms)[4]—that is, on local indigenous cultural turf, largely outside the sphere of influence of non-Aboriginal institutions. Such narratives do not need to satisfy criteria imposed by a foreign power. In form, content, language and function, they are products of Aboriginal agency, and are designed entirely or primarily to meet Aboriginal people's needs.

How Aboriginal agency works in non-indigenous institutions is another question, however, one that involves considering the intercultural political dynamics of Aboriginal life narratives. All indigenous Australian life writings are to some extent collaboratively produced. Although theoretical conceptions of authorship in general have changed in recent decades,[5] the traditional romantic-individualist concept of the author as an autonomous agent is manifestly inappropriate to the circumstances under which Aboriginal people have produced accounts of their lives, both now and in the past. This is not to say that Aboriginal authorial agency has been annulled: there is textual evidence to suggest that indigenous agency, both now and in the past, has managed to elude, contest and/or appropriate the power invested in those institutions within which their life narratives have been produced, transmitted, interpreted and put to work.

To appreciate these tactical aspects of indigenous life narratives, it is necessary to view writing and storytelling as modes of political and/or economic action rather than merely a means of codifying information. As 'tactical histories', indigenous life narratives play a set of 'clever tricks . . . within the order established by the strong'.[6] By looking initially at a selection of different forms of early indigenous life writing, and then at a recent book-length biography— Ruby Langford Ginibi's *Haunted by the Past*[7]—some insight can be gained into the transformations of Aboriginal life writing over two hundred years, and into the tactical means by which indigenous authorial agency has worked within colonial power relations.

LIFE WRITING AS TRADE GOODS?—BENNELONG'S LETTER

While indigenous oral anecdotal traditions have existed for thousands of years, Aboriginal people's participation in the process of life writing begins in 1796, with Bennelong's letter to Mr Phillips, a steward of the British Home Secretary, Lord Sydney, whom Bennelong had met while visiting England three years earlier. Bennelong produced the letter collaboratively, by dictating it to a scribe. Although the language suggests that Bennelong's words were recorded verbatim, there is no external evidence indicating whether or not the scribe prompted or altered Bennelong's utterance.

Sydney Cove
New S. Wales,
Aug 29, 1796

Sir,

I am very well. I hope you are very well. I live at the Governor's. I have every day dinner there. I have not my wife: another black man took her away. We have had murry doings: he spear'd me in the back, but I better now: his name is now Carroway. All my friends alive and well. Not me go to England no more. I am at home now. I hope Sir you send me anything you please, Sir. Hope all are well in England. I hope Mrs Phillips very well. You nurse me Madam when I sick. You very good Madam: thank you Madam, and hope you remember me Madam, not forget. I know you very well Madam. Madam I want stockings. Thank you Madam; send me two pair stockings. You very good Madam. Thank you Madam. Sir you give my duty to Lord

Sydney. Thank you very good my lord, very good: hope very well all family. Very well. Sir, send me you please some Handkerchiefs for Pocket. You please Sir send me some shoes: two pair you please Sir.

Bannalong[8]

Like other tactical texts, Bennelong's letter appears to obey the rules. It conforms to the norms of colonial letter-writing in three respects. First, it opens with a series of remarks about the health of the writer and good wishes for the health of the recipient. Second, it offers news—it narrates a fragment of Bennelong's life: having decorously mentioned that he lives in and dines at the Governor's house, Bennelong briefly recounts the violent conflict between himself and Carroway, who has speared him in the back and taken his wife. Third, it adheres to the colonial convention of asking for particular items to be sent from England. By reporting on health, conveying news and requesting material goods, Bennelong's letter observes colonial epistolary norms.

Yet, in certain regards, Bennelong's textual practice disrupts the colonial institution of the letter: it does not address the same interlocutor throughout. At the beginning of the letter, the word 'you' refers to Mr Phillips, the letter's official addressee, of whom he requests 'anything you please'. Further down, Bennelong mentions Mrs Phillips, and begins addressing himself to her, asking her to send him two pairs of stockings. He then refers to Lord Sydney, to whom he directs his good wishes and thanks for an unspecified gift or favour that has either been received or is anticipated. Finally, Bennelong returns to addressing Mr Phillips, asking him to send him some handkerchiefs and two pairs of shoes.

It is possible that this departure from the European norm of one-to-one address is not an incidental error. As I have suggested elsewhere,[9] Bennelong's practice of addressing several people in the same letter emerges from an orally based paradigm of social relations. Bennelong dictates his letter as though he, and everyone he speaks *about,* are in each other's physical proximity, and can thus be spoken *to,* as was usually the case (subject to traditional avoidance patterns) in precolonial Aboriginal societies.

It has been suggested that indigenous autobiographies 'are not a traditional form among native peoples but the consequence of contact with the white invader-settlers, and the product of limited

5

collaboration with them'.[10] This does not mean, however, that traditional indigenous textual practices, and the social relations within which texts do their work, play no part in shaping indigenous life writings. Certain practices, for example, might be read in terms of both indigenous and non-indigenous cultural traditions. How do we decide, for example, whether Bennelong was observing the colonial convention of asking for goods to be sent out from 'home', or deploying his letter within a traditional indigenous cultural economy of reciprocation and exchange wherein the letter—as a carrier of news and a reminder of kinship obligations—functioned as a type of trade-good that obliged its addressees to send the writer gifts in return?

Indigenous principles of reciprocity and exchange work on the basis of both obligations to kin with whom one is in a particular relationship, and personal knowledge of an individual. When Bennelong reminds Mrs Phillips of the time she nursed him when he was ill, he asserts a quasi mother–son bond that obliges her to give him material gifts. Similarly, when he writes, 'I know you . . . Madam. Madam I want stockings', his statement and request may seem incongruous and blunt by European standards but in indigenous cultural terms it effectively affirms a long-standing acquaintance with Mrs Phillips that, for Bennelong, again obliges her to supply him with goods.

It might be argued that Bennelong situates Mr Phillips and Lord Sydney in a somewhat different kind of kinship relationship, offering news and paying his respects on paper in return for material goods. Although polite pleasantries like 'how are you?' were not part of traditional cultural practice, he may have been attempting to assimilate such English rituals into an indigenous cultural economy of exchange. While in England, Bennelong is likely to have noticed that polite greetings were a powerful bonding agent in British society, particularly where relationships of patronage were concerned. Patronage systems are based on quasi-familial relationships of obligation and exchange that resemble indigenous kinship relations in certain regards. By providing news and paying his polite respects to Mr Phillips and Lord Sydney, Bennelong may have been situating them as patrons in a quasi father–son or uncle–nephew relationship that obliged them to give the requested shoes, handkerchiefs and unspecified gifts in exchange for words on paper.[11]

Bennelong's letter may also be viewed as a hybrid cultural technology he adopted in order to integrate foreigners into an indigenous kin-based system of reciprocal obligations. If he believed letters were a medium of exchange, Bennelong may also have reasoned that by writing to three people in a single letter he could situate them all in a relation of obligation to himself. Far from being a 'mistake', his practice of addressing three different people in one letter may have been a tactical manoeuvre, a means of obtaining multiple gifts in exchange for a single, news-carrying, kinship-affirming object. Moreover, it can be argued that a letter addressed to three people is qualitatively analogous to a manuscript printed in multiple copies for a multitude of readers. Bennelong may therefore be viewed as a literary ancestor of today's commercially published indigenous writers who situate their readers as quasi kin while at the same time entering into a commercial relationship with them.[12]

LIFE WRITING AS JOURNALISM—THE *FLINDERS ISLAND CHRONICLE*

Much early Aboriginal writing was produced under close surveillance in colonial institutions. The Aboriginal writers knew their work would be read by white authorities and evaluated as evidence of their assimilation of European values and beliefs. One critic, Mudrooroo, has called this practice 'writing for the governor's pleasure',[13] and in the case of the *Flinders Island Chronicle*, the first Aboriginal newspaper, there is evidence to suggest that George Augustus Robinson, Commandant of the Flinders Island Aboriginal Settlement (to which all Aboriginal people in Tasmania had been moved between 1831 and 1834), played a large part in deciding what was written, both through direct editorial intervention and as an authoritative imagined reader whose criteria of acceptable writing had to be met.

Published irregularly between September 1836 and December 1837, the *Flinders Island Chronicle* was handwritten and hand-copied in English by two young Pallawah men, Thomas Brune and Walter George Arthur. One of the aims of the paper was to provide a 'brief but accurate register of events'.[14] The *Chronicle* recorded aspects of day-to-day life on the island, such as church services, the arrival and departure of ships, illnesses, deaths, food shortages and hunting. The paper also promoted civilisation and Christianity by urging people to read the Bible, wash with soap, cease hunting rats and mice to supplement their rations, and show more gratitude for

Robinson's generosity and benevolence. 'Accuracy' was preserved through Robinson's reading and correction of the proof sheets generated by Brune and Arthur, which were then hand-copied for sale to the very few Aboriginal people who could read.

Given Robinson's editorial involvement, it is difficult to gauge the extent to which the Pallawah journalists were able to express their own perceptions and interpretations of events, or whether they felt compelled to write what Robinson wanted to hear. Since the proofs were copied by hand, however, they may occasionally have been able to evade Robinson's editorial scrutiny. While some editions of the paper praised the Commandant's projects, others documented grim aspects of life on the island, including details that Robinson might have preferred to suppress. It seems likely that these writers occasionally subverted the censorship process by adding extra material after Commandant Robinson had 'corrected' their proof sheets. In the penultimate edition of the *Chronicle*, for example, Brune writes: 'I got rite to you the same things over and over again. Commandant has directed me to work and if I dont attend to it I must be put in to gaol.'[15] In the previous edition, he had written: 'I am much afraid none of us will be live by and by as then as nothing but sickness among us. Why don't the black fellows pray to the king to get us away from this place.'[16] The final sentence is missing from other copied versions of this edition in Robinson's papers.[17]

LIFE WRITING AS POLITICAL AND LEGAL SUPPLICATION

On 17 February 1846 Walter George Arthur and seven other Pallawah men put part of Brune's suggestion into effect by sending a petition to Queen Victoria. Since my discussion focuses on several distinct sections of the petition, I shall quote it in full:

> The humble petition of the free Aborigines Inhabitants of V[an] D[iemen's] L[and] now living upon Flinders Island, in Bass's Straits &c & &c.
> Most humbly showeth,
> That we Your Majesty's Petitioners are your free Children that we were not taken Prisoners but freely gave up our Country to Colonel Arthur then the Governor after defending ourselves.
> Your Petitioners humbly state to Y[our] M[ajesty] that

Mr. Robinson made for us & with Col. Arthur an agreement which we have not lost from our minds since & we have made our part of it good.

Your Petitioners humbly tell Y[our] M[ajesty] that when we left our own place we were plenty of People, we are now but a little one.

Your Petitioners state they are a long time at Flinders Island & had plenty of Superintendents & were always a quiet and free People & not put into Gaol.

Your Majesty's petitioners pray that you will not allow Dr. Jeanneret to come again among us as our Superintendent as we hear he is to be sent another time for when Dr Jeanneret was with us many Moons he used to carry Pistols in his pockets & threaten'd very often to shoot us & make us run away in fright. Dr. Jeanneret kept plenty of Pigs in our Village which used to run into our houses & eat up our bread from the fires & take away our flour bags in their mouths also to break into our Gardens & destroy our Potatoes & Cabbages.

Our houses were let fall down & they were never cleaned but were covered with vermin & not white-washed. We were often without Clothes except a very little one & Dr. Jeanneret did not care to mind us when we were sick until we were very bad. Eleven of us died when he was here. He put many of us into Jail for talking to him because we would not be his slaves. He kept from us our Rations when he pleased & sometimes gave us Bad Rations of Tea & Tobacco. He shot some of our dogs before our eyes & sent all the other dogs of ours to an Island & when we told him that they would starve he told us they might eat each other. He put arms into our hands & made us to assist his prisoners to go to fight the Soldiers we did not want to fight the Soldiers but he made us go to fight. We never were taught to read or write or to sing to God by the Doctor. He taught us a little upon the Sundays & his Prisoner Servant also taught us & his Prisoner Servant also took us plenty of times to Jail by his orders.

The Lord Bishop seen us in this bad way & we told H[is] L[ordship] plenty how Dr. Jeanneret used us.

We humbly pray Your Majesty the Queen will hear our prayer & not let Dr Jeanneret any more to come to Flinders Island. And We Y[our] M[ajesty]'s servants & Children will ever pray as in duty bound &c &c &c

Sgd. Walter George Arthur, Chief of the Ben Lomond Tribes, King Alexander, John Allen, Augustus, Davey Bruny, King Tippoo, Neptune, Washington.[18]

Western commentators have often foregrounded the symbolically transgressive, openly indecorous aspects of the writings of subordinated groups. They highlight those moments when members of oppressed groups violate due process, commit unlicensed speech-acts, or break conventions of genre, grammar, tone, voice or narrative.[19] For many oppressed peoples, however, overt transgression is a luxury they cannot afford. Their vulnerability demands forms of risk-averse behaviour that may be misread (both by authorities of the day and by researchers who come after) as a sign that they have been ideologically manoeuvred into submission. James C. Scott has argued that the outwardly deferential behaviour of powerless peoples is a mode of self-protection and camouflage, a 'ritual of homage' that keeps the subordinated group from harm.[20]

The etiquette of official communications is invariably imposed by the politically dominant group. It is an institutionalised product of, and means of perpetuating, a particular power structure. To violate such etiquette would have been entirely counterproductive for the Flinders Island petitioners. By adopting a submissive tone and observing all the correct formalities, the Pallawah petitioners created a rhetorically effective frame for their narrative of Jeanneret's previous reign of terror. Given the possibility of Jeanneret's return, the act of writing and sending the petition was risky enough in itself. Although the petition was supported by Superintendent Milligan, it so incensed Jeanneret that, when he did eventually return to the island, he persecuted those involved in writing the petition. He imprisoned Arthur for seventeen days in an effort to make him renounce the petition, and told the petitioners, according to Arthur, that they would 'all be hung for high treason for writing against him'.[21]

Given that Jeanneret's return was always a possibility, and that the account of his misdeeds could trigger outbreaks of revengeful fury, it is perhaps not surprising that the Flinders Island petition was hyper-correct in its strict conformity to norms of process, presentation, tone, and language. In these regards the petition bears the stamp of the governmental administrative and legal institutions within which it was produced and put to work. Although Arthur was capable of penning the petition himself, he chose not to do so, fearing perhaps that his handwriting, spelling or language might detract from the authority of the document. These were legitimate concerns for a colonised people writing to the British monarch from a tiny island on the other side of the world, in a climate of racial opinion that presumed alphabetic literacy was a primary criterion of rationality, cultural advancement and full human status.

Arthur therefore wrote, on behalf of himself and his fellow signatories, to Dr Joseph Milligan (the Flinders Island superintendent whom Jeanneret was to replace), requesting him to ask the catechist, Mr Clark, to draw up the petition to the Queen.[22] The terms of address employed by Clark—phrases such as 'we humbly pray', 'we humbly tell Your Majesty' and 'we Your Majesty's servants & children . . . as in duty bound'—are part of a formula designed to reassure Queen Victoria, and all who governed in her name, that the petition was not a proclamation of rebellion. At no point did the petition question the legitimacy of colonial rule *per se*. Instead, it focused on Jeanneret's abuse of the powers invested in him. Its political leverage derived not from a demand for Aboriginal sovereignty or political autonomy, but from an invocation of moral values espoused by English abolitionists, philanthropists and other influential sections of British society.[23] As a tactical document, it played British colonial authorities at their own moral game. The petition worked by highlighting the discrepancy between officially espoused humanitarian ideals and the recent historical actuality of Jeanneret's abuse of his powers and neglect of his responsibilities as superintendent. The political force of this petition derived both from the content of the narrative of Jeanneret's previous actions, and from the tactically correct way in which that narrative was framed.

The Flinders Island petitioners' narrative of Jeanneret's misdeeds is a communally generated story about the community's experience. In this regard it falls within the category of communal life writing. Yet this communal voice is no more autonomous than the voices of the journalists who wrote for the *Flinders Island Chronicle*, because the document was created with the help of, and for the eyes of, a series of officials occupying positions of institutionalised power. The petition was clearly written with those others' sense of propriety in mind. The entanglement of indigenous voices with non-indigenous officialdom is thus more complicated and impersonal than a voice-centred model can account for. Clark was the instrument through which Arthur and his fellow petitioners generated a document that conformed to the discursive norms of political supplication. Their story of Jeanneret's misdeeds, packaged in its proper discursive frame, was handed by Earl Grey, Secretary of State for the Colonies, to Queen Victoria in March 1847,[24] and it might have been a decisive factor in the removal of the Pallawah people from Flinders Island to the Oyster Cove settlement near Hobart later that year.[25]

LIFE NARRATIVES AS EVIDENCE

Fragments of Aboriginal autobiography are also included in transcripts of proceedings of official inquiries and court cases. In some of these, however, individual Aboriginal voices are mediated and circumscribed in highly complex ways. Such entanglements of voice are illustrated in the transcripts of the case of *Regina v Nipper*, heard in the Supreme Court of Western Australia, 13 April 1898. The Aboriginal defendant, Nipper, had been accused of shooting two other Aboriginal men, Monday and Jacky, the latter fatally. Nipper had his own quarrels with Jacky and Monday, yet a number of Aboriginal witnesses testified that Gerry Durack, a member of the famous squatter dynasty, had given Nipper a revolver and told him to shoot Jacky and Monday, whom Durack believed were spearing his cattle. The following is a transcript of Monday's testimony under examination by the Crown Prosecutor:

> *Monday*. affirmed. Does not speak English. Wheelbarrow Creek. Know Jacky Know Nipper. Going along road saw Nipper and talked to him & said go to Durack's camp in W Creek Find Sambo that night Sambo go away, Durack came up Got off his horse & broke spear & womerah. Go to packhorse got out Revolver & gave it to Nipper. *Durack said shoot Jacky first & then shoot Monday*. Drive them over mountain. *I understand what Durack say*. Nipper drove into mountains me only and Jacky. Women went right way. Shot him left loin & right forearm. Nipper shot me in shoulder.[26]

Although each testimony is clearly labelled with the relevant witness's name, a multiplicity of mediating voices renders the notion of 'individual voice' problematic. First, the scope of the Aboriginal witnesses' narratives is constrained by the questions that are put to them by legal counsel. The extent of these constraints is difficult to ascertain because the questions are not included in the transcript.

Second, the questions and answers are filtered through the voice of an interpreter, 'Joe', who is probably Aboriginal. The interpreter's input is both mutable and difficult to quantify: some of the Aboriginal witnesses can at least partially understand spoken English (including Durack's instructions to Nipper), but they cannot or will not speak English (or repeat Durack's instructions) when asked to do so in court. Third, the interpreter's version of the witnesses' stories is recorded in note form by defence barrister Richard Haynes and his assistant, who do their own sifting and paraphrasing of the interpreter's words. Fourth, the police officer who arrested Nipper (after himself inflaming hostilities by giving Nipper one of Jacky's women) alleges that some Aboriginal witnesses care more about pleasing the questioner than about telling the truth.

In the transcript of Aboriginal accounts of the shooting of Jacky and Monday, then, we have a set of quadruple-voiced narratives where the voice of the witness cannot be extricated from those of the questioner, the interpreter and the transcriber. In complex, highly formalised dialogic contexts such as this, Aboriginal and non-Aboriginal voices are so inextricably entangled that it is difficult to know precisely who is saying what. Nipper was nonetheless found guilty of manslaughter and imprisoned for five years.

The voices of Aboriginal witnesses were not always so thoroughly obscured, however. In 1884, a number of Aboriginal prisoners at Rottnest Island gave evidence to a committee to inquire into the treatment of Aboriginal prisoners. In the committee's report, each prisoner's evidence forms a single paragraph, as though each testimony were delivered as a monologue, without input from those conducting the inquiry. Yet although the length of the testimonies varies, they are all structured in a similar manner. Each begins with a statement about where the prisoner comes from, and proceeds to identify his crime, whether this is his first term of imprisonment at Rottnest, whether he likes the island, the food, the blankets and so forth—always in the same order. This parallel structuring suggests that instead of being spoken as monologues, the testimonies were in fact dialogically generated, with the same questions being put to each prisoner in turn. The voices of the questioners, however, have been erased from the official record in spite of (or because of) the fact that such a process effectively restricts the scope of each prisoner's testimony. Questions can operate as a means of suppressing or containing information, rather than as a means of bringing the whole truth to light. The Aboriginal witnesses who testified at this inquiry were

confined to specific topics, decided in advance by the officials conducting the investigation.

One prisoner, however, managed effectively to circumvent these
constraints. Identified only as 'Benjamin', he seized sufficient
control over the proceedings to articulate a grievance not scripted in
advance by the questioning process. No matter what he was asked,
Benjamin managed to steer his narrative around to the terrible
journey he was forced to make on foot, naked and in chains, from
Eyre Sand Patch to Albany. After answering the initial questions
about home country, crime and length of sentence, he stated:

> I walked from Eyre Sand Patch to Albany naked, with a chain
> on my neck. My neck was sore from chain. I knocked up from
> the long walk. Policeman Truslove no good. He hit me for
> knocking up. Policeman Wheelock a good fellow, nothing sulky.
> I like ship, I was not sick. I do not like walking so far. I came
> with a bullock chain round my neck from Eyre Sand Patch to
> Albany. When it rained my neck was very sore from the chain.[27]

In response to questions about blankets and medical care,
Benjamin told his story a third time, working the narrative around
again to the hardship and humiliation he had endured:

> I have same blanket I came with a fortnight ago. I had a cold in
> Fremantle. The Doctor saw me at Fremantle, when I was ready
> to come to Rottnest. I was ill, and when I got here I was very ill.
> My trousers and shirt I came from Albany in are now in the
> Prison. I gave them to a native this morning. I did not get any
> from the Prison. What clothes I have on were obtained by inter-
> change with other natives. I had no clothes given me from Eyre
> Sand Patch to Albany. I was quite naked all the way, no clothes
> or blanket.[28]

Aboriginal people in Victoria also managed to get across what
they wanted to say by breaking out of the question-and-answer
method of inquiry. At a 1881 parliamentary board of inquiry into
conditions at Coranderrk reserve, witness after witness patiently
answered the commissioners' questions about rations of tea, meat,
sugar, flour, tobacco, clothing and so forth, but while these matters
were important, discussing them crowded out other matters that
troubled the Coranderrk residents. By submitting written narratives

to the inquiry—which they or one of the officials read out to the commissioners—they seized a measure of control over its agenda, raising issues overlooked by the commissioners in their ordinary lines of oral questioning. Caroline Morgan, for example, had Thomas Dunolly write out the following narrative for presentation to the inquiry:

> This is my evidence. Coranderrk, November 16th 1881. I have asked Mrs. Strickland [wife of the reserve manager] for a pair of blankets for my sick boy. She told me that she must write to Captain Page [the Secretary of the Victorian Board for the Protection of Aborigines] first. Then I told her, must my little boy be perishing with the cold till you get a letter from Mr. Captain Page? . . . So my sick boy was dying. He asked Mr. Strickland to send to Mr. Captain Page for some eggs [as none could be obtained locally]; so Mr. Strickland said he would see. So when Mr. Strickland came up and visited him, the sick boy asked him again about the eggs, and Mr. Strickland said, 'Well, my boy, if I send to Captain Page he would laugh at me for the idea of sending for eggs to town from up country' . . . Caroline Morgan X[29]

Mrs Morgan's narrative alleges, in effect, that reserve administrators were using the 'proper' administrative process of writing as a means of slowing the wheels of the bureaucratic apparatus built ostensibly to secure the welfare of Aboriginal people. Yet, by its very existence, her document shows how Aboriginal people were also appropriating writing and life narrative for their own purposes. By preparing written statements in advance, they were able to derail the constraining dialogue, and create a space to speak at greater length about issues of their own choosing.

As well as conforming to the proprieties of formal communications with the inquiry commissioners, Morgan's narrative also observes traditional Kulin protocols of communication. Like other women, she wrote on behalf of herself and her family. Only senior men, led by William Barak, clan head of the land on which Coranderrk was established, had authority under traditional law to write on behalf of the Coranderrk community as a whole.[30] Nonetheless, by providing different kinds of testimonies in writing, the men and women of Coranderrk acquired a degree of control over how their views were represented in the official minutes of evidence.

LIFE WRITING AS LITERATURE

Much of today's indigenous life writing is motivated by a similar desire to get Australia's hidden black history onto the written record. Having been produced through and within the institutions of 'literature', the book-length indigenous life writings of the 1980s and 1990s give more space for the exercise of Aboriginal authorial agency than was usually achieved in nineteenth-century letters, petitions, journalism, and court and inquiry testimonies. Yet 'literature' is by no means a free discursive field where colonial power relations play no part in determining the form and content of narratives. As indigenous life writings move into literary genres such as autobiography, biography, poetry and fiction, the 'governor's pleasure' reasserts itself in the shape of audience tastes and market preferences. To cover their costs, commercial publishers must sell thousands of copies of each book they publish and, although there is considerable market demand for Aboriginal life writings, the 'general situation of acceptance', as Stephen Muecke and others have noted, 'tends to hide a more complex series of apparatuses of exclusion and co-option'.[31] The shift into literature should not be viewed as an unequivocal liberation into a politically autonomous or culturally separate Aboriginal textual space; it is more accurately understood as a shift from one colonial discursive regime to another.

From within the space of literature, Aboriginal life writing has certainly challenged the conceptual and methodological foundations of the academic historical disciplines as traditionally practised. Yet, if consumed as 'literature', indigenous life writing can be readily transformed into an aesthetic object or mere entertainment. The potential political impact of indigenous life writings can be dissipated or deflected by aesthetic and touristic modes of consumption.[32]

The tastes and cultural values of dominant literary audiences impinge on indigenous life writing not only at the moment of reading but also during the prior stages of composition and editing, when the power of the dominant audience is brought to bear on Aboriginal writers by literary agents, editors, book designers, and other mediators and collaborators. There has been some controversy about the politics of black/white collaboration at the writing stage. Mudrooroo has argued that texts written in collaboration with non-Aboriginal people are less authentically Aboriginal than those written single-handedly by Aboriginal authors.[33] Some

16

Aboriginal life narratives—for example *I, The Aboriginal*—have indeed been 'de-Aboriginalised' to attract a mainstream readership and conform to white literary norms and expectations. But certain Aboriginal authors prefer to work with an editorial assistant who, while preserving the integrity of the author's voice and story, assists in producing a manuscript that needs little subsequent editing. Such collaborative processes may be viewed as a tactical move, a way of 'in-sourcing' or supervising part of the editorial process, thereby maximising the Aboriginal author's control over the text that finally appears on the bookseller's shelves.

THREE-WAY COLLABORATIONS—RUBY LANGFORD GINIBI'S *HAUNTED BY THE PAST*

In recent years, indigenous authors have begun writing and/or editing the life histories of family members and friends.[34] A number of life writings have been produced in three-way collaborations between two members of an Aboriginal family and a non-Aboriginal editor, for example *Auntie Rita*.[35] Ruby Langford Ginibi's *Haunted by the Past* was also produced through a process of collaboration between Aboriginal family members with white editorial assistance—Ruby and her son Nobby (the main biographical subject), and myself.

Like a number of other indigenous authors, Nobby began to write his story while serving time in prison. When he became bogged down, Ruby took over the task. She did a good deal of writing while Nobby was still behind bars, but after his release in March 1996 he was able to sit down with Ruby and record some of his early memories and prison experiences on tape. Ruby and Nobby had been separated for many years by prison walls. Making the book together gave them both a chance to share certain parts of their lives for the first time. While Nobby tailored his story so as not to upset his mother, Ruby presented her son's story in a manner that demonstrated her complete faith and trust in him.

Ruby wanted me to help her produce a manuscript that conformed to white norms of spelling, punctuation, paragraphing and narrative structure, yet which allowed readers to hear her own voice(s). Under no circumstances was I to 'Gubba-ise' her text. My working with her at her home in Granville every week enabled her to maintain control of her text in a manner that would not have been possible if all of the editing work had been done by the publisher alone.[36]

After working with Ruby for a year or so, she started to call me 'tidda' (that is, sister) and invited me to call her this too.[37] But with Nobby, the subject of the book, the relationship and the politics were more complicated. I did not meet him until after his release from prison, by which time I had already been working with Ruby for eight months and was in a position to see into all sorts of intimate details of his life. This power–knowledge imbalance made me feel somewhat awkward. I suspected that from his point of view I represented the literary police. Ruby wanted Nobby to talk about certain parts of his life on tape. So much of his life had been spent behind bars that there was a lot that Ruby herself didn't know. At first Nobby was quite reluctant to speak into the tape: he had been taped by police a number of times in the past. Some of the taping for the book was done in my presence, not because we had especially planned it that way, but because Nobby happened to drop in while I was at Ruby's place, and she grabbed him and sat him down and made him talk while she had him there.

Some of Nobby's prison writings have the same hyper-correct aspect as the Flinders Island people's 1846 petition to Queen Victoria. For example, his parole application letter of 24 May 1989 begins: 'Sirs, I respectfully ask your compassionate consideration to granting me parole.'[38] *Haunted by the Past* incorporates official documents from Nobby's police, prison and court records; Ruby uses these documents both to move the story forward and to convey a sense of how, within the institutions of the legal justice system, Nobby's fate was being determined by the kinds of stories that people in authority were able to write about him and that he was able to write about himself. Ruby wanted to retrieve control of the meaning of her son's life from the hands of the law enforcement authorities and the criminal justice system. She recontextualised the official records inside a wider story of Nobby's life, and the lives of other Aboriginal people, so that he could no longer be dismissed as a 'criminal' but could be understood both as a unique human being and as an Aboriginal man whose life had been shaped by a chain of historical events going back to 1788.

In terms of tone and content, *Haunted by the Past* is not written 'for the governor's pleasure'. It is stridently critical of an array of aspects of non-indigenous society. Yet in terms of narrative structure, language, punctuation and paragraphing, it is written with the norms and expectations of a mainstream readership in mind. Before the text could do its intended work of (as Ruby puts it) 'edu-ma-cating' the public, the story had to be able to attract a suitable publisher and a viable mainstream readership who would hear Ruby's story out. *Haunted by the Past* thus establishes an ambivalent, mixed relationship with 'the governor', that is, with the book's primarily non-Aboriginal readership. Although Ruby says some things that 'the governor' might find offensive, she brings non-indigenous readers close in two distinct but related ways.

First, as well as being Ruby's 'tidda', one of my roles as Ruby's editorial assistant was to be a surrogate stranger—a representative of 'the governor' or the mainstream reading public—who must be given sufficient pleasure to ensure favourable reviews and high levels of consumer demand. Ruby liked working in the physical presence of someone who could anticipate the needs of strangers and serve as a sounding board. Reading over her drafts, I would talk with her about points of potential readerly confusion or matters of decorum, such as whether she wanted to leave the swearing in (which she did), even though it might limit the book's chances of being included on school reading lists. The second way in which Ruby disarms 'the governor' is by bringing readers imaginatively into her bodily proximity. This face-to-face, dialogic relation is perhaps reflected most obviously in her use of the word 'aye?',[39] which is both a marker of oral enunciation and an almost irre-fusable invitation to agree with her. 'The governor' is thus imaginatively positioned inside Ruby's social circle. Readers are invited to stand with her—*at* her side, and *on* her side.[40]

SHARING HISTORY?

This study of early and recent indigenous life writings looks at one category of texts through which indigenous Australians have sought to get their truths across both to legal and government authorities and to the wider reading public. Patterns of connection, as well as differences, link early colonial and more recent forms of Aboriginal life narrative. Although indigenous Australians are less tightly con-strained today than in the past regarding the ways they put their stories into words, it is still true to say that the means of reprodu-cing their enunciations, disseminating them and ascribing authority to them—the processes necessary to making indigenous knowledge public and politically effective—continue to be controlled in large measure by non-indigenous individuals and institutions. Today's book-length life writings, like the hundreds of narrative fragments generated by indigenous Australians from as far back as the late eighteenth century, must still work tactically within a cultural, political and moral order established by a foreign power.

2

Stories for land
Oral narratives in the Maori Land Court

Ann Parsonson

One of the most significant sources for the study of the Maori past, and Maori understandings and constructions of the meaning of that past, is the minute books of the Maori Land Court. The court was established in 1865 by a colonial government anxious to institute a judicial process that would identify individual owners of Maori land and thus ease the purchase of millions of acres of land for British settlement.[1] Direct negotiations with chiefs representing the interests of their various communities in blocks of land the government wished to buy had often proved difficult (and indeed had triggered war in Taranaki in 1860), and collective control of the land was perceived as the obstacle to its acquisition. The job of the court was to establish 'who according to Native custom own or are interested in the land', extinguish customary title and substitute Crown-derived titles which would put the power to sell into the hands of individuals. In countless hearings conducted in the latter part of the nineteenth century by the court in order to establish eligibility for certificates of title, hapu (sub-tribes) and iwi (tribes) were required

21

initially to prove their rights by arguing cases before Pakeha judges.[2] To do so, they had to bring their oral traditions and histories out of their customary tribal context and into a court which was an instrument of government policy. Oral narratives were pressed into service as evidence, as each claimant descent group had to decide who would speak for them and what aspects of their history to present that would both identify them with their land and define them in relation to other groups, who might be claimants for the same or adjacent lands. This essay will examine ways in which those giving evidence on behalf of their various hapu drew on oral traditions and histories to shape their cases in court.

A case study of Pirongia East and West, a subdivision hearing in 1888 within the vast Rohepotae (King Country) block in the central North Island, which had itself first come before the court two years earlier, provides some understanding of the ways in which claimant groups navigated a course through the shoals of the court processes.[3] The court was obviously an ambiguous venue: the circumstances seemed familiar in that they involved discussion of the past by Maori who were related, often quite closely, and well known to one another; yet they were unfamiliar, too, in that they involved new adversarial processes.[4] Each group of claimants appointed and instructed a kaiwhakahaere (conductor)—tribal leaders fought successfully to keep lawyers out of the Rohepotae hearings[5]—who had to run their case on a day-to-day basis, calling on, advising and questioning their own witnesses, and cross-examining those of opposing parties. Although traditional sanctions must have operated to some extent—given that nearly all those present in court were there to support the various claims being argued[6]—the demands of the court processes also meant that oral traditions and histories were being marshalled and interrogated in quite unfamiliar ways.[7]

Over generations such histories had been moulded and passed down within kin groups; their purpose was not to keep a chronological record but to 'maintain the mana of one's ancestors and community'. Thus, it 'was not the duty of the storyteller and community to take into account another group's perception of the same event'.[8] In the court, however, different histories became conflicting evidence, and everyone was aware that a judge who was an outsider was weighing their histories against one another and trying to reconcile them, and that one man had unprecedented power to make decisions as to final divisions of the land among those he deemed to be entitled.[9] The consequences of court judgments for all those whose land was involved were far-reaching.

The King Country was a region where the pressures of the Court were felt particularly acutely. Over the past 30 years Waikato-King Country had been the heartland of the Kingitanga (Maori King Movement), which embodied Maori aspirations for autonomy and protection of the land. Within five years of the raising of the first King—the ariki Potatau Te Wherowhero in 1858—British troops had invaded the Waikato, spearheading a military occupation that was followed by massive confiscations of land. Thousands of Waikato people, their homes overrun or destroyed, withdrew into the lands of their Ngati Maniapoto relatives. By the early 1880s, however, Ngati Maniapoto were facing sustained government pressure to 'open' their territory, and their attempts to negotiate an alternative to the Land Court process (which was widely feared as the first step to land alienation) met with only limited success.

These circumstances clearly shaped participation in court hearings in this region. The Kingitanga remained a strong force, despite the decision of Ngati Maniapoto leaders that there was no alternative but to proceed with the Land Court; the arrival of the second Maori king, Tawhiao, on a visit to Otorohanga in 1888 was enough to cause the judge to cancel the day's hearing, observing that there would be little point in continuing because there would be 'very few natives' in court.[10] Tawhiao had prohibited involvement with the court in the postwar years; but his recognition of the dilemmas it posed for Kingitanga supporters is embodied among his tongi (sayings) reassuring the people that, if some needed to take a different path to protect the land, the Kingitanga would remain as a source of sustenance to which they could return.[11]

Tawhiao's concern about the nature and impact of the court was widely shared. Among the 'principal men' who shaped the Rohepotae hearings were the Ngati Maniapoto leaders Wahanui Te Huatare, Taonui, Rewi Maniapoto, Hauauru Poutama, and Wetere Te Rerenga. But Wahanui, after his initial appearance to make the *prima facie* case on behalf of the five tribes who were joint claimants,[12] attended the court infrequently during the first Rohepotae hearings in 1886. His kaiwhakahaere reported from time to time on his ill health, and sought adjournments. In the end Wahanui made just two appearances over two months, each for a day only, and his replies to cross-examinations made it clear that he intended to distance himself from the hearings. (He implied that he had not kept in close touch with the proceedings, and was therefore unable to give an opinion as to whether the evidence of other witnesses was 'strictly correct'.)[13] The court, quite simply, was not a comfortable place to be.

Who, then, did speak for the land in court? Clearly those who were most knowledgeable in tribal traditions were not always those who gave evidence, or participated most fully, as Wahanui's limited involvement indicates.[14] King Tawhiao's prohibitions may well have meant that some kaumatua (elders) who might have spoken did not; others may have decided they were not prepared to reveal tribal knowledge on the court's terms. Sometimes reference is made in court records to elderly people who were to have spoken but were too unwell to come, or to witnesses who did not arrive when expected. Some kaumatua may never have been called on to give evidence, either in deference to their knowledge and the need to protect it, or because of their frailty. Whatever the imperatives of court hearings, in other words, they did not override all cultural considerations.[15]

It seems that senior women were seldom called on, though there were women of great mana (authority, control, influence) and knowledge, widely recognised as such, who might have spoken; land rights descended through women as well as men, and women of status could vest land in others. Why, then, are the voices of women seldom heard in court? Tom Moke, of Ngati Mahuta and Ngati Hikairo, a descendant of some of those kaumatua who were prominent in the Pirongia case, remembers his grandfather Paahi Moke saying that 'the old people decided that women should not be there', perhaps because they were more apprehensive of the potential influence of women in court than of their exposure to the cultural challenge of its processes. Forthright and formidable, senior women might have had difficulty supporting some of the strategies of their male relatives.[16]

Whether because all these circumstances left something of a vacuum, or because the court was a forum in which they could feel more at home than their kaumatua did, there was one prominent group in the Rohepotae hearings: the sons of the Pakeha traders— only a handful of them—who had settled many years before on the west coast harbours, or in the interior, and had married into the local communities. These younger men—John Cowell (Hone Kaora), John Ormsby (Hone Omipi), Thomas Hughes (Poupatate) and his brother William (Wiremu Huihi), Walter Searancke (Hari Whenua), James Edwards (Hemi Erueti), Louis Hetet's sons and

William Turner's—were bilingual and bicultural, and played an important role in shaping cases in court. They gave evidence in many cases, and sometimes acted as kaiwhakahaere. According to the old people, however, they had their own agenda; there was in fact a pact among them not to challenge one another's cases before the court in order to make sure that each got part of the lands. And that created problems for the kaumatua 'who understood what the younger ones were trying to do, but didn't like it'.[17]

The court thus highlighted, or perhaps engendered, particular generational and cross-cultural tensions. In discussions that took place after the first Rohepotae hearing in 1886, which had resulted in judicial recognition of the rights of the five claimant tribes (as well as those of some counter-claimants),[18] it became clear that while many kaumatua may have been suspicious of the court there were those who saw it as an opportunity. The Pirongia East and West case arose after lengthy discussions outside the court between two of the iwi, Ngati Maniapoto and Ngati Hikairo, failed to settle the internal boundary between them in one part of the Rohepotae block. After some days Ngati Hikairo decided to return inside in the hope of securing a better hearing there; the very presence of the judge encouraged such a solution. From that point other groups of claimants—Ngati Ngawaero, Ngati Matakore, and Ngati Maka-hori[19]—outlined their own claims, and the case turned into a full-scale subdivision of the Pirongia lands.[20]

In court each group of claimants was obliged to establish the nature and the history of their own relationship with the land. In the Pirongia region there had been substantial continuity of that relationship for many generations; although the people had not totally escaped the effects of the large-scale movements of war parties throughout Aotearoa in the wake of the early nineteenth-century spread of European influence, their lives had been much less disrupted than those in many parts of the country. Take tupuna (rights to land passed on through whakapapa (genealogies)) was thus the main take (basis of rights transferred from one generation to the next) brought before the court, linked always with noho tuturu ('continuous occupation', as the court put it, over many generations),[21] and with mana and kaha or atete ('power to hold' or, as Wahanui expressed it, 'the power I have held to maintain my position').[22]

Take tupuna required the naming to the court of particular tupuna (ancestors) from whom land rights were derived. This in itself meant that claimants had to consider how to interpret their past to the court. Rights could descend through both male and female forebears; and some rights may have been 'kept warm' in recent generations rather than others, though in the normal course of events those who were entitled might activate rights even if they had not been exercised lately. There were many who might have claimed through more than one line of descent, depending on how they chose to explain the derivation of their rights, and their choice might also be influenced by the way in which other groups of claimants were shaping their cases.[23] In the first Rohepotae hearing in 1886 Wahanui gave the name of the principal ancestor (Turongo) from whom the broad Ngati Maniapoto claim derived, thus laying the basis for more detailed tribal claims within the block. Then, as the lands came before the court for further division, claimants and various counter-claimants each gave the names of tupuna under whose maru (protection) they derived their rights to the specific parts of the land whose rohe (boundaries) they gave, supporting their take (basis of claims) with whakapapa. (It was the tupuna who were important to the bases of cases, not the hapu; subsequently the various hapu who were considered to be included by their descent from those tupuna were listed.)

Traditional narratives were given in court to support the take brought forward. For take tupuna, kaumatua relied on traditions of first settlement and naming of the land, handed down over many generations. The details of these narratives might differ, but their essence was the same: they had passed into tribal tradition. Traditions relating to tupuna who had lived their lives in particular regions would be brought forward only by those whose whakapapa clearly entitled them to do so. As Te Oro Te Koko put it during the Pirongia subdivision hearing, 'the present time is one when the land of each ancestor is being disclosed by their descendants'.[24]

All those speaking also gave evidence of their 'occupation' of the land, or rather, of the exercise of authority which enabled them to 'occupy' successfully. They provided the names of pa (fortified villages) and kainga (unfortified settlements), bird-catching places and eel weirs, and also often gave stories of the tupuna with whom they were connected. Relationships with the land in more recent times were proved by oral histories relating to gifts of eels or fernroot or canoes, transactions entered into with Pakeha, or successful challenges to opponents' rights to make canoes or gardens—all acts in which the speakers themselves, or their matua (elder relatives), had participated.[25] Knowledge of this sort of evidence of 'occupation' was also specific to kin groups among whom it had been passed down; although certain gifts or disputes might be widely known, different hapu preserved their own histories of them. All of these kinds of narratives, plucked from different contexts, were woven together into a series of sworn statements, the object of which was to convey to the court the strength of the case being made.

The requirements of arguing a case in court had a marked effect on the histories that emerged. In traditional narratives, the prime purpose was to record relationships among the people, to tie everyone in by whakapapa, and to honour the mana of the great ancestors of the past. All those purposes are still evident in the court histories, but they are often overlain by an urgent awareness of the need to demonstrate to outsiders the basis of land rights. Differences in the way the traditions were told are evident if we contrast them with those gathered together, translated and edited as *Nga Iwi o Tainui: The Traditional History of the Tainui People* by two leading Maori scholars, the late Dr Pei Te Hurinui Jones of Ngati Maniapoto and his kinsman Professor Bruce Biggs. Traditions such as those recorded in *Tainui* are centred on the understanding of tribal relationships, and marriages among rangatira (chiefly) families that would shape tribal politics and alliances and responsibilities over many generations. They are very human stories about the ancestors, the circumstances in which they were born, received their names, grew up and fell in love, lived their lives, and met their deaths. Their memorable utterances, waiata (songs), tauparapara (protective chants), and ngeri (short haka) fill the pages, with details of insults offered and avenged, and reconciliations. The 'cultural imperatives of kinship and revenge', in Biggs' words, were 'burned into the minds' of tribal historians.[26] Although there are occasional references in the narratives to lands being divided between a chief's children, or new lands settled, the focus is less on the land than on relationships among the people. Even in traditions which can be dated to the eighteenth and early nineteenth centuries, when land disputes are more frequently mentioned, they feature simply as the context in which the narrative is set.[27]

In court evidence, however, the emotional intensity of the stories has often disappeared, the dialogue survives only in snatches, and waiata, though sometimes sung, are seldom recorded in the minutes. There is also little reference to beliefs—to the significance of spiritual understandings—though these so often provided explanations for why the old people acted as they did. Allusions to them were often filtered out, as they still are; the most important matters are not to be shared in the public record. And that of course is a reminder of a fundamental shift that was taking place in the court: histories that until then had been passed on only within customary contexts were being transferred out of the Maori world and written down by Pakeha officials. As Tom Moke has remarked, 'these accounts [are] significant for what they don't say . . . It's very mechanical, [the old people's] approach to it'; they regarded the court 'as an imposition, that they were being forced to justify what to them was for them only', and they saw it 'as a threat'.[28]

This reduction of traditions to a more singular narrative is evident in the approach of some kaumatua to the waka (canoe) traditions, which they gave to establish their earliest connections with the land. These traditions of the voyage of the ancestral waka had been passed down over generations, and were known throughout the tribe. Various versions might be told, which placed different emphases on the first journeys across the land and on the names given to mountains, lakes and rivers by those who made those journeys. For example, Te Oro Te Koko of Ngati Ngawaero gave the court this narrative of the voyage of the ancestral Tainui waka under its captain Hoturoa, and Rakataura, the tohunga (spiritual leader), who together bore responsibility for its safe arrival. The narrative emphasises Raka's inland exploration before the canoe had even reached its final destination, as Hoturoa himself acknowledges when he comments on the discovery of Raka's footprints:

Raka[tāura] was Hoturoa's companion in the canoe. Raka was a 'tohunga karakia' [expert in protective chants], his place was in the nose of the canoe & Hoturoa occupied the stern; their canoe sailed from [Hawaiki] and landed at Tāmaki [Auckland]; the people went ashore and Raka went to Puketāpapa [Mt Roskill], after he had gone Hoturoa had the canoe dragged over to Manukau on the West Coast. Raka thought he fixed the canoe [so] that it could not reach Manukau, he performed some religious service and Hoturoa thought he could not drag it across and therefore they had to take it back to Tāmaki . . . Raka . . . went to Tahurikōtua at Aotea & from there he went to Harehare at Kāwhia; Raka had twisted feet: he returned from there to Karioi, the tūāhu [altar] he had there was called Tūāhupapa; whilst he was there the canoe 'Tainui' was seen out at sea, it landed at Matatua [sic for Moeātoa], Kāwhia, where they saw Raka's foot prints on the sand; when Hoturoa saw these marks [he said] 'ah this is the fellow Raka', Hoturoa took up his abode at Kāwhia and Raka at Karioi which is between Kāwhia and Raglan.[29]

Subsequently, Te Oro Te Koko continued, Raka's descendant Kahu[30] travelled inland after the birth of her child Rakamaomao, naming all the places as she went, from Pirongia (Te Pirongia ō te Aroaro ō Kahu, 'the scented pathway of Kahu'), to Mangawaero (Te Manga Waero-ō-te-Aroaro ō Kahu, 'the stream in which Kahu's dog-skin cloak was washed'), to Kakepuku (Te Kakepuku ō Kahu, 'the hill over which Kahu climbed'), to Te Aroha in the Hauraki district (Te Aroha ō Kahu, 'the yearning of Kahu for her husband and home'), to Whakamaru (Te Whakamaru ō Kahu, 'the shelter of Kahu'), to Rangitoto (Te Rangitoto ō Kahu, 'the black lava of Kahu'), to Pureora (Te Pureora ō Kahu, 'the life-giving ritual which aided Kahu's recovery from illness'), to Puke-ō-Kahu ('the sacred mountain of Kahu') where she died.[31] The succession of names (which could be understood only in relation to one another) acted, like many Maori place names, as 'survey pegs of memory' (in Sir Tipene O'Regan's words), releasing 'whole parcels of history to a tribal narrator and those listening'.[32] Here they recorded a journey crucial to the identity of the descendants of Kahu and Raka with their land.

If there is a mechanical ring to a narrative like this it is partly because of the way it appears to have been edited. Te Oro Te Koko did not feel obliged to relate the waka tradition in full which, as we know from other accounts, might have given the reasons for the tension that had developed between Hoturoa and Raka, the names of Raka's companions on his overland journey, the words of his karakia, and the origin of the names given by Kahu on her journey. But, like other kaumatua, he paused to spell out the meaning of his narrative for the court. He concluded his account of Raka's journey overland with the statement: 'the reason Raka was in a hurry to get over[land] first, was to get possession of the land.' Of Kahu's travels, he commented: 'she named those places for her descendants.'[33] Similarly, Rihari Tauwhare (Riki Taimana Waitai) of Ngati Hikairo and Ngati Paiariki, who attributed the first journey inland from Kawhia to Rakataura and his wife Kahukeke, explained in the course of his account: 'land & women were a matter of great importance to the maories in those days.'[34] Deliberate interpolations like this are a reminder that kaumatua were always conscious of the transposition of their narratives into a new cultural context, and of the judicial weight being brought to bear on their statements.

Stories told in court about tupuna of more recent generations also focused on the derivation of land rights, though they often also preserved the essence of traditional narratives. They were filled with detail and explanations for why the ancestors acted as they did. Te Mapu Tahuna of Ngati Ngawaero gave this history of a crucial marriage six generations earlier between his own tupuna Kuo, and Paiariki (which involved the establishment of an important tribal relationship), and of a gift of land made at this time to Kuo by her father Upokotaua. The story of the gift, in a context in which Ngati Paiariki were also claimants before the court, underlined the point that it was made to Kuo, not to Paiariki who became her husband:

> Paiariki had no claim to the land, when he got to Kāwā he went to a house called Tūranganui, he went there for the purpose of seeing Upokotaua's daughters, as he had heard that they were very fine women; when he arrived there he sent his companion to have a look at them and he found the younger one the most attractive. Kuo was her name; the elder sister then got angry. Kuo sent for some food for her husband but the elder sister would not send any, the person returned & said the food was withheld, Kuo shed tears as there was no food for her husband & Upokotaua her father found her in tears & he said to her why are you crying for, she replied they have refused to give me some food for my husband. Upokotaua gave her a portion of land commencing at Kāwā & extending to Pirongia & Paiariki's mana was over that portion from that day, that being the portion where the food was refused to Paiariki viz preserved birds and eels.[35]

The flow of this narrative was uninterrupted, but Ngati Ngawaero kaumatua then faced the challenge of interpreting it to the satisfaction of the court. Their claim ultimately derived from their tupuna Motai, a teina (relative of a junior line) of Turongo,[36] hence Te Mapu Tahuna's explanation that the gift to Kuo had not destroyed the title of his tupuna Motai to the land, as 'Paiariki only had the mana over the land'.[37] Te Oro Te Koko, when pressed, further explained the distinction: '[Paiariki's] "mana" is over the people only . . . [he] had no claim on the land.'[38] In other words, his tupuna had recognised the mana of Paiariki, and valued the relationship formed with Paiariki's people, but while Paiariki was entrusted with the active leadership of the people within the area gifted, and thus the protection of their land and interests, the land itself had not passed out of the hands of Upokotaua's people.[39]

All those who stood before the court gave a great deal of evidence about their 'occupation' of the land. Histories of rohe marks and tohu (special landmarks) made by their tupuna, which spoke every day of their presence on the land, were important to their descendants and to their collective identity. Only those entitled by descent had such knowledge. Ngati Matakore claimed rights to part of the land before the court through Punga, Tipi-ā-Houmea, and their sister Tukitaua, who had lived nine generations before; Ngati Matakore kaumatua Te Rauroha Te Ngare thus talked about their tohu, about a boundary mark named Te Apunga-ō-Tukitaua— 'that place gets its name from Tukitaua having kneeled down there'—and another named Tātua-ō-tū-te-Ākau—'Tūte Ākau himself [son of Tukitaua] gave it that name, it was named after a bend in the Turitea stream, & he called it after his belt'.[40] Other tohu included Te Moko-ō-Tipi, a small hill—'it took his name were [sic] Tipi was tattooed, he gave a number of names to places—one was called Te Pekenui ō Tipi it was a tree for snaring birds'—and Waiwhakaata-ā-Tukitaua, a pool of water in a log, was used by Tukitaua as a mirror.[41] Thus, as often happened, a strong association with the land was recorded in whakapapa which, like the origin of place names, would be passed down in oral histories. Rihari Tauwhare of Ngati Hikairo similarly spelt out the significance of tohu for the court when he spoke of some tawhero roots 'carved to represent images of Hihi and Toataua, these two people were twins, the roots are entwined to suggest twins'. And he invited the court to go and look at the carvings on these roots and two others, adding, for the court's benefit: 'they were made so that people travelling may know that the carvings represented the owners of the land.'[42] (The fact that Judge Mair spent a number of days examining tohu on the land, deciding that they had an important part to play in his final decision, is a reminder too that histories would undoubtedly have been given to him in their proper place, on the land itself, though paradoxically these are not recorded.)

Such mediation of tribal knowledge to the court was also apparent in evidence given about places where the old people had their noho kainga (unfortified settlements), pa, and urupa (burial grounds); where they had hunted or fished or planted food, caught their eels or birds (snaring them in trees, or by water where they came to drink); and where they made their canoes. In these parts of hapu evidence we are very conscious of it being presented specifically for the purposes of the court. Knowledge of all the places on the land with which people had their own associations was compressed into lists of names, and it was given publicly (though names, of course, did not reveal locations!).[43] Such knowledge would, in the normal course of events, have been passed on to younger relatives chosen as kaitiaki (guardians, protectors) of that knowledge, according to the timing of the old people, as they went to take their birds or eels. Nor would it have been just knowledge of mahinga tuna (eel-catching places) or mahinga manu (bird-catching places) that was given; the histories of all the places passed, and traditions about those tupuna who lived there, would also be told.

Some kaumatua spoke in court, however, as they would have on the ground. Rihari Tauwhare paused in his list of pa to explain important hostilities, and their resolution, at Nawenawe pa. And Te Wi Papara, who gave the names of many waka, and the place where each was made, often also gave their history: on one occasion before the British wars, he said, three named canoes and three without names had been included in a wedding present made to Ngati Tipa (from the lower Waikato River); and he related the circumstances of the marriage, and of the journey made by Ngati Paiariki to 'take the canoes & the woman'.[44] In a longer account, Te Oro Te Koko, listing his mahinga manu, explained the significance of one in particular—Paewhenua—which was disputed, and had become a well-known boundary mark. 'Pukehoua was another bird catching station', he told the court, '& it was through that that the name Paewhenua became known'. In the time of his ancestors Hie and Ruatemarama there had been a dispute between their people, living on one side of Pukehoua hill, and other hapu, Ngati Horotakere, Ngati Puhiawe and others, on the north side. In the course of the dispute they discovered the tree which was 'favoured by the birds' but they agreed to make it a boundary between them, 'one people to own one side of the tree and the others on the other side'. He went on to explain how this had come about:

At that time the tree had no name; after that a bird, larger than a pigeon came into this district and Ruatemarama was sitting under the tree and one of the birds alighted there & he killed it with a spear, the bird was called Tauwharepū, that name was given because the point of Ruatemarama's spear was made from the bone of a man named Tauwharepū; when he speared it the spear went right through it and stuck into the branch of the tree and he called out 'see how powerful the point of the spear is' . . . The meaning of the word 'Paewhenua' [ground level] is because Ruatemarama speared the bird from the ground without having to climb the tree & that name was afterwards given to the boundary.[45]

This story, which had clearly been passed down among Te Oro's people, honoured Ruatemarama's feat and recorded his successful taking of utu (compensation) on a former occasion (hence the bone on the tip of his spear), though it passed over the spiritual significance of the appearance and killing of the great bird. As told in court, it connected the naming of the tree to Te Oro's tupuna, and emphasised the origin of rights.[46]

Histories of gifts made and returned were always of great importance in the narratives told in court, as they were outside the court. Some were of gifts made long ago, passed on from one generation to the next because of their significance. Others were recalled by kaumatua as having taken place in their own lifetime. Such accounts were important both because of the relationships and obligations that were recorded in them, and because of the recognition of rights involved in return gifts, for receipt of the return gift was an acknowledgment from outside the community of whose who had played the most important role in connection with the original gift.

One such account was given by Te Wi Papara, of Ngati Hikairo and Ngati Paiariki; as he gave the names of his weirs, he stated: 'Some of the eels taken from my weirs were given as presents.'[47] In the course of a series of peace-making visits between Tainui and Ngapuhi after the battle of Matakitaki (1822), an incident took place when a Ngapuhi chief named Ruku was somehow omitted from customary distributions of food, and was 'very much annoyed'. Tainui were anxious to conciliate Ruku, and Te Puhia of Ngati Te Kanawa went to Ngati Ngaupaka to get some special foods for him. Ngati Ngaupaka gave eels from their weirs, Te Tarere in the Mangawhero stream, Te Karaka in the Waipa, and Te Para in the Moakurarua stream. Later, when Tainui returned the visit, Te Puhia was among the chiefs who went north, and Ruku made a gift in return: 'Ruku gave up his pākehā named Armitage to these people to be a pākehā for them at Kāwhia.' In turn, Te Puhia and his people gifted their waka Te Ahirahaki in which they had travelled, and Ngapuhi returned a gun which was named Te Ahirahaki after the waka. Te Wi Papara continued: 'I have that gun in my possession now, it is a single-barrelled flint gun; as a return for the food & canoe and the slave that was given to Te Kauau [sic][48] a cask of powder was given.'[49] The immediate importance to Ngati Ngaupaka of the named gun was that it was evidence of recognition by others of their established rights to catch eels in certain places. Te Wi Papara's narrative was not given in the context of a history of the arrival of Ngapuhi taua (war parties), the struggle at Matakitaki and the peace process that was entered into subsequently; rather, it was prompted by the pa tuna (eel weirs), and it focused on a series of gifts that embodied both relationships within Ngati Maniapoto, and the extension of relationships between Ngapuhi and Tainui.

Relationships among people remain the key to narratives of the years of the nineteenth century in which the lives of those who spoke in court and those of their senior relatives had been lived. They were not narratives which traversed the major key events that were part of the wider tribal memory, though various of these events were often referred to in passing: the departure of the whole of Ngati Toa from Kawhia harbour to re-establish themselves further south; the incursions of Ngapuhi taua from the far north in the course of their great expeditions of the 1820s; the arrival of the Pakeha traders from the 1830s and of the Wesleyan missionaries in the early 1840s; the British invasion of the Waikato, war, and confiscation in the 1860s. All these events were, in the context of the Pirongia hearings, merely a backdrop well understood by all present. However, they were called on either to provide context for the stories that were told, or specifically to help meet the Pakeha preoccupation with chronology.

Those who gave histories relating to their own or their parents' lifetimes constantly attempted to date the events they spoke of. Even older speakers wove in references which would help locate the period or even the year of occupation in particular parts of the block: 'I . . . myself lived on the land from childhood until I was a man', said Waretini Tukorehu, 'I was a child living there when I saw first european books';[50] Te Anga Toheroa stated: 'It was when the mill was first built at Mangarewarewa that I first saw [Ngāti] Te Waha, that was also the first time I saw [Ngāti] Paiariki, it was about subsequent to the first time of the measle epidemic';[51] and Hone Te One gave the judge some idea of the timing of important matters in the life of his grandfather, the great leader Whakamarurangi, by reference to his own birth at Matakitaki before the fateful battle there against Ngapuhi, explaining, in a few words which come from a tradition less concerned with dates, '[t]he time of the fall at [the pā] Mātakitaki I was old enough to run about and I was old enough to know my father & mother's names but not old enough to know what fear was'.[52] Such comments reflect a determination to communicate in a non-Maori forum in terms to which the judge could readily relate.

Yet, while the histories told in court about these years tended to unfold in a roughly chronological sequence, their purpose was not to provide a broad outline of tribal history. Because the claimants to the Kopua-Pirongia lands were closely related and were concerned with clarifying their respective rights before the court, their histories illustrate the exercise of rights on particular occasions, the derivation of those rights, and their recognition by others. They were histories specific to particular communities, and they embody different memories and different interpretations.

Various hapu histories were given, for instance, relating to the temporary move of Waikato to Te Kopua around the time of the Ngapuhi intrusion in the 1820s, when the prime concern of all Tainui was to mount a strong defence against the northerners. Each of the hapu spokesmen recorded the particular relationships between their own old people and Waikato leaders that explained why Waikato lived at Te Kopua, and each referred to gifts made to Waikato after they had returned home, so that the tapu on the land might be lifted. Waikato acceptance of those gifts testified to their acknowledgment of the rights of their various hosts to make them. Ngati Matakore, for instance, recorded that six head of cattle had been taken by Ngati Ngawaero to the great Waikato leader Tawhia Te Rauangaanga, which in their account represented land occupied by Waikato on the east side of the river, while Waikato's occupation of land on the west side had derived from Ngati Matakore's own earlier gift of the land to Tawhia's mother Here, a descendant of Matakore.[53] Along with the cattle, a horse named Takahiparu, representing the land extending to Te Kopua, was also given to Tawhia by Te Taiepa of Ngati Makahori, 'and [Tāwhia] brought it to us [Ngāti Matakore] to let us see it; after we had seen it we returned it to him. Tāwhia drove the cattle & that horse to Waikato'.[54] Thus, in the Ngati Matakore history, Tawhia, by bringing the horse (which represented rights to particular lands) to them, also acknowledged their rights in those lands himself.

In many of the Pirongia histories, considerable emphasis was also placed on the details of early transactions with scattered Pakeha settlers when they first took up residence in the region. Whether this reflected the importance of these new kinds of transactions locally, or the key roles of the settlers' sons in the court hearings, which meant that both they, and other witnesses, tended to give weight to the transactions, is hard to say. But different histories were also preserved about these transactions. As with gifts, they involved questions of rights and recognition of rights, connected with the distribution of payments.

The first major transaction in the area was the purchase of land at Te Kopua by the Wesleyan missionaries. (We know from official sources that the Wesleyans made a down payment of £4 for land in 1840; the transaction was finalised in 1847.)[55] Te Wi Papara's account conveys a great deal about the details that had been preserved about the transaction in the Ngati Ngaupaka history: the names of those who initially participated in the transaction, the opposition of Ngati Ngaupaka and the way in which it was expressed, the resolution of the matter, and the distribution of payment received from the missionaries in a way that left no doubt as to whose land the missionaries were living on.

'I remember the sale of Kōpua to the Missionaries', said Te Wi Papara; it was made by Te Oro, Te Warihi, Takerei (Tawhia) Te Rauangaanga and others; Takerei received the payment, £30, and took it to a settlement up the Waipa River above Ngaruawahia. But, Papara continued, 'none of the people who soled [sic] the land had any right to it, 30 acres was the area sold, but the portion the sellers intend[ed] selling was a very large one . . . the real owner of the land was absent at that time . . . namely Te Meera'.[56] The sale, he charged, had been made without consultation:

> When Te Meera heard of it he came over and quarrelled with Te Oro & party about it and he proposed to come to blows about it & took up a tomahawk to strike Te Oro [in fact his brother-in-law], but no blows were struck and [they] confined themselves to wordy warfare; after that Te Meera portioned [off] a piece which the Missioners should have & placed a stone there, the latter is now in my possession; while he was laying off the rohe the Rev Mr Buttle inquired who the old man was & was told that is the man who owned the land.[57]

When he had finished, Te Meera sent his son to Takerei Te Rauangaanga to repossess the payment. It, too, was carefully divided.

Te Meera gave £5 to Te Huatau (who gave it back to him); then he kept the money for a couple of years, until he was able to buy a horse 'the progeny of which he intended to distribute among the co-owners of the land'. The names of the animals marked their connection with the people who had rights there. The horse was called Mere Aina, 'after our sister'; the first foal was called Panurua and was given to Moriwhaiti and his father Te Huatau; the second, a filly, was called Hariata (after a daughter of Mere Aina), and was given to her; the next was called Matuakore and went to Te Wi Papara. The whaka-papa provided to the court shows the close relationships among those mentioned; they were all cousins, descended from the marriage between Te Ra and Ngaupaka.[58] John Ormsby, in his evidence, under-lined the importance of the transaction in the community's memory:

> all our people say that Te Meera took no part in it [the trans-action], but it is a well known fact that when he heard of it he came over with his tomahawk to quarrel with Te Oro & [others] . . . another matter greatly spoken about was Te Meera reducing the area of the portion sold to 35 acres at Kōpua . . . he refixed the rohes & dug them on the ground; possibly it was after that that he took part in the sale.[59]

All those who had rights to the Kopua/Pirongia lands preserved accounts of their entitlement to leasing payments (reti) in their oral histories; these, too, were histories owned by particular kin groups. The arrival of leases, which brought substantial economic returns, highlighted tensions over land occupied by Pakeha. Two hapu in particular disputed the land from this time, and their disputes are reflected in their histories. According to Ngati Makahori, rents were charged from the time Te Toenga returned from Sydney and demanded payment from the Wesleyan missionary for grazing: 'he told Te Taiepa & some others that it was a pākehā custom to charge rent. Rev[erend] Mr. Buddle agreed to pay & 3 bullocks (cows) were given as payment, the people reared them and eventually they had 50, some were stock from the three & the others were for yearly payments of rent.'[60]

After the initial agreement, a more formal arrangement was entered into by one of Buddle's successors, Reid. According to Ngati Matakore, the land Takotokoraha was leased to Reid to run his sheep on by the three hapu, Ngati Matakore, Ngati Makahori and Ngati Ngawaero, who made a single arrangement with him. The rent was paid in sheep and divided in three, one third for each hapu.[61] Ngati Makahori also acknowledged that payment was made to all three hapu, but stated the dispute started when their matua wanted part of the payment given to Ngati Matakore, 'but the latter did not agree'.[62] From this time the trouble had not let up, though there had been a determined tribal attempt to mediate in the matter of the lease payments. Te Anga Toheroa stated that disputes between Ngati Matakore and Ngati Makahori had continued from the time of the old people; 'our quarrel now is about tōtara on the Moakurarua stream, the log belongs to them [Ngāti Makahori], but I took it, then they came and burnt it, that is part of the same quarrel since the time of our elders'.[63] Yet some recent resolution had been found, evidently in the traditional form of a marriage.[64]

Histories of disputes were in fact frequently related in order to show that kin groups had held their ground and not backed down in the face of challenge or provocation. These were histories which had been passed on because it was important that younger generations knew the history and outcome of confrontations with their neighbours which often involved the right to valued resources. John Ormsby's account of a dispute at Te Kopua between his people and Ngati Ngawaero shows that rights were defended in the late nineteenth century just as they had been in earlier generations—by confrontations, not necessarily involving bloodshed, in which each party mounted a strong physical assertion of their rights.[65] Although the means to hand were less traditional, the narratives are easily recognisable. According to Ormsby, the roots of this dispute, too, were to be found years before, stemming from the time before the wars of the 1860s when several villages (named Nineveh, Babylon and Jerusalem) were formed near the Wesleyan mission. Te Mapu Tahuna of Ngati Ngawaero had agreed some fifteen years before the court sitting to give up land which they had occupied during those years, returning to their own cultivations. But some of the young people of Ngati Ngawaero decided to stay at Te Kopua and make their gardens. The news spread fast throughout the district. Ormsby's account continued:

as soon as I heard of it I yoked up my pair of bullocks & went also to plow there. Te Roha Ēnoka was my companion and by the time that N'Ngawaero got on the ground my ploughing had far advanced. N'Ngawaero had two pairs of bullocks and they were there in great force. About midday Te Maapu said we better stop the plowing & discuss the matter, but I objected & no discussion took place & plowing went on. [T]owards evening a native named Te Tūpara had heard of the dispute, he came over to act as mediator (of Ngāiterangi), he went from one to the other and the result was that [Ngāti] Ngawaero agreed to stop plowing, and we took our plows away.[66]

Subsequently a long-term arrangement was worked out whereby Ngati Ngawaero were to cultivate the northern end of Hiruharama (Jerusalem), and Ormsby's people were to cultivate the southern end. (Ormsby added that he had not been present when this arrangement was entered into but, as he put it, 'as the arrangement had been entered into, I was not justified in upsetting it'.)[67] The ploughs and bullocks might not have been traditional, but the manner in which both sides maintained their position—and eventually co-operated to resolve the dispute, accepting the involvement of a mediator from an outside tribe (Ngai Te Rangi of Tauranga)—was entirely so. The dramatic way in which the confrontation was conducted would doubtless have ensured that the story survived in the oral record, as so many had before it.

These latter histories are a reminder that disputes could occur in any generation, and could either be vigorously pursued, left in abeyance for a time if tensions were felt to be running too high, or resolved. In a society of close-knit communities the presentation of court cases was itself part of the continuing history of the people and their relationships with each other. As decisions were made about the shaping of those cases, whole histories of alliance, antagonism and obligations had to be taken into account, and those decisions themselves and their outcomes would be recorded in the oral histories. Frequent uneasy responses during cross-examinations ('I did not hear that . . .', 'I do not know that . . .') testify to witness preferences not to contradict the evidence of others directly.[68] And outsiders may never know the extent to which kaiwhakahaere or individual witnesses 'edited' their evidence as they spoke, in acknowledgment of the importance of preserving, or not allowing the deterioration of, relationships that would continue long after the court had left the district.

If Maori edited the histories they took into the court, however, they shielded whole bodies of knowledge altogether from it. As Sir Robert Mahuta has explained, Waikato in the difficult postwar and confiscation years were engaged in a deeply spiritual quest to understand their predicament of enforced and evidently permanent exile from their homes. Drawing on the experience of the children of Israel, Tawhiao, a prophet king, shaped a vision embodied in his ohaoha or tongi which have guided followers of the Kingitanga ever since. In tribal hui (meetings) Tawhiao's vision of salvation and interpretation of the history of the Kingitanga gave strength to generations. The belief system and values of the Kingitanga were enshrined in their own oral narratives, transmitted on the marae (traditional tribal meeting grounds); here knowledge was owned by the people, it could not be appropriated by outsiders.[69] In Land Court narratives, there is little hint of the political and spiritual significance of the Kingitanga to the people of Waikato–Maniapoto. There are occasional mentions of hui, and occasional references to the role of the Kingitanga in helping the people to relocate in the post-confiscation period. But there is no echo of the oral narratives that embody Kingitanga understandings of their fate, 'encrusting meaning around events'.[70]

Yet the old people—those whose lands were outside the confiscation areas—could not escape the court. Either they stayed away and lost their land, or they attended, gave their evidence, secured a Crown certificate of title, and took the first step to major land loss. To read histories that, despite their narrow scope and rigid format, cannot conceal a vibrant tribal past, and to realise that the stories of that past were playing their role in deciding the final fate of those who told them, brings its own sadness.

3

Crying to remember
Reproducing personhood
and community

Fiona Magowan

In northeast Arnhem Land, men and women frequently comment that 'Those who sing, "know"'.[1] Accomplished singer and clan leader Wilson Ganambarr had firmly advised me of the importance of 'knowing' through song shortly after I began fieldwork at Galiwin'ku (Elcho Island) in 1990 in search of women's song traditions. I had asked him whether I might be able to learn songs performed by women, and he had advised: 'You must first learn my songs [manikay], my uncle's songs, my mother's mother's songs and my mother's songs from me in that order and then you may learn women's songs.' Four months after Wilson had begun teaching me ritual songs,[2] as men would perform them, he declared: 'Now you know all my songs, you can learn women's songs.'[3] I was greatly surprised at his assessment. Although he had spent many days telling me the stories of the songs and singing their ritual texts, I had not been asked to perform. What did it mean, then, for an outsider and a novice like myself, and ultimately for Yolngu,[4] 'to know'?

41

For Wilson it was sufficient, it seemed, that I could detect core song words and, at the appropriate times, rise from the sheet in the sand, knees bent, my eyes fixed on the ground in front, swaying my hips rhythmically to the clapstick beat. On this occasion, I raised and lowered my forearms in line with my body in rapid succession, keeping strict time with the ironwood ring of the clapsticks. As the song of the seagull died away, I stood up straight to my dhuway's (husband's) shouts of 'Barrku' (Far out!), accompanied by much raucous laughter from the young men.[5] Although it was inappropriate for a single, young woman to attempt to sing his clan songs, I had shown that I could dance, a skill and obligation required of all women to encourage men to sing longer and enhance the vigour of their performance.

By the time Wilson dismissed me from his tutelage, I had listened to and recorded many hours of his singing and, perhaps more importantly, I had danced when the occasion arose. However, finding women who were now willing to teach me their only mode of ritual song performance—crying-songs, or ngäthi manikay as they are called—was much more difficult. Those who were old enough, and respected enough, were seldom willing to perform outside of a ritual context and, though word travelled quickly around the community that I was looking for a suitable teacher, it was a couple of months before Murukun, a senior Djambarrpuyngu woman from my mother's mother's clan, offered to teach me her crying-songs.[6]

In this chapter I will explore how Yolngu come to know about themselves and others through story and song, and examine how Murukun was able to assert her right to teach and cry through song, as a mode of transmitting and transposing personal and collective knowledge across clan lineages and disparate locales. The dissemination of social knowledge via song knowledge, I argue, is a means of narrating one's own lifeworld[7] and those of others, shaping a sense of personhood, obligation and affiliation for both singer and listeners. Both stories and songs serve to remake the ties of storyteller and singer to their listeners at every performance—ties that are necessarily partial, fragmented, negotiated and flexible, despite a rhetoric of cohesion and consistency. It is not my aim to recapture the 'full history' or indeed an entire 'life story' of Murukun, even were she able to recount all the events that might be considered testament to her being; rather, this reflection on Yolngu singing and storytelling is an analysis of how Yolngu come to know themselves and others in the present through the emotional weight of remembering and

42

forgetting their pasts in song. I will consider how storytelling provides a basis for songs; how narrative techniques of storytelling, and corresponding linguistic principles in song structures, generate an illusion of narrative cohesion; how landscapes of crying-song knowledge are presented simultaneously as ones of action and consciousness, relating ancestral, personal and group-orientations and carrying augmented status for women; and finally how the sentiments of crying-songs are especially and solely employed by women to shape individual testimony, group cohesion, differentiation and affective connections to kin and land.

SINGING STORIES

In Yolngu life, stories (dhäwu) are often told in song as a means of making sense of the world and everything in it.[8] Wilson's insistence that I should learn his songs first was a way of telling me his stories. Thus, I learned his clan songs and stories simultaneously, as a mixture of practical skills that included knowledge of the landscape; the anticipated outcomes of hunting and gathering exploits; and acts of ancestral intervention. His songs always paralleled his storytelling as he used one genre to support the other in order to validate the 'facts'. Wilson's story and song versions were born of personal, collective and ancestral experience, and gave rise in turn to new experiences in their telling as he attempted to locate me in the web of Yolngu knowledge.

Ranging across a vast area of more than 3000 square kilometres in northeast Arnhem Land, Yolngu relate their personal histories as ancestral stories and ancestral songs, each reflecting the other, creating a series of life events—albeit necessarily fragmented, partial and elliptical—that are intimately related to others both locally and further afield. The freedom to travel via plane, boat or four-wheel drive to over 50 homeland centres generates a continuing sense of the interconnectedness of daily life with relatives living elsewhere. As stories are told about the practical difficulties of journeys between places, as well as the ancestral journeying of megafauna creatures of long ago and the trials and tribulations they encountered on the way, the landscape acquires significance through the cartographic marking and mapping of experience and event.[9] Storytelling is, therefore, embedded in ancestral creation but animated by contemporary action, such that the cartography of country is also a cartography of the mind. Places are spoken or sung into being through the imagined worlds of the storyteller, singer and listener, the places chosen depending partially on the response of the listener as the legitimator of the emergent narrative.[10]

The ability to condense long journeys over vast tracts of land through telling stories is a means of journeying from place to place and from one group to another in practice and in the imagination. The stories and songs that Wilson narrated described various aspects of his related clan regions and their seasonal cycles through particular colours, smells and sounds of the flora and fauna throughout the year. Each song would focus on an animal or bird, plant or natural element evident in either the 'wet' or the 'dry' season, signalled by the formation or dispersal of clouds, the strength, direction and feel of the winds, and the colours and availability or scarcity of bush foods and animals. His songs were not restricted to the Galiwin'ku environment only, but extended across the Arnhem Land locale divided into five inland regions: sand dunes, mangroves, open forest, rainforest, and the swamp. When the songs moved to the sea, Wilson changed subjects to the travels of Yolngu and ancestral beings in canoes or praus to catch shellfish, turtle, crabs, stingray and other marine life. Today, hunting and gathering still take place at homelands for much of the year, until the tracks become impassable due to the heavy rains of the wet season. These ecological zones are the basis for clusters of songs, the subjects of which mainly focus on individual species, their actions and attributes.

By evoking all the shapes, colours and sounds of the environment, singing recalls to memory the actions of the ancestors in the form of deceased relatives. In each song, the ecosystem is grouped into sequences of song subjects, such as water, trees, leaves and winds, thereby comprising 'poetic event clusters'. The songs of the landscape and seascape are committed to memory by seeing in sound. This sonic imagery allows Yolngu to transcend imaginatively the bounds of landscape by poetically mastering natural images, turning them to their own social ends in musical metaphor. The ability to imagine these poetic event clusters in the mind's eye is critical to effective recall. The speed of the current, the height of the waves or the strength of the wind, are not just recalled to the tempo of a particular tune, but a singer will visualise the actual movements of birds or animals and their corresponding calls. A large number of adjectives in songs describe these sensory elements of the environment, such as the sloshing of canoes through water, creating a performative discourse of nature that embodies social relations.

For Yolngu, then, the auditory and the visual are co-dependent, and the recall of hundreds of tunes is necessarily reliant upon the sounding of ecological images in the mind's eye, a form of synaesthesia.[11] These images, furthermore, are premised on a moral link with the ancestral past that is suffused in, and emergent from, a sensory engagement with the environment. This, in turn, encodes a politics of sentiment, or a sense of eco-place.[12] This means that in such songs ancestral conscience is not simply located in objects as inanimate containers of fixed social meaning, but that, instead, ancestral land and sea forms are recreated and embodied as identities of relatives, living and deceased. Emotional catalysts for remembrance are thereby located in a poetics of eco-place in which the environment is the vehicle for motivation to joy, sorrow, guilt, nostalgia, empathy, antipathy and resistance. These senses of the environment, it should be noted, are not static or fixed, but flow through time as one generation dies and the next is born, each memory building upon and adding to the one before. The personalised meanings of the environment communicate, then, in particular ways to the singer, and more generally to listeners who share knowledge of the song texts.

As each area and all the species in it are marked with important ritual names and owned by clan members, to know the ecology is to know the land and the names and identities of those it sustains. Consequently, to tell stories is to give away knowledge of an area, and this requires the right to impart information about ancestral action. This may not be undertaken lightly or by those who are considered too young to 'know', or those who have not inherited the right either through patrilineal or matrilineal affiliation. The right to locate stories of birds and animals in different areas will depend on the connections of the storyteller to the region and subjects of the narrative. Understanding authorial relativity further entails knowing strings of ancestral and family histories as stories reflexively locate the singer who adopts a strategic position within the grid of relational knowledge, situating him or herself and others according to his or her rights, personal affinities and antipathies.

In narrating a story, this strategic positioning of an individual may be structured by repeating a theme and reinforcing it with variations. For example, in order to stress relative authority, a speaker may repeat part of a sentence within the sentence, where semi-intoned passages list names of relatives or clans in order of their importance, each repetition punctuated by a pause. The leader of the Ngaymil clan told the mythology of Elcho Island like this: 'This area is Elcho Island. It is owned by the Ngaymil, D̲atiwuy and Murrungun clans. The island is called Murrunga by the D̲atiwuy, Ngaymil and Gunbirri clans. These people are Murrungun Yolngu of the D̲atiwuy, Ngaymil and Gunbirri clans.' His first statement placed his own clan at the head of the list of clans, indicative of his right to speak for the land. However, his clan is only one of a complex of clans who share rights in the island through the morning star ceremony.[13] When he lists D̲atiwuy in the third sentence, he still acknowledges that his brother, Wilson, holds equal rights in the story. And Gunbirri join these two clans through the journey of the morning star across their lands, indicated by the collective term, Murrungun. Narrating one's country, then, is a way of narrating oneself and others, providing shifting and enduring perspectives on experience that are both personal and projected.[14]

Yolngu stories are necessarily local and localising, and consequently there is no view of the universe as a single undifferentiated strand of collective memory. Instead, each story is positioned against the one before and in relation to song series that others are known to hold. Indeed, during the process of narrating a story, Wilson would often break into song to stress the interconnectedness of one place with another, citing related place names side-by-side in the song text. In treating the two genres as interchangeable, he drew attention to the fact that dhäwu and manikay are based on a continuum of contemporary social action from the mundane to 'miraculous' occurrences which often involve a merger of ancestral actions from the distant past as present events.

By shifting from practical narrative to ancestral story, Wilson would effect a temporal transition from one state of affairs to another, from immediate concerns to emotional attachment and social obligation. By invoking such a 'chronological dimension of narrative',[15] he could create a sense of social order from disconnected experiences. Although the events of Yolngu song took place in the past, they are narrated in the present as if they are presently emergent. These 'landscapes of action and landscapes of consciousness'[16] allow storytellers to bring past events into morally apprehensible contemporary social action and emotion. Landscapes of consciousness thereby activate collective memories in the present, creating a sense of bonding between those who knew and loved the deceased and who will continue to remember them into the future.

A story is, therefore, much more than a series of events to be told; it is a moment of expressive embodiment, the manifestation of personal attachment and past regret. To be located within the story-paths of memory is to be able 'to know, speak, act, invite, deny, share and ask' as individuals and groups come to be situated in a complex of authorial relativities,[17] and where not to sing is tantamount to a declaration of war on one's neighbour, and not to tell is to deny connection—an affront to the relationship, and a rejection to varying degrees of familial ties depending on the age, status and proximity of kin ties to the deceased.

Thus, narratives mediate knowledge of the self as much as knowledge of others, as well as knowledge of the other as self. Their intersubjective construction renders them highly effective as a means of strengthening social control, depending on the degree of narrative cohesion that is understood and accepted. The embodied other is learned as narrative form, where gestures, gaze, facial expressions and other modes of bodily comportment validate and authorise the listening experience. So, just as a knowledgeable storyteller has the authority to cry and narrate, so lack of age and authority can silence those who would dare to ask, or even desire to cry.

THE STORY-PATHS OF SONG

As I have already suggested, the idea of recounting life stories as somehow totalising entities is not part of Yolngu consciousness; instead, key images and events are highlighted in strategically conscious manoeuvres that place the storyteller and listener in a particular relationship to each other. These images and events are logically ordered in song series, though the route may change direction at any time to travel through another clan's country. Thus, there is no absolute beginning, no ultimate point of origin, but rather multiple possible origins that create a mosaic of life sequences.

Sequences of ancestral subjects comprise song-paths (dhukarr) of storytelling that are geographical, mytho-poetical and commemorative. The spiritual sense of 'path' implies the ancestors' ways of coming and going, where dhukarr are the footprints they left behind on their journey; dhukarr is also the way of doing things—it is the path of speech or song that inscribes the memories of people into places.[18] The journeys that singers relate turn places into biographical accounts of genealogical and ancestral actions and creative events.

47

Every journey is hautological in that its features are marked by movements in the environment that are echoed in ancestral and human
ways of being, talking and moving in the world. As two or more
song-paths intersect, so their signification and interpretation become
increasingly complex. Intersections allow singers to compose in ways
that enable them to be located within their own group, whilst also
becoming temporarily enfolded into another. The same principle
occurs in speech when 'calls' communicate and identify both people
and ancestors. For example, when relatives are visiting another country, they must make themselves known to the ancestral custodians of
sacred areas belonging to other kin. Speaking of Yawurryawurrngur,
where the two creator ancestral sisters emerged, a woman of the
Gälpu clan, Yälurr, said: 'The spirits must know you, or else they'll
kill you. In order to have a successful day's hunting you must call out
to the spirits at their areas like our beach area at Nyokamirr on
Galiwin'ku, where they will give you a lot of shellfish.'

Calling out to spirits invokes their essence whilst enabling men,
women and children to mingle spiritually with their environment as
their voices blend with the ancestral identity at that place. In turn,
the identity of the place becomes a corporeal extension of their personhood and part of the larger genealogical map of the clan that
incorporates the presence of members, living and deceased, who
have visited that site. This reconfiguration of people-as-places and
places-as-ancestors in the sea and land can be heard in all ritual
songs.

BIG SONGS, SMALL SONGS

Both men and women's ritual song images cover the entire range of
hunting and gathering techniques and practices, and are replete with
references to the Yolngu life cycle of birth and death through their
embodiment of the ancestral world of spirit beings. In ritual,
women's crying-songs associate the singer with the deceased, whilst
enticing others to experience the power of the ancestral being, as
'representations are believed to be imbued with power and also carry
a heavy affective load, not least because people conceive of themselves as of the Being in their very essence'.[19] Crying-songs are the
only ritual songs for women showing respect for the deceased, and
provide a means of grieving for personal loss. They are performed
spontaneously in the isolation of the bush or privately at home as

well as in a public ritual context, and they form one of Yolngu women's most distinctive contributions to ritual performance.

As there are no formal lessons to learn the art of crying, young women sit close to their mothers and grandmothers during times of mourning, listening to the style and structure of the singing. My sister, Gäwiny, commented: 'Women wail little by little. Some songs are learned from listening, some from tape and some from teaching.' With the introduction of tape recorders and hi-fi equipment, men and women have the chance to recapture the songs of particular occasions and to learn them in more informal contexts. Like young men, girls do not practise crying within earshot of men; they may attempt some crying-songs while out gathering bush fruits or playing in the sand dunes.[20] Young and old women will dance together during rituals, but it is only the senior women who will sing as only they are able to structure the texts correctly. A woman of the Wangurri clan explained: 'Women will pick them up from the men when they sing songs. Only old women will sing, not young girls. Young girls just cry real tears, yaka manikay djama [they don't create songs].'

While women may know all the song subjects in any song series, they are not required to perform them all. Women mainly perform songs of each clan's ancestral beings (yindi wangarr), whose songs are referred to as yindi manikay (big songs). The minor songs surrounding the main ancestral subject are called nyumukuniny manikay (small songs), which complete the song cluster. Women will sing minor subjects to establish the ancestral location and its environment. Each nyumukuniny manikay that precedes or succeeds the song of an ancestral being constitutes a focal point in its own right, though its purpose is to indicate the presence of the ancestral being. In ritual, women will cry one main song subject that links a person with an appropriate seasonal event related to their ancestral identity. Yälurr remarked:

Milkarri [crying] is the other way of telling a story.[21] You don't have to cry to a certain point, like from the land to the sea. You can stop on the land or on the sea. When you feel the wind blowing from any direction you can cry that wind. If women are out collecting shellfish or when they see a fire burning, they will sing gurtha, fire. They think to themselves, 'that's my tribe burning in that area'. At other times when there's fruit coming up, the wild green plums, munydjutj, remind them of their ancestors, as does the roar of the thunder. When they see a turtle, it reminds them of someone who was a good hunter. When the beautiful red sunset comes, they will cry if someone has died, just as when a new moon comes up or if they hit a snake belonging to another person's clan because they feel they have hurt a dear relative.[22]

Women's memories of people-as-ancestors and people-as-places are framed in images composed from a core stock of song names, structured in the appropriate order. They do not sing the movement motifs of birds and animals in the men's driving rhythms, but they share the same core of onomatopoeic names that indicate their movements. They can choose the order and composition of names, freely improvising and combining them on each performance, without the punctuated rhythmic structure.[23] Although the multiple synonyms for song names obscure rather than reveal all the possible connections implicit in calling to mind the identity of particular individuals, they allow those who 'know' to remember in their own personal and intimate way.

The act of singing reformulates absence as presence by bringing into being the presence of those who are absent. Through singing, in other words, absence becomes presence, and the memories of individuals or groups can be added to, and expanded upon, depending on the ability of the singer to perceive natural shapes, colours, sounds and movements from the flow of the land or sea. In this way, as Simon Schama remarks, 'memory . . . forms part of the landscape itself'.[24] The evocation of the deceased comes to be remembered by ancestral association with nature where the singer can allude to affective links with the deceased by implicitly revealing, without directly telling, the most personal details of their affiliation.

A respectful act of remembrance, then, is the ability to express this nexus between a singer's affective knowledge of another person with all their sociopolitical, personal and interpersonal connections, whilst retaining the right to mask particular personal details. The ambiguity of evocative imagery in song names allows for multiple remakings and remembrances of the person as uniquely polyphonic reflections upon the personal connections and experiences that the listeners had with the deceased. If these songs of the environment were not sung, memories would fall prey to instability and loss and, thus, the absence of song would be the absence of memory.[25]

SHARK SENSE AND SHARK KNOWLEDGE

Over the course of sixteen months, Murukun delighted in singing her entire song knowledge for me. She would start at 8 am and often sing through the day until 6 pm. She would determine the song series each day, some days combining a mixture of Dhuwa and Yirritja clan songs,[26] on others concentrating on part of one song series. Instead of working through the entire series, she would often repeat 'song clusters'. I recorded these clusters on numerous occasions to check the meanings and improve my own performance.

Periods of instruction were interrupted when funerals intervened, but these opportunities allowed me to record Murukun in her own ritual contexts and put my learning into practice. As singing occurred most frequently at funerals, I would sit beside her, listening to her construction of the text. The obligation to participate as a sign of love and respect for the deceased was strong. Her singing was both personal and public. One minute we would be sharing an amusing incident as the female mourners waited for men to indicate that they should cry, and the next Murukun would break out into loud sobs, wailing in her deep metallic tones. Murukun would sing for either close or distant relatives and was keenly aware that her brothers and uncles were expecting her to cry because she had a 'clear sound' ('däl rirrakay', a hard noise). As she was a renowned singer 'who knew', other women would also sit near and listen to the song names describing images, such as the tern flying over the sea, and their evocative power would prompt other senior women to join in singing.[27]

While I regularly learned crying-songs from Murukun in the artificial confines of her house, there were many other occasions during which I was to experience crying-songs as an emotional response to life's events. As she would recall those who had died recently or recount the domestic difficulties her daughter was encountering in Darwin, she would burst into sobs of song. These were intensely moving and deeply affecting moments. Other times—major family disputes, the illness of a relative, the birth of a baby,[28] children fighting, or a wrong marriage between teenagers—would result in similar emotional outbursts of song. These outbursts were frequently triggered by the sight of natural phenomena such as the light of a new moon or the sound of a white cockatoo. Once when we were out gathering pandanus to make a mat, I returned to find Murukun crying—the sight of the flowering red kurrajong bush in the undergrowth had reminded her of a baby that had died recently.

Plants, animals and all elements of the natural world were potential catalysts for her emotional responses, evoking memories and sorrow about those who were no longer alive. Thus, the environment could alter her mood from expressions of sorrow to joy and vice versa, but this emotion was always channelled through her crying-songs.

The crying-song of Murukun's own being, personality and clan identity is that of the shark, a major (yindi) ancestral creator whose form and actions carved out the cliffs and the rivers at its sequence of sacred areas in its clan homelands. The song incorporates specific images of the shark habitat and its creative movements in each performance where each verse relates to one aspect of the shark: its body; its creative actions; the colour and quality of the water in which it lies; and its personality traits. When Murukun explained the meanings of the shark song, she began by referring to its creative propensities, locating it at different clan homelands, describing its movements and actions at each place, and listing their names. Inscribed in the imagery of the shark journeying across the land are the ontological properties of the shark such as its angry personality and its potential danger for humans. The song also alludes to the birth of baby sharks, a metaphor for the birth of Djambarrpuyngu clan members, and in the naming of these images there are deeper connotations of marriage and clan links. Murukun noted:

> Mana is for all of us Djambarrpuyngu.[29] It made the creek at Garrata, Gurala and Benyanbi. It tossed its head, called Gululuwänga, Gadulkirri, Wadulnyikpa and Bukuwadawada, making the creek. Its fin, emerging from the water, is called Gudapiny Gara.[30] The shark is called Wadulnyikpa, Gululuwänga, Gadulkirri, Milan, Darrkamawuy. Bul'manydji is the name for the whole shark but there are many names for the body parts.

Names are a key factor in singing with knowledge. Those who 'know' are able to sing deep names that may otherwise be restricted or seldom used in daily conversation. Singers assert and are attributed status and authority within their clan and among other women by demonstrating particular skill at combining a range of names, especially when they include names that are more obscure, or infrequently heard. These names are known as bundurr or 'power' names and all evoke a sense of those deceased and living as both places and ancestors.

In every version of the shark song I heard,[31] Murukun identified core themes that could be divided into three alternating images: A: Creative actions—the form and movements of the shark; B: Muddy water with the shark inside; C: The fin of the shark sticking out of the water, a danger sign, warning Yolngu of the presence of the shark. These three images can be isolated as distinct sections, as Murukun made it clear that names used in the various lines of each section should not be composed randomly throughout the song. She would correct me for singing a shark name adjacent to a name for the muddy water. Although the water turns muddy from the creative actions of the shark, the names for the creator ancestor should be sung together and, similarly, water names should be listed together until these images are firmly established. While the order and number of the names within a song is flexible, each image should be clearly established and then repeated. Only at the end may more than one image be combined as a summarising statement. The song alternates these shark images as follows, A B A : 2A 2B : 3A : C : A B & C. The A:B format is repeated, before segment A introduces idea C. The last two lines combine all three ideas as a final coda.

Mana—Shark song (version 1)

A   Wakalam ngarra marrtji
     (I swim along slowly)

A   Wanthun ngarra marrtji wanthuna
     (I see with my eye as my head turns from side to side)

A   Yindi Garakara Buku-milanbuy
     (The big shark called Garakara Buku-milan)

A   Gululuwäga Gadulkirri Wadulnyikpa
     (These are my names, Gululuwänga Gadulkirri Wadulnyikpa)

B   Bon ngarraku gapu Madjitmadjitthurra
     (My water is called Bon Madjitmadjitthurra)

B   Ngurrnanawänga ngarrany marrtji dhuwal
     (This water covers me as I swim along)

A   Wakala yindi Garakara Djulkamawuy
     (The big shark Garakara Djulkamawuy moves slowly and ponderously)

Yä (humming)

2A   Wängam ngarra marrtji buma ngarra dhuwal
     (I make this place as I go)

2A   Yindi Garakara Nyekuymirri Wadulnyikpa
     Gululuwänga
     (The big shark called Garakara Nyekuymirri
     Wadulnyikpa Gululuwänga)

2A   Nyekuymirri Wadulnyikpa
     (and Nyekuymirri Wadulnyikpa and Gululuwänga [I am
     going to make this place belonging to Gundangur
     Djambarrpuyngu])

2B   Bäy ngayi ngarraku gapu Madjitmadjitthurra
     (For this is my water Madjitjmaditthurra)

2B   Ngurrnanawängan Bonmirringur Djarrarranmirringur
     (The muddy waters also called Bonmirringur and
     Djarrarran)

2B   Murrupumirringu
     (and Murrupu cover me)

3A   Dhiyal ngarra marrtji Guluwu djandimirriyangal
     (I toss my head slowly from side to side as I go)

3A   Garakara yindi Darrkamawuy Milanbuy
     (The big shark, Garakara Darrkamawuy)

C   Ngarrtjam dhu Mamaduku
     (My fin is the sharp spear, Mamaduku)

C   Yalwarryalwarryu
     (Yalwarryalwarr)

A   Wanthun ngarra marrtji yindi Gululuwänga Gadulkirri
     Wadulnyikpa
     (I look from side to side as I go. I am the big shark,
     Gululuwänga Gadulkirri Wadulnyikpa)

B&C Djipthun ngurrnanawanga
     (My fin stands out of the muddy waters)

In this song, the shark's bundurr is Gululuwänga, Gadulkirri Wadulnyikpa, names of the Gundangur subgroup who identify with it and the land to which it belongs. By invoking the names of the shark, Murukun brings the essence of ancestral and human relatives together as one. In addition, a single name can encapsulate a complex of metaphorical ideas about people-as-place. For example,

54

Wanda refers to a Djapu outstation on the mainland but it also means the head of the ancestral shark and is a metaphor for the deepest knowledge of the clan to which only the male elders have access. From yet another perspective, the name inspires images of the semicircular beach area at Wanda.[32] The beach area is the shape of the shark's head where it came to rest, and the area where clan members sit together singing in their sacred shades.[33]

In all her songs, Murukun would position herself in relation to her clan ties to the ancestral song subject,[34] the shark, since her identity is partly derived from the form, shape, size and personality of this main ancestor of the Djambarrpuyngu clan. The seaways song series of the Djambarrpuyngu clan travels through a marine ecosystem that leads up to, and focuses on, the ancestral shark, but the clan comprises six subgroups whose lineages are closely related and who all share rights to perform the shark song. As a senior woman of the Ngurruyurrtjurr Djambarrpuyngu subgroup, whose land is at Djarraya, Murukun is specifically associated with the King Brown snake, Därrpa, but as a member of the Djambarrpuyngu clan she holds rights to sing the shark song that belongs primarily to the closely aligned though geographically distinct Gundangur sub-group, whose land is at Garrata. Shared rights are considered to be socially and politically advantageous and are established through the ancestral narratives of these creatures travelling from place to place, connecting clans, subgroups and their homelands. Ancestral links thus extend each subgroup's rights and obligations to different regions, joining geographically disparate groups in clan decision-making at funerals and other ritual events.

Shortly after I had begun working with Murukun, a tragedy struck the island. A nine-year-old girl playing on 'Mission Beach' got caught in a riptide. Unable to swim and out of her depth, she could not struggle back to shore and drowned. The community was in mourning. Her father, a senior man of the Djambarrpuyngu clan, held the funeral at his house. Songs were performed to carry the child's body to the funeral shade beside the house. Once the coffin was laid under the blue tarpaulin, women started to wail. Murukun sang the song of the shark, recalling her memories of the child and those of her clan who shared the child's identity but who had died previously. By crying, Murukun located the child in relation to the multiple identities of her already deceased relatives. Her song was situated beyond herself and yet within herself, 'constructed both within and without',[35] evoking her grief and enfolding others into it.

The crying-song of the shark for this funeral, as for others, was an intentional act of personal and group remembrance-as-emplacement in the country of the deceased's ancestral origins. Murukun spoke of how she had seen the girl at the school the day before, playing in the yard. She remembered how she had wanted some rrupiya (money) for the shop. As she recounted this sequence of events, she took up her crying-song of the shark at another Djambarrpuyngu homeland. This brief song details the shark and his creative movements at particular homelands:

Mana—Shark song (version 2)

A   Dhuwandja ngarra wan'thun
     (I am tossing my head)

A   Ngarra dhuwal Gululuwänga Gadulkirri
     (I, the shark called Gululuwänga Gadulkirri)

2A   Wänga ngarra marrtji buma
     (I create different places as I travel)

B   Dadalngu Gurrungalngalnydja
     (at Dadal and Gurrungalngal)

B   Benyanbi Wandanyngurnydja
     (Benyanbi and Wanda)

The four place names, Dadalngu, Gurrungalngal, Benyanbi and Wanda, link the two other clans sharing the mythology, Datiwuy and Djapu, to Djambarrpuyngu via the names of their clan lands, Gurrungalngal and Wanda respectively. Multiple names of places and shark body parts conjure up rich images of rivers, coastal swamps and adjacent stringybark forests common to each shark clan. When this song was complete, Murukun changed the song subject and began to cry the names of other creatures that interact directly with the shark, such as the brown pigeon (ngapalawal). This pigeon, found in the trees near the creek where the shark lies, calls out 'gukuk gululululululu' to warn Yolngu that the tide is full in and that it sees the form of the shark. He espies the shark's shadow in the muddy water with its fin appearing ominously from the shallows. In this cry of the bird, Murukun added her own voice of mourning, re-emplacing her memory of the child in the land and evoking sentiments of her own personal loss and grief as well as the absence of other shark clan relatives. Her crying-song was a medium by which she could transcend the 'mystery' of why the accident occurred, whilst simultaneously releasing grief and legitimating her personal relationship to the deceased.

SHARK MEMORY: ME IN THE I OF THE SHARK

As Murukun came to see the child's form in the shape of the shark, in the colours and shadows of the water, and in the contours of the creek in which she lay, her own identity merged with that of the child. In some sense, she was briefly part of the child, where the notion of 'I' collapses into 'me', each becoming 'subsumed in the other as deity'.[36] However, this subsumation is always partial with an interplay between singer and deceased, or between several deceased relatives who share the same identities. Identities ebb and flow even though the shark, like the child, is invisible, the impression of the shadow under the water indicating its sacred site. Visible ancestral forms are often held behind a veil, obscuring but still implying the presence of ancestral essence. Out hunting at other times, when the creek is muddy and the water is fairly calm, Murukun will remember deceased relatives by crying this song, reinvoking their images in the water, whose muddy reflections conjure a stream of consciousness about their lives.

The song technique of recalling the image of the shark ensures a continuity of deceased relatives in the seascape. In the making of her song, Murukun would often make and remake her listeners by inserting careful references to places related to them through the ancestors. Her life story was also theirs, neither a singular event, nor a soliloquy told in isolation for the listener; rather, she sang to enfold the listener into the group though the story, creating them in the making and strengthening their position in her own and their lifeworlds. She could take the listeners with her by evoking nostalgic memories of their homelands by structuring events in a logical topographical sequence. Framed in topographically familiar sentiments, the landscape then comes to embody a sense of loss, loneliness or abandonment for the relatives of the deceased. Places such as these would be avoided for some time immediately after a death, as visiting or even mentioning them evoked for the mourners particular times and circumstances associated with the deceased. Colours of personhood, uniquely constructed and remembered in the minds of the mourners, are thus imposed upon the fragments of place. Only certain memories, concerns and expectations persist as shards of images, creating unique patterns of landscape that come to generate fragments of experience, to be stored and layered as part of the moral fabric of society and the possibilities of experiences past, present and future.[37]

A single song image, then, can hold a multitude of personal and extended meanings where the song names of the shark in its sacred nest at each subgroup's homeland constitute 'place-memories' and reflect a complex relationship between the affiliations of those still living and those of the dead whose identities are embedded in the homeland.[38] These place-memories enable relationships of considerable time-depth to be retraced and the memory of past leaders to be handed down to the next generation. Holding the country is about holding the songs, a duty that requires considerable knowledge of the topography in which place-memories reside and where each song constitutes its own localised grid of remembrance about people and places. Performing place-memories through crying-songs serves to deflect the anguish of personal grief about an individual's death, by engaging others in a process of communal catharsis, which is why the same shark song can be sung for all the members of the same clan on their deaths.

Through the performative skills of memorialisation and remembrance, then, songs structure Aboriginal knowledge and interpretation, whilst allowing a community to mourn. Furthermore, songs and the meanings they evoke enable Yolngu to establish personal affiliations both locally and regionally, strengthening, contesting, recalling and reaffirming existing connections to close family and extended family over a wide geographic area, providing a generational grid of place-memories. Void of the judicial and religious power of song, Yolngu communities would fragment and their ability to exchange, engage with and interact across large distances would cease to operate as a system of respect based on a balance of obligation and reciprocity. The continuity of ritual song prevents a loss of identity and emotional attachment between homelands and clans, as place-memories order the weight of the bond between relatives and their loved ones.

Remembrance is always a ritualised event, seeking temporary closure with regard to the memories of those left behind until the passing of the next kin. The historical present allows singers to mark the passing of relatives as if intimately related to the singer's living world, and as if they can once more be united with their loved ones. For example, the creative actions of the shark may be seen to be finite, generating an illusion of narrative cohesion, but its metaphors of moral action continue in the present. The obligations to pay respect to the deceased and to grieve appropriately are embodied in the death of the shark itself. This process of transposing self onto others renders the boundaries of past and present fluid, as the singer's lifeworld is captivated in the dynamism of the shark in the here and now. The ancestral shark is no longer alive, yet the person-as-shark takes on the creative actions of the shark, whose superhuman action becomes embodied as ancestral consciousness in the mind of the singer.

CRYING TO REMEMBER

Heart-wrenching strains of grief echoed against the back walls of the police station on Galiwin'ku, in March 2000, their melodic contours outlining the familiar song of the shark. Murukun's daughter, an exceptionally gifted linguist and police-aide, sat in the shade with her head bowed, her body shaking in the agony of loss. I, too, had returned to pay my respects, to join her in a lament of love for a brilliant mother and teacher and had brought some of her recordings and a photo album for her daughter. Together we flicked through the pictures of absence, images of Murukun in happy times: making damper at Dharrwar, her shark homeland on Galiwin'ku; dancing to instruct me on these red haematite cliffs; showing me how to make pandanus mats; or out hunting for mangrove worms and witchetty grubs with other women. Our tears of loss turned these pages of history and memory jointly and individually, as the song of the shark and the sounds of Murukun mixed with our tears of remembrance. In Murukun's absence, her voice and her songs continue as place-memories of love, pride, pleasure and privilege through those and for those who were a part of her lifetime. In our melancholy our song-paths of memory were constructed from the inside-out, from our memories of Murukun through the shark song; yet, her identity will not be lost or forgotten, even when subject to temporary absence, since that absence is a presence that comes from within the land and the sea.

As I cried for Murukun, the images of places that were hers flowed easily to mind, heavy-laden with emotion, quite unlike the emotional detachment I had often experienced early on in learning these songs. No longer did I have to try to remember, for my crying carried the pain of remembrance and shaped my memories and the stream of ancestral consciousness that poured from me. Her memory was within me and part of me; the bonds of laughter and learning had become a resting place for my experiences of her and her songs, ready to be released at this final time. This shared time of crying opened myself and her daughter to aspects of our own unre-solved grief and pain about the suddenness of her death. Yet, our singing took us beyond grief to experience a realm in song about ancestors and sea-life, place-memories of safety, assurance and ultimate return that are now a part of Murukun and her abiding heritage. We were each extending into each other's narrative whilst allowing our images of Murukun's ancestral world to extend into us.[39] In my grief, I could at last form her song as an enduring part of myself, as an experience of her relation to me as self and not-self. The song was a passage and rite of reminiscence, but rather than rendering oblivious the pain of loss it contained, it made it real, fashioned it into a tribute and honour and gave her a sense of eternity for as long as her memory abides in me. Memories, then, do not begin with the utterance of song, or end with the completion of it as resonance, as song is not a finite or complete process. It is a moment of utterance, a moment of recognition, a glimpse of invoking things past as a fragment of the present, where memories persist as a sense of eco-place in which the resonances of people-as-ancestors and people-as-places return to the ancestors in song, to be recalled again at the next funeral by crying to remember.

4

The saga of Captain Cook Remembrance and morality

Deborah Bird Rose

Strong stories change the way people think.[1] Hobbles Danaiyarri told that kind of story. In his lifetime he helped shape political, cultural and historical consciousness among Aboriginal people in the Victoria River District of the Northern Territory of Australia. And with the publication of some of his work, he has shifted the consciousness of many more people, even including some of the pastoralists whose way of life was built on his and his people's suffering.

Hobbles Danaiyarri was a deeply philosophical man with an interest in history, race relations and morality. I met him in the Aboriginal settlement of Yarralin in the Northern Territory in 1980 when I went there as a novice anthropologist to conduct field research for a PhD.[2] Hobbles took me in hand, as did a number of well-regarded senior teachers. Almost immediately he started telling me about Captain Cook, injustice and alternatives. Having worked as a stockman for most of his life, he spoke from his own experience of 'Captain Cook's law'. Alongside his station work, Danaiyarri was one of the main bosses for a ceremony line relating to young men's initiation. He travelled from the desert areas of Western Australia through to the desert, river and saltwater country of the Northern Territory. He observed, he assessed, he told stories, and sometimes he exhorted. He was an activist as well as a philosopher, and his activity was aimed primarily at unsettling people's acceptance of unjust structures of relations between 'white' and Aboriginal peoples.

The Captain Cook stories were the vehicle for his analysis of European political economy, as it has affected Aborigines, and the causes and effects of colonialism. The saga represents Captain Cook as the archetype of all early Europeans. As the first, he is credited with initiating and establishing the law that governs relations between Aboriginal people and 'white' people. The saga is not so much about Captain Cook *per se* as it is about colonial relationships. There are two sets of characters: Europeans and Aborigines. Europeans, both Captain Cook and his successors, are represented as invaders, Aborigines as indigenous landowning people. The relationship between them is shown to be unjust and immoral. Europeans initially dominate and attempt to destroy Aboriginal people; later they attempt the domination and destruction of Aboriginal culture. In Yarralin life, Captain Cook sagas are the most succinct summation of this European–Aboriginal relationship of domination and destruction. Almost every instance of European action which appears to fit this relationship is defined as an instance of Captain Cook's law, and the most outstanding actions are incorporated into versions of the saga. In this way the saga of Captain Cook is ongoing because the relationships it describes and analyses are ongoing too.

Danaiyarri dictated this narrative in March 1982. It is the introduction to a full history of the region that he told me in sections during March and April that year. I taped his narratives, and the transcriptions are taken directly from the tapes. The full document constitutes the core of an Aboriginal history of the region. In this introductory section Danaiyarri offers a moral analysis of the structure of domination. Later segments take up events in much greater detail.[3] Danaiyarri was a fluent speaker of Gurindji, Mudbura, Ngarinman, Kriol, and Aboriginal English. He spoke Aboriginal English in order to present the saga to a non-Aboriginal audience; when the saga is recounted for an Aboriginal audience it is usually told in Kriol. I have used English spelling in my transcription. However, since Danaiyarri's English has some Kriol characteristics, the

English spelling may sometimes encourage incorrect interpretations, and so I have included translations in brackets where I think this may assist people who are unfamiliar with Aboriginal English.

THE SAGA OF CAPTAIN COOK

Right. Well, I'm speaking today. I'm named Hobbles Danaiyarri. And I got a bit of troubling. Long way back beginning, I think, right back beginning. When him been start, that Captain Cook, still thinking about to get more land. From London and Big England, that's his country. Lotta man in Big England, and they start there and looking for nother land. And get the sailing boat and get a lotta people and have a look at it: Australia. And when that Captain Cook been come through down to Sydney Harbour, well he's the one been hit the Sydney Harbour. And lotta people, lotta women, lotta children, they're owning that city. That's his country. And he don't askem, that man. Too frightened. He never look whitefellow coming longa his place and start a fight. And he don't askem for land. He don't say 'good day'. No. He say to him, ask him, 'This your country?' 'Yeah, this my country.' 'Ah, yeah!' He didn't askem really. 'Pretty country', Captain Cook reckoned. 'It's a good country. Any more people around here?' 'Yeah, plenty people round here in Sydney Harbour!' That mob still in the bush, looking for a bit of fish and tucker. And lot of food old people getem.

He got a bit of jetty. And putem out those people, takem out them guns, and bullock, and man. And roll up all his swag and a bit of food, everything. Captain Cook been shooting there for, I think, nearly three weeks' time. Shooting all, all the people. Women get shot, kids been get knocked out. That means Captain Cook getting ready for the country, going to try to take it away. But he's the one been start up shooting them there now. Three weeks' time and pack his gear and put it in the sailing boat and keep going right round follow the sea. Every pocket him go in and have a look around on another people. Same thing. Shooting right round like that and every pocket some fellow been running away.

When him got to Darwin, that's the biggest place. Lot of people been there, another people. He's belong to Darwin mob. People been born in this country. Whatever building up in

Darwin now, he belong to Aboriginal. Darwin only been sit down no house, nothing. There the people been havem lotta food again. Lotta fish and lotta tucker. Getembad [get], people been getembad anything, crocodile, anything. Makembad [make] spear. And Captain Cook come up, see that old fellow sit down makembad spear there, hunting fish. And he don't ask him. Same thing. Ask him one bit of a story: 'By Christ, that's good land here. Your country, it's big one? Many people around here?' 'Oh, lotta people round here. We big mob people here', he said. 'Big big mob Aboriginal people. This we country. We never look whitefellow come through here. That's first time you coming. We can be ready for you. Got a big mob spear. We don't want whitefellow!' He start to hear that story. Captain Cook been hear that story. 'Get ready for this, old fellow. We might start here!' [He] Start to put the bullet in the magazine, start to shooting people, same like Sydney. And everything: 'Really beautiful country', Captain Cook reckoned. 'That's why I'm cleaning up people, take it away. And after that I'm going to sailing boat, pack up gear, and gone [keep going, enjoy freedom of movement].' He gone every bit of pocket and leave that sailing boat there and walk around. He might see two or four or six people on that country. Country for that every one of them people. Captain Cook been jealous [envious]. And he clean up and they been come running around.

When him been shooting and going back, straight back. Follow that sea right around again. Right over to Sydney Harbour. Straight back. Captain Cook reckoned, 'I been want to clean that people right up. That's good country. I like to put my building there. I like to put my horses there. I like to put my cattle there. I going to take all my book to make a bit of an office in Sydney Harbour'.

All right. When him been start to building Sydney Harbour, that means he get all the books from London, Big England. Bring a lot of man, coming back again and bring lotta horse and lotta man longa big sailing boat. Loading boat. Bring lotta horse and bring lotta rifle, bullock.

'When that people been settle down, if you can see people little bit cheeky [hostile], you might be hitem them. And if you ready, all right, come up with the horses. Some of them no good, fight for land!' They been fight for land. No good whitefellow come up here, he'll have to reckon with these blackfellows. And some of those whitefellows been get a spear [killed by it]. That's one big country longa Northern Territory. They been get a spear. When that old people come up, gotem horse, and that Captain Cook been sendem over. Sendem over here shooting lotta people. Some couldn't get a man, followem up, and that's why these Aboriginal people make an army. They been shooting all over, people gotem horse. Horse been galloping all over Australia, hunting all those people. Still, people been running away, still. Can't catch up. Horse can't gallop over rough place or them caves. And this country, sandstone country, people been plantem meself [hiding themselves] there.

That's right. We been ready for whitefellows all right. They don't wantem come up whitefellows through here. And they been really, really cranky [angry], my people. They been knock some of them whitefellows now straight away. Hitem with spear, killem. They been fight whitefellow. Blackfellow been fight, and another whitefellow been shot the whole lot. Because they been have a spear, and whitefellow been have a rifle. That been beat him. If whitefellow been come up got no bit of a gun, couldn't been roundem up, killing all the people. They never been give him fair go. I know Captain Cook been little bit wrong for these people. 'This no more blackfellow country. No more. Belong to me fellow [it's our] country', he said. That means, to bring all buildings, houses. They bring all the buildings now. 'I'm going to put my place. Anywhere I can put him.' He start to put this station. Him bring lotta book [law] from Big England right here now. They got that book for Captain Cook from England. And that's his law, book belong Captain Cook, they bring it Sydney Harbour. And lotta government got it in there from Big England.

Gilruth, he's the one been in Darwin, nother government bloke took over from Captain Cook. Lotta man there, man from Big England. Same book he been havem. And that Captain Cook, when them two stations [Darwin and Sydney] been get big enough, that means all belong to Captain Cook.

Right. And my people been start to work around, old people. And really frighten for the white people coming from Big England. They didn't ask. And they been really, really sad, poor buggers. And when that Gilruth, well Gilruth [had] the same book from the Captain Cook. All right. Anybody sick, anybody sick in the guts or in the head, Captain Cook orders: 'Don't give him medicine. Don't give him medicine. When they getting crook [sick] old people, you killem him first. When they on the job, that's right, you can have them on the job. But don't payem him. Let him work for free. While we run that station. Any children come round, you can have the stockman killem him. We'll still hold that people and don't letem go. Any man come sick, boy, anything like that, blind man, don't give him medicine. You take him in a dry gully and knock him [kill him]. And after that, women, women got a bit of a baby, don't let him grow that baby. Just kill that baby. And whatever man been work, people round there eating tucker, tucker with the kerosene, flour with the kerosene [food placed in discarded kerosene tins].'

Start up they been catching him, catch him when him running away. They got a bit of a trick. Captain Cook got a bit of a trick again to catch him. All right. Get all the police station, every way on Wave Hill and all on Timber Creek, Police Hole. That station been move around, circle around. That means policemen been circle around. That's Captain Cook orders to move around a little bit. They got that book all over from Captain Cook: 'You might see him blackfellow anywhere longa this country, you'll have to get them together and if them too wild, and shootem whole lot.'

When that manager now for Wave Hill, he got that same book. Same book from Captain Cook. Whatever book been through belong Sydney Harbour, going back to Darwin, and Darwin book been through all this way. When they getem whole lot people there, they getem in the work. 'Big mob you can getem and putem in a bit of a job. Otherwise, you'll always get trouble. If they stop out that way [remain in the bush], might be somebody, stockman or somebody else, killingem bullock, that means he'll have a lot of trouble.' But still and all, some fellow, people mine, they can't look at him whitefellow. They been frighten. Really. Hard days if you got a trouble. One day he's knocking a bit of bullock, you know, that's causing trouble. You running away from job, you stealing, that's trouble now. Because Captain Cook order: 'You got to clean that people up, right up. And put all my whitefellows on top. This my country. Good people this I bring in one day. They all ready for the Aboriginal people. He's the wild one. No good keep this land. Anyway, you the boss. You askem up in Darwin—Mr Gilruth.'

All right. Askem Mr Gilruth and Gilruth said, 'All right, you just getem in one mob people. Getem together, putem in. But nother thing, no school house, nother thing, no hospital. But they can be work for free. But no money come in. He can't make any wages. He going to work for bread and beef'. That's the Gilruth order. Old Gilruth been tell him: 'Every man, whitefellows you gonna kill these people right up. And you can have, top of that, couple of men, or big mob men, make him bit of prisoner. If you putem on a job, make them prisoner. Make them work for you. All right. Because you can't findem bit of a truck, let them carry on their shoulder. Whatever big house, they can knock a big tree, big post, and cart it [on the shoulder]. All the man can die. No matter. And no pay, just maybe the beef. Whatever dead bullock, him dead longa road, sick one bullock on the road, they'll have it. Every time when that load been coming up from Depot, that's for the people to carry. Whatever they cutting posts right round, make a yard, they cartem on shoulder. If him sick and tired, he don't liftem that thing, kill him right there.' And lotta people been work round, my people. That means we're prisoner. They been have a lotta building. One on Wave Hill, [and one on] Victoria River Downs. Get lotta people up there, Aboriginal.

And still that book never finish. He still belong to Gilruth and Gilruth been have that book from Captain Cook. That's why grow along and building up. And that man, this one Gilruth, said to all the people, Aboriginal: 'This not your land. This mine. This here my building. Here my cattle and horse. This my land.' Really, belong to him [Aboriginal people], it's just for Aboriginal. But that book was go new way, coverem over.

Same book. Not only one book, book all over. And he still got it today. Sort of a, cut at one end [truncated]. But still we got it today. But I think that was finished now for the Captain Cook. And belong to Gilruth. That time been gone. It's finished now. But really, it [the land] belongs to Aboriginal people. Captain Cook and Gilruth, that two fellow been on Darwin, been on Sydney Harbour, all right. I think you two fellow been stealing this country. You, Captain Cook, and Gilruth. They really crook men. Steal it and make it them land. Because why Gilruth didn't ask them what people been live over to Darwin. And Captain Cook went longa Sydney Harbour and people been live over there. And why didn't you ask them? You, Captain Cook, when you come through. When that Captain Cook been bring you bit of a man in Darwin, put your manager, company. Because

I know you Gilruth, in Darwin. He's the manager. I think they been take the wrong book. Steal. Kill my people no reason. You, Captain Cook, and Gilruth, you kill my people. You been look around, see the land now. People been here, really got their own culture. All around Australia. Really Australia, because Aboriginal people with different, different language. Different, different language, lot of people.

And right up to Gurindji now we remember for you two fellow Captain Cook and Gilruth. I know. Why didn't you look after London and Big England? Why didn't you stop your government, Captain Cook? You're the one been bring him out now, all your government from Big England. You been bring that law. My law only one. Your law keep changing. I know you keep changing lotta law. You, Captain Cook, you the one been bringing in new lotta man. Why didn't you give me fair go for my people? Why didn't you give it me fair go? Should have askem about the story. Same thing, I might go on another place, I must askem. I might stay for couple of days. You know. That's for the me fellow Aboriginal people. But you, Captain Cook, I know you been stealing country belong to me fellow. Australia, what we call Australia, that's for Aboriginal people. But him been take it away. You been take that land, you been take the mineral, take the gold, everything. Take it up to this Big England. And make all that thing and make your big Parliament too.

Nother thing. Captain Cook coming back big boss now. Bringing nother lot government belong you. Still you been bring your book, and follow your book, Captain Cook. We know you government. When you been bring it over to Sydney, there people been work it up, government been work it up. You reckon, 'white man's country'. That's the way that Captain Cook and Gilruth been make a lot of fault. Blocked up this country and trying to get this people not to make some money. You know that story belong to Gilruth: 'You can make money for we mob. Whatever stock camp, or contract, or anybody work around there and make some money for we mob. For we mob. Not for him. They can just have their bit of a tucker, flour and sugar. And bit of swag, and he can use his boots and hat. When he gotta start up work he can be use them. He can be use them when he's going stock camp and start up musterem cattle. And he can be brand them and when he's coming back to get pay or something like that, well, he can't get pay. Whitefellow get pay, not black man. They can't get pay.' Because he can't get pay because whitefellow gonna get pay. They gonna get a lotta money from Aboriginal people. That's why this manager up here, Gilruth, tell it to every manager: 'Don't give him the money, don't give him a pay, keep the money for white people. They work for you to make the money.' And that mob there, whatever company owning manager, they been tell that manager and that mob, all my people: 'You can be work just for flour and sugar and bit of matches, bar of soap. That's all.' And crook one bullock, crook one cow, they knockem killer [beef for local consumption]. 'They can be work behind, behind, but don't letem get money. Don't givem wages. Just let them work for you and me.' That's what Gilruth been tell him. 'Work for you and me. We the one own the land', Gilruth said. And that's why, Gilruth been make a bit of a big building over Darwin, from Darwin find lotta air strip and everything.

And we got the story from old people. I know. The government been come up. Captain Cook been come up. Really bad man. They never been give a fair go them people. Well, he's got a big building now up in Darwin, up in Katherine. He started building up now. And my people here, they don't got a building. Nother people and nother people still wondering about for land. But this the one I'm telling you today, to the government: that time for Captain Cook and Gilruth, that was gone. And this is the one that's troubling for the really Aboriginal people. I know. I know Captain Cook been stealem country and bringem out boat people and start to clean my people. And still he been put his law. Still Captain Cook been say for Gilruth. And all round Aboriginal people round that country. Because you, Captain Cook, walk around trying to knock all my people. But givem a fair go for them my people, Aboriginal people. They want to get a land, they can get the land. Because I'm saying, we the one on the land. Sitting on the land, Aboriginal people. You got nothing, all you government. Well, this the land. We might as well get it. For every people, not for you. For we mob. We remember. We thinking. Because we got all the culture. That Dreaming place, important one. You don't know. Because that's why we worry. Not you the boss. Me, Aboriginal people. We want to try to get it, this land. This land, he no got a lease. He's only the freehold. He's the freehold altogether. When that Captain Cook been come in stealing the freehold, people been free, sitting about on land belonging to him. Well, the same thing I want it. It's the freehold all over, people been havem.

We the one boss for the land. Because I know. You been coverem up me gotem big swag [concealing the people and the truth]. Government been coverem up me. Coverem over. That's why he been pinch it away, that land. Because we know you mob now. But anyway, I can tell him. You'll have to agree with us, agree with the people, people on the land. You gonna agree because Aboriginal owning.

THE PROBLEM OF THE IMMORAL LAW

I use the term 'saga' in order to distinguish these narratives from the Dreaming myths.[4] While the form and structure of the narratives is thoroughly in keeping with the form and structure of Dreaming mythology, there is a crucial difference between the two forms of narrative: the saga is set in a time frame that is conceptualised as part of the present (ordinary time), whereas Dreaming myths are set in a time frame conceptualised both as the past and as a concurrent present. The latter are source of moral principles, and moral action is judged by reference to these principles, which are deemed to be permanent rather than subject to change and negotiation. Captain Cook's law, by contrast, is seen as immoral, and this presents Danaiyarri and others with a problem: how to account for immoral action that is reproduced through time and thus appears to endure, just as Dreaming law endures. I contend that Yarralin people's logic requires that the Captain Cook saga be kept in ordinary time—that it not be allowed to become part of the Dreaming past.

For Yarralin people, the concept of law is synonymous with morality: that which is encoded as lawful behaviour is, of necessity, also defined as right or good.[5] Actions that are defined as wrong or bad are not encoded as law. The saga of Captain Cook describes European actions that Yarralin people judge to be based on laws and at the same time immoral. Yarralin people's experience over the last one hundred years has thus presented them with what, in their view, is a critical problem: an immoral law. The saga explores the implications of this problem, examining in detail the injustices instituted under this law, and showing how Europeans have managed to perpetuate this law.

The Captain Cook saga contains many implicit assumptions

70

about Aboriginal moral law. Indeed, one of the main points of the saga is to contrast Aboriginal with European law. Because the saga was developed by and for Aboriginal people, Aboriginal law remains implicit while European law is made explicit. It is not possible to analyse the saga adequately without making explicit some of these basic moral principles. Aboriginal law, as Yarralin people taught me and as they demonstrate in the course of their lives, is complex and far-reaching. Here I present a brief summary of their moral law and moral principles.[6]

The concept of Dreaming asserts the propositions that all parts of the cosmos (animals, humans, sun, etc) are alive; all parts are conscious, that is, capable of knowing and acting; and all parts are related to other parts, either directly or indirectly. I have identified four principles that I believe form the basis of Yarralin people's concept of morality: balance, symmetry, autonomy and response. All these principles relate to an ultimate belief about the meaning of life. Yarralin people see the nurturance of life as the ultimate achievement of the Dreaming and as the moral basis to current life (not merely human life).

The four principles depend on a structure of separate and related parts. One significant base unit, or part, is 'country': bounded geographical units to which people and Dreamings belong and which they own. Countries are connected through Dreaming actions that provide a logic for relationships between countries and groups. Everybody has rights of ownership that include the right to exclude others. The principle of balance indicates that no part shall overcome other parts but rather shall act upon another in such a way as to contain but not destroy it. The related principle of symmetry indicates that, when and if parts of the system oppose each other in a hostile or potentially destructive manner, boundaries must be drawn in such a way that parts (countries, groups) are equal or symmetrical. In Yarralin life hostility among various human parts is frequent, pervasive and unavoidable. Moral actions consist of defining human groups in such a way that the opposing parties to hostilities are symmetrical.

Autonomy, as a moral principle, indicates that no part of the system is subservient to, or dominated by, any other part as an enduring structural principle; there are no inter-group relationships of dominance or subservience. The principle of response prevents autonomy from becoming anarchy by indicating that each part of the system must pay attention and respond to other parts. These principles are manifested most clearly in social life through the process of 'testing'—of seeking to push the limits of autonomy, to elicit a response, to define the limits of the other, to balance force with counterforce. The point of such negotiations is to find and maintain a (forever unstable) balance.

The process of testing and responding, in Yarralin people's thinking, is not intended to destroy. The principle of response asserts that parts of the system must remain interdependent. The principle of symmetry assures that like must oppose like. The principle of autonomy assures that there are no final winners or losers. The only situations in which everybody wins are those situations in which nobody wins.

As I understand Yarralin people's thinking about morality, they are asserting that these moral principles are universal. They recognise different laws, of course. They say, for instance, that Aborigines in saltwater country and in desert country have different laws for young men's initiation (this use of the term law refers to songs, myths, and organisation of labour and events). Yarralin people are quite aware, too, that Europeans have many different laws. But their view of moral principles is that they are universally applicable, universally recognisable, and need no justification.

The saga of Captain Cook is told in implicit dialogue with this system of morality. Captain Cook represents a figure who both develops and acts upon law but whose law has no basis in morality. I must emphasise, however, that while the saga gives ample evidence of a law implemented by ruthlessly immoral people, Yarralin people do not regard Europeans as lacking the ability to make moral judgements. Yarralin people's desire to have their history and the saga presented to a European audience rests precisely on their conviction that Europeans *do* have a moral sense. And, indeed, Captain Cook's law would probably not be formulated as it is in the saga if Yarralin people had not had experience of Europeans who were appalled by, and protested against, the conditions of Aborigines on cattle stations.

Captain Cook's law can be succinctly summarised as the law that might makes right. More specifically, the saga shows it to be a law of domination and destruction. Propelled by his vision of what he wanted to do with the country, Captain Cook denied all previous claims to ownership. In order to make a social reality of this denial he implemented new laws: Aborigines could be killed with impunity, they could be forced to work to establish a European economic base, and they could be denied basic services that were available to Europeans (housing and medicine, for example).

The saga offers a catalogue of injustices inflicted on Aborigines (longer versions providing more comprehensive catalogues) and shows that these injustices were not random but part of systematic processes of invasion and conquest. It is clear from the saga that Aboriginal labour, the land, and the minerals were all used by Europeans to develop their political economy—to 'make themselves strong'. The wealth of the Northern Territory is shown to have been developed by Aborigines, circulated among Europeans and funnelled back to England. It was used to increase the power of England, to enforce laws advantageous to Europeans and to strengthen the ability of the Australian government to extract more land and labour from Aborigines.

According to the saga, what was being built out of Aboriginal labour was 'government'. In Aboriginal cattle-station English the meaning of the term 'government' is not identical to its meaning in standard English. For those of us who were raised and educated in western democracies, the term government has complex connotations of power flowing upward from the people, of being a system whereby the interests of the people are represented, of laws and actions acquiring moral force because they represent the will of the people. Of course, we all know that this ideal is flawed and that to be powerful in the West is to be able to serve the interests of the few at the expense of the many. But regardless of the realities of power, our concepts of government are closely bound up with our concepts of representation.

Yarralin people see government differently. From their point of view, government was, and may still be, something inflicted upon them from outside, which they are powerless either to change or evade. When Captain Cook was building up his government, represented in the saga as buildings and offices, he was building a relationship to Aboriginal people that was based on utter inequity. Europeans could do the most cruel and unjust things to Aboriginal people, and they were powerless to respond. Their only way of evading Captain Cook's law was to escape to areas that were not accessible to Europeans. As the saga makes abundantly clear, however, the entire country was deliberately made dangerous for Aboriginal people. The result was that, having lost their land through violence, Aborigines were forced to work to increase the power of Europeans. The product of their labour was used to perpetuate the conditions of their labour; to reproduce the relations of production, in Marxist terminology. Danaiyarri equates their position in the relations of production with that of prisoners (slaves would be an equally valid term): people deprived of all rights and freedoms, forced to work for others only.

One important point, which is dealt with explicitly, can be seen as the answer to an implicit question—did Captain Cook know what he was doing? That is, was he ignorant, or was he guilty of informed and wilful defiance of moral principles? The answer in the saga is that Captain Cook was not ignorant. He is shown encountering human beings who provide him with all the information he needs to know precisely what he is doing. In his encounters with Aborigines Captain Cook was presented with all the evidence necessary to demonstrate that the people he met were, in fact, owners. He met people living in the country, eating food from the country and demonstrating their superior knowledge of the country through running away and hiding. In Yarralin people's thinking, he could not have failed to realise that he was dealing with people who had an undeniable moral right to be where they were. Nor could he have failed to realise the undeniable fact that he did not have the right to be there. His denial of Aboriginal ownership was, therefore, not the result of ignorance but of a total disregard of fundamental principles. Yarralin people find this aspect of Captain Cook's behaviour extraordinarily puzzling. In the saga it is stated many times, 'he should have asked', meaning that he should have asked permission to be there. When I asked Yarralin people what would have happened if Captain Cook had asked properly, I was told that either he would have been denied permission and therefore would have gone away, or he would have been allowed to stay but only on terms decided by the owners of country.

While Yarralin people recognise the existence of different languages and cultures, they also expect all humans to recognise and act on the same fundamental principles, to act in general with respect for life and country, to be involved in maintaining the world as a life-giving system. Yarralin people recognise individual aberrations from these expectations; madness, cruelty and hyper-aggression are not confined to Europeans. What they do not expect is that aberrations will form the basis of law.

I have suggested that Yarralin people's morality derives from four major principles. While these are not explicit in the saga, Captain Cook's defiance of them is quite overtly stated. The principle of balance indicates that no 'part' (person, group, species) must destroy any other part. In killing Aborigines, taking their country, denying their rights of ownership, and making himself strong through forcible acquisition of Aboriginal land and labour, Captain Cook clearly demonstrated himself to be in defiance of the principle of balance.

The principle of symmetry indicates that where there is hostility, or opposing views, like must oppose like. Captain Cook's disregard for this principle is seen most clearly in the inequitable confrontation of technologies: 'that [rifle] been beat him. If whitefellow been come up got no bit of a gun, couldn't been roundem up, killing all the people. They never give him fair go.' In other versions of the saga it is suggested that Captain Cook should either have given the Aborigines rifles or put aside his own rifles and faced his opponents with spears. That is, if he was determined to fight, he should at least have ensured a fair fight.

In similar fashion, Captain Cook is shown to violate the principle of autonomy. This principle indicates that each 'part' (group, country, species) is its own 'boss'; that there are no inter-group relationships of dominance or subservience. Captain Cook's law, of course, states that Europeans are bosses for Aborigines ('put the whitefellows on top'), that Aborigines do not have equal rights or autonomy.

The principle of response indicates that any part may test itself by pressing against other parts, and that other parts have both the right and the obligation to respond. In the saga, Aborigines respond to Captain Cook in a moral fashion; they state and demonstrate their ownership of the country and fight to protect their autonomy. Captain Cook's invasion depends on obviating any possibility of response that would lead to balance. Rather, Aborigines became virtually powerless to respond.

Captain Cook's law is thus shown to operate in defiance of moral principles. The saga highlights the difficulties Yarralin people have had in trying to understand the workings of this immoral law. It is stated, for example, that Captain Cook killed people in order to steal the country and to replace the original law of ownership with his own law. At the same time, the saga asserts that Captain Cook killed people 'for no reason'. I think these contradictory assertions must be read as indicating that Captain Cook had no moral reason for killing people.

Yarralin people have lived under this law for many years, but they are still at a loss to really understand how it can be. It is not that they are unacquainted with cruelty, greed, jealousy and violence in their own culture. But, in their view, these aspects of human life do not form the basis of law. According to their logic, Captain Cook's law must be a different *kind* of law. Primarily, the difference between Dreaming law and Captain Cook's law is stated as a difference in time. Dreaming law originated in Dreaming time and is conceptualised as unchanging; Captain Cook's law is specifically set in ordinary time, defined in part by the conceptualisation that that law is always changing. As Danaiyarri states, 'my law only one. Your law keep changing'. It is also stated that Captain Cook's law has been truncated ('cut, at one end'), and it is predicted that it will be terminated ('that time for Captain Cook and Gilruth, that was gone'). Thus, while the saga makes it clear that Captain Cook's law is not an individual aberration, it is posited as a historical aberration. It is not a moral principle, but a moral disaster.

Dreaming law is thought to exist because of the responsible actions of all parts of the cosmos. In contrast, Captain Cook's law is thought to exist because of a massive series of lies. One of the basic points of the saga is that the immoral law could only be perpetuated through extreme control of the people who constituted the living proof of its immorality—his law had to be enforced through physical strength because it could not be enforced through moral strength. The analysis of conquest rests on the assumption that at least some Europeans make moral judgements that are similar to those made by Aborigines. It appears to be assumed, for instance, that killing babies will be recognised as an immoral act without any need to make explicit precisely why this is so. The catalogue of injustices can be read as a list of wrongs that do not need further explanation. The saga goes beyond a mere list of injustices, however, applying moral principles to Captain Cook's law and showing its fundamental immorality.

The saga asserts that there was a concerted attempt to conceal the true facts of the law ('coverem up me gotem big swag'). The implication of this assertion is that Captain Cook's law does not have a moral basis among *Europeans* and that in order for it to persist it has to misrepresented. Therefore, it is up to Aboriginal people, who know the truth about Captain Cook's law, to tell Europeans what it is really all about. By naming the oppressors and analysing the oppression, Aborigines demonstrate that Captain Cook has not succeeded in establishing his 'book' as the single expression of either law or memory. Although Aboriginal people are partially concealed by the power of European society, and are often ignored and despised, they continue to be the people who know. They know the principles of morality, the true relationships of conquest and oppression, the true basis of the strength of European society.

This particular narrative concludes with a statement about the power of remembrance. The knowledge that Captain Cook's law tried so hard to destroy is neither dead nor forgotten. The true owners of country are not dead, nor have they forgotten moral principles. Captain Cook's law has not succeeded in concealing moral principles, nor has it succeeded in concealing its own true nature. Remembrance is asserted as a primary contemporary engagement with injustice ('we remember for you two fellow Captain Cook and Gilruth. I know'). This is an engagement that refuses to submit.

The goal for the future, in Yarralin people's thinking, is a moral Australia. This means either that Europeans will all have to leave, or that they will have to abandon Captain Cook's law in favour of moral law. Almost all of the Aboriginal people I know regard the first option as both impractical and not highly desirable. The second option, that of the creation of a moral Australia, is the one most frequently (almost unanimously) put forward in this region. Danaiyarri states that prior to Captain Cook all the land was freehold. He uses this term to mean that it was both owned and inalienable. People, too, were free at that time. They were autonomous in their own country, in the sense that no country, or group, was able to dominate others. The call for land is a call for autonomy of landowning groups, and thus for a restructuring of political and economic relationships.

In another version of the saga, Danaiyarri states:

Right. Now we can, we can have a friend, friend together now. I'm speaking about now. We can come together, join in, make it more better out of that big trouble. You know, before, Captain Cook been making a lot of cruel, you know. Now these day, these day, we'll be friendly, we'll be love meself [one another], we'll be mates. That be better. Better for make that trouble.

Aboriginal people in the Victoria River District do not expect to re-establish moral law through immoral means. The goal is not to destroy European Australia. Rather, it is to bring it back to moral principles. Yarralin people expect this to be accomplished through moral persuasion. They believe (in the face of regular evidence to the contrary) that, once Europeans know and understand Aboriginal morality and realise the potentially disastrous consequences of their own immorality, they will voluntarily try to make things right. Their own logic gives Yarralin people few options. Their morality is directed toward life, towards the maintenance of living systems. This is a large part of what is meant by still having culture: to continue to recognise, and act on, principles of morality.

For Yarralin people it is inconceivable that the current state of affairs, their oppression under Captain Cook's law, will continue indefinitely. It is not just that they do not want it to; it is that it cannot. In defying moral principles, Captain Cook's law defies the ultimate goal of maintaining life-giving systems. In Yarralin logic, such defiance cannot have a long-term future. The saga is not millenarian; it does not predict the necessary end of the world, nor does it predict a radical transformation of the world. It does not aim to transform human nature, to eliminate violence, greed and self-interest. Rather, the saga seeks to re-establish the recognition and implementation of moral principles, to reinstate freedom and autonomy for all Australians through what might be called a multicultural system of autonomous and interrelated parts.

CONCLUSION

The Captain Cook saga is history, moral philosophy and political economy, as well as an engagement with the conditions of life under a law of severe domination. It describes and analyses the establishment and implementation of this law. The saga defines the temporal limit of this immoral law (ordinary time) and asserts that the law must come to an end. Finally, the saga issues a warning: destruction comes from this immoral law, and the law must be changed. The saga enjoins European society to recognise and act upon moral law. Such a recognition would, of course, substantially benefit Aboriginal people, resulting, at the least, in a fuller recognition of their rights to land.

For Yarralin people, the saga is a vehicle of remembrance; it is one of a number of ways in which Captain Cook's law continues to be recognised as a law of oppression. Remembrance embodies the principle of response. It is thus articulated as a form of action that engages with injustice. Or, as the sociologist John O'Neill puts it,

'Remembrance is the bodily infrastructure of political knowledge and action. It holds injustice to account and sustains the utopian hope that underlies the will to freedom and equality'.[7] The many recent shifts in Australian society and culture have confirmed that, far from being the consolation of the powerless, remembrance is an active force for social change.

5

Encounters across time
The makings of an
unanticipated trilogy

Judith Binney

It was an invitation to speak about my 'trilogy' of books in July 1997 that first jolted my personal memories into an articulated form, for while the three works in question were born one from the other, they were neither planned nor constructed with such a purpose in mind. The 'unanticipated trilogy' grew from a series of personal dialogues over time, and from the discovery that family oral stories may provide crucial keys to unlock histories that have been previously unacknowledged in the public arena. The three books are very different in their formats, but they all arose from talking with Maori elders about their 'recent' past—fragments of their collective colonial experience.

The first book, *Mihaia* (Messiah), published in 1979, is a co-authored study of the Tuhoe prophet leader, Rua Kenana. It was constructed around early photographs, whose existence had been previously unknown to most Tuhoe (and indeed to most people). The second book, also co-authored, is *Ngā Mōrehu: The Survivors*; published in 1986, it narrates the histories of eight Maori women, largely in their own words. *Redemption Songs: A Life of Te Kooti Arikirangi Te Turuki,* published in 1995, is a study of the prophet and fighter who stands confronting them all—in historical time, and in their imaginations.[1]

I was first invited to speak about the three books at a conference entitled 'Lives, Stories, Narratives', held at Monash University in Melbourne; now I have been asked to turn this address into written prose.[2] In so doing, I have largely retained the informality and personal viewpoint of the spoken form, because I am tracing a personal voyage of some eighteen years. The first book was launched in 1979, at the tiny marae (community space and meeting house) at Tuapo (Matahi), where Rua is buried; the last biography was launched in October 1995, at the equally small marae at Te Wainui in the eastern Bay of Plenty. This book, republished simultaneously in Australia and Hawai'i two years later, has now launched itself on an unknown journey in foreign lands.[3]

In New Zealand there has been extensive debate about the writing of Maori history, just as there has been about Aboriginal history in Australia. What might sometimes appear to be prescriptive demands—that indigenous history 'belongs' to the voices of its own people—reflects the ways in which the written histories have been mediated and narrated. Above all, this argument indicates the failure of published history (at least until recently) to enter into other ways of seeing, and the failure to respect the integrity, and the purposes, of oral accounts, which carry but also shape memory in indigenous societies. The three books have been part of this debate in New Zealand, and have been influenced by and constructed within this debate.[4]

Maori hostility to being studied—that is, as an object of European intellectual inquiry—had already modified the practice of anthropology in New Zealand even as the discipline was being developed. When academic writers took over the *Journal of the Polynesian Society*, which had been published since 1892, the articles that once were contributed by Maori dwindled, and from the 1930s the *Journal* visibly alienated that audience. The strength of Maori feeling about the independence of their culture earned it at least a grudging respect; when the discipline became professional in New Zealand during the 1950s and 1960s, anthropologists almost invariably went 'off-shore' to the Pacific to locate their indigenous communities. For their part, historians, locked into documentary research, tended to assume there would be little historical knowledge left to recover orally from Maori which would not be unreliable, or unable to be verified from written sources. As the use of te reo, the language, shrank in both the Maori and Pakeha worlds, fewer and fewer people could read the large number of Maori documents which had been archived; at the same time Maori, when they had a choice, tended to withhold material from public deposit, seeing nineteenth-century written documents as belonging to their tipuna (ancestors) and sometimes, therefore, burying them with the dead, or entrusting the manuscripts only to their descendants. Such manuscripts were being treated (and often still are) as tapu (protected or sacrosanct) material.

By the early 1970s, although it still seemed possible for European-trained historians to look at Maori and European relations, and also to practise what was then called 'culture-contact' history, largely using European sources and thus writing history 'under western eyes', it was viewed as not only difficult but also probably unwise to try to reconstruct Maori history, which included the post-1800 Maori past. The view that this multi-layered, indigenous history belonged to the voices of their own people was widespread, spurred on by the failure of much written history to present historical explanations which were satisfying to Maori readers. Written history was failing because the general writings had not acknowledged that there existed different ways of seeing, depicting and transmitting crucial events. Conversely, while written tribal histories existed (at least for some regions), they in turn failed to engage in any discourse that translated beyond localism and particularism.

New Zealand's history was mostly penned without a Maori audience, and it neglected most orally composed sources—the narratives and the songs, the living korero (talk). Yet oral transmission of knowledge shapes memory and, therefore, history. Oral history in turn becomes communal memory. The methodological structurings for oral knowledge are still strongly retained in those societies, which, like Maori, became literate with colonisation. Because the marae remains the centre of most Maori activities, orality survives. The endurance, and then the vast revitalisation of marae over the last 25 years, quite simply ensured the survival of Maori conceptu-alisations—Maori ways of doing things, remembering things and depicting things. But academic history largely shut out these local, autonomous and varied knowledge systems, seeing them as mainly problematic. Given these contested issues, I think you will believe me when I say that the trilogy was 'unanticipated'.

It all began with a box of photographs. There were two remarkable bundles, one dating from 1908 and the other from 1916, and both collections had been partly published in a popular magazine of the time, the *Auckland Weekly News*. The photographs depicted the Tuhoe prophet leader, Rua Kenana, and the community that he founded in 1907 at Maungapohatu in the Urewera, the mountainous heart of the North Island. This settlement was assaulted in April 1916 by armed police, and when I say 'assaulted' I am using the legal judgment from Rua's subsequent Supreme Court trial. In March 1916, the police commander had tipped off an Auckland newspaper, the *New Zealand Herald*, to expect a colonialist triumph over a 'dissident' Maori leader, hence the surprising presence of a press photographer. The assault left two young Maori men dead, one of them Rua's son, Toko, shot by the police. Toko's death remains unsatisfactorily explained in the police testimonies; instead, there is clear evidence of a litany of orchestrated voices as the police officers protected themselves against possible criminal charges. This armed expedition left a permanent legacy of distrust among Tuhoe, which still surfaces. In 1998, a demand for an apology from the police was again articulated: representatives of the surviving family have asked for a police 'acknowledgement' that Rua's 'gunpoint arrest' was wrongful, and that Toko's death and (a recent assertion) the rape of Rua's eldest daughter were criminal acts.[5] The extent of the long-standing legacy of distrust is perhaps best indicated by Tuhoe's stated belief (in the 1970s) that the force was made up not of the police but of their wartime substitutes—criminals.

Many people are recorded in these photographs, and all were labelled casually as 'Rua's followers'. There was no way of knowing who anyone was, except by taking the photographs 'home'. Thus, in 1977, I set out diffidently with photographer Gillian Chaplin in search of the people behind the images. We expected to do no more than ask if anyone could identify the elders. Instead, we found that the photographs unlocked memory. They brought forth so many associations, of both pain and pleasure, that our encounters with Rua's people became a transforming experience. The photographs conveyed a past which had not died in either individual or collective memory. They became the means by which a people's history was recovered, together with their understanding of it.

Some of the people with whom we talked were not literate. But the photographs they could read, and they read them with an attention to detail that revealed their precise and personal knowledge. Few of them had seen any of the photographs before. Taking the photographs to them was as if we were bringing the tipuna to visit.

Some of the oldest people talked directly to the photographs. Materoa (Harimate) Roberts, who was brought up by Rua's first wife, Pinepine Te Rika, sang a tangi (lament) to the photograph of Pinepine, and then she spoke to her: 'Hello Mum!' Materoa turned to us. She said how she had always narrated her dreams to Pinepine, and she talked to us, and to her:

> 'Look, Mum, I dreaming I've been picking up charcoal for my kai. E kai haere ana au i te ngārehu [I am eating charcoal]' . . . And she says, 'Why girl, why?' And I say to her, 'Everything you say to us is come, right now. The people is start selling Maungapōhatu'.[6]

Some of the photographs carried painful associations. The group photograph taken of Rua's arrest was crumpled and stained with tears, and we had to reprint it several times. It recalled for everyone 'the War', and they meant the police assault and three-day occupation of Maungapohatu, not World War I. Bringing back this photograph

The arrest of Rua, 2 April 1916. Rua is fourth from left, his tie twisted. His eldest son, Whatu, stands next to him. His second son, Toko, had been shot by the police. (Photograph by A.N. Breckon, C.C. Webb Collection, Alexander Turnbull Library, Wellington)

spurred people to discuss their knowledge with us—outsiders. We had provided the opportunity for the people of Maungapohatu to reopen their history. And they told it, using us as a vehicle, to reach their mokopuna (grandchildren), most of whom were, in the late 1970s, living in the cities.

We also found that the photographs offered a means of testing written sources, and our informants. For example, the police stated that the women of Maungapohatu had never been held prisoner, despite the women's testimony in court. One photograph, which had never been published but which came from one of several private collections that we subsequently located, showed the women of the community seated together on the ground guarded by two armed police. The long shadows indicated that several hours had passed since the morning's shooting. Our informants were able to identify most of the women. In explaining who they were, or suggesting who they might be, they often explained their own relationship to them. By consulting widely from family to family we came to know

The women under police guard, 2 April 1916. One of the police has a drawn revolver in his right hand. (Photograph by A.N. Breckon, John B. Turner private collection, Auckland)

Te Akakura Rua (left), with her sister Putiputi, on the verandah of their father's derelict house at Maai, near Maungapohatu, January 1978. (Photograph by Gillian Chaplin, collection of the author)

the networks of relationships and who were the more accurate informants. We came to know many histories, which had previously been private.

One of our most important visits was the occasion in January 1978 when Gillian Chaplin and I returned to Maungapohatu with two of Rua's daughters, Te Akakura and Putiputi. The experience was profound for both women, and their very different responses to visiting their father's derelict home is captured in Gillian's photograph. Te Akakura, who had lived in Auckland since the late 1940s, was the elder daughter of Rua and his pre-eminent wife, whose name she bore. Her pride and her powerful personality can be seen; as her father had told her, 'You are of your blood'.[7] Puti was the daughter of Rua's second wife, Rehe, a quiet woman who for many years ran a little shop selling sweets and tobacco at Maungapohatu. Puti's visible sadness reflects her recollections of the many years she lived at her father's home, first as a child and then as a young married woman (unlike her sister). The photograph taken that day of the two sisters was seminal for us, for it came to stand not only for our great debt to Rua's children, but also for our growing awareness that private histories may reveal a larger history. This photograph was one of the seedbeds for the second book, *Ngā Mōrehu*.

If *Mihaia* was about the recovery of a history, *Ngā Mōrehu* was about the construction of history. It contains the life stories of eight women whose lives interconnect, and are partly shaped by the Ringatu faith, which was founded by Te Kooti Arikirangi. Rua had extended Te Kooti's teachings and had, thereby, created a schism within the faith. The use of photographs in this book was different, for many were private photographs belonging to the women. The photographs did not unlock memory; they were a part of their living memory. Further, *Ngā Mōrehu* retained the structure of orality. It told the independent stories of the individual narrators as they chose to construct the narratives. We did not try to incorporate their accounts into a history whose themes we had identified and organised; rather, we maintained the integrity of each story, largely as it was told. Each woman gave her history and that of her family, establishing thereby their connections with Rua—or the prophet who stood directly before him, Te Kooti. Of the eight women in the book, two are daughters of Rua, one is his daughter-in-law, and one is Te Kooti's great-granddaughter.

This book had, in fact, originated as a quest for Te Kooti. Talking with the women, and most particularly with Te Akakura, we began to wonder if we could attempt to demonstrate the ways in which the lives of contemporary individuals and their whanau (extended families) flowed, like the fan of a great river delta, from the history of the two prophet leaders and their teachings, yet also retain the distinctive experiences of the individuals.

We were sent by Tuhoe to Te Kooti's family. This meant a journey into a different tribal district—another area of mana (authority) and a different set of experiences. Te Kooti belongs to Rongowhakaata, from Poverty Bay, on the east coast of the North Island, an area that is tribally quite distinct from the Urewera. Journeying here, we became ever more aware of the importance of whanau, the family and the reciprocal obligations deriving from its embrace, which is primary for Maori. Seeking ancestral history inevitably means tracing family history, as it is understood that only the family, the lineal descendants, may properly tell their ancestral history. And thus we learnt, too, that whakapapa (genealogies) not only structure and link families, they activate political decisions and explain decisions, and are utilised strategically—although not always in a predictable manner.

We first met Te Kooti's great-granddaughter, Hei Ariki (Tihei) Algie, whose mother was the child of Te Kooti's only known son,

Wetini, in 1982. From Tihei we learnt, unexpectedly, that she had only discovered her relationship to the prophet as a schoolgirl, at about the age of fourteen:

> I didn't know anything about Te Kooti. I used to hear how he was a rebel and all that, and I didn't think I was connected with him ... But then we were asked to write about Te Kooti at school. I was in Standard Six. And I didn't *know* ... I went home and talked about it, and was told to forget it. 'Don't worry about it! It is over! Finished!'. I went back and told my parents that my headmaster was threatening to strap me—because I didn't know anything about Te Kooti. I asked them—*then*. My mother said, 'Oh well, it is too late now'. And she started telling me who we were, who he was. My grandfather was there, and she said, 'That is his son, sitting over there'.[8]

Tihei's suppressed family history was not simply the product of the settler, small-town environment of Gisborne, where Te Kooti had been born and which had collectively interpreted him as a rebel and 'murderer' of innocents. It was also the product of her own family history. This history was as much political as it was personal. Wetini had been taken from his father as a small boy in 1868, and brought up by one of his father's leading tribal enemies, Te Mokena Kohere, who was a senior chief of Ngati Porou and tuakana (elder male relation) to Te Kooti. The Ngati Porou chiefs had mostly chosen to ally with the government, although they were fighting for their own, autonomous reasons—primarily to protect their land from government confiscation. They hunted Te Kooti without mercy in the last phases of the wars, from 1868 to 1872. Then, in 1883, Wetini married one of his father's former wives, Oriwia Nihipora of Ngati Kohatu from inland Wairoa; Oriwia's previous marriage to Te Kooti had been arranged by her kin, and she had stayed with Te Kooti throughout the wars and for ten long years of exile afterwards. Tihei's family descends from Wetini's marriage with Oriwia: both blood and betrayal link her back to Te Kooti. When we enter into dialogues such as these, all stereotyping—Maori and Pakeha—and all historical assumptions explode. The alienation of Wetini was a weapon in a protracted civil war among East Coast Maori, and his adoptive family was, and is, one of the most senior families on the Coast.

We were sent from family to family. Only the families knew who it was that we should see. Just as we were sent to Tihei, we were sent to Te Aomuhurangi Te Maaka Delamere-Jones. Te Maaka was one of the very few women tohunga (religious leaders) in the Ringatu faith, and a daughter of the former Poutikanga (Sustaining Pillar) of the Haahi Ringatu (Ringatu Church). It was from the women that we first learnt the crucial stories, the family narratives, which connected their whanau, through their immediate elders, to Te Kooti.

It was from Heni Brown, another of the women in *Ngā Mōrehu*, that we first learnt of her great-grandmother, Meri Puru, who, with her father, was sent to Chatham Island (Wharekauri) as a prisoner in 1866. Meri became a tapu woman because of her lengthy association with Te Kooti; when she was buried, in 1944, she was placed face down, her long black hair crossed across her back, in precisely the same manner as Tuhoe's ancient daughter and taniwha (water-guardian), Haumapuhia, lies in the waters of Waikaremoana with her long flowing hair rippling the lake. Meri Puru was buried thus so that her mana—her authority and power—flowed into the earth and did not disturb the living. Yet all the anthropological literature insisted that women were not tapu.

The thread which linked the women in *Ngā Mōrehu*, was Te Kooti's teachings, although not all are of the Ringatu faith. As the oldest of the living Maori scriptural faiths, its teachings are concerned with the recovery of Maori autonomy. The Ringatu faith was born in 1866–68, the period of its creator's imprisonment on Chatham Island when he was deported without trial as a 'spy', but Te Kooti elaborated it in later times of peace, when Maori were seeking to recover control over the growing web of land laws, in which all Maori families found themselves entrapped. This faith, founded in the scriptural promises to Moses and the exiled children of Israel with whom the people identified, developed pleromatic ways of reading history: that is, their narratives are told in a manner which seeks the fulfilment of earlier sayings or predictions. The faith also took hope from the New Testament promises, which they interpreted for their own generations, while history itself was narrated (and understood) in ways which sought to find 'transhistorical' meanings for human events.

In 1986, the histories told by the eight women provoked feminist as well as Maori autonomist comment. One publicly voiced criticism of the book seemed (to me) pedantic—that, as Gillian and I were not the authors, whilst the women were, our names should not have appeared on the title page. The criticism failed to recognise the dialogic nature of the narratives. People who knew the women individually, however, commented that they could hear the cadences of their voices as they read their stories, and this particularly delighted me since the spoken voice does not easily translate onto the written page. By choosing to tell their narratives, the women all hoped that younger people, and particularly Maori, would benefit. Their narratives transcended the personal, and the women knew this as they spoke. They were telling communal and political histories through the stories of their lives.

I placed their narratives within a kete (basket), an introduction, which contextualised them, historically and regionally. There was an underpinning of notes—some dates and references to the larger historical issues that the personal narratives touched upon, ranging from the illegal exile of the prisoners to Chatham Island in 1866, to the payment of family benefits in the 1970s. This method explored memory without interfering with it. Elisions of memory occurred, but I found I had no reason to question the sequences of events, the selection of what was important to the women and the observations they made, although their notions of causality were often very different from my own. Memory is now sometimes depicted, historiographically, as a minefield, littered with silences and unexploded secrets. But the women's stories were richer by far than the scanty written sources, and the narratives were supported, not undercut, by complementary archival material—including the potentially 'dangerous' ones, such as school records and birth, marriage and death registers. At the end of the project there was no doubt in my mind that the narratives had illuminated a world that could not be recovered any other way.

Ngā Mōrehu grew sideways from my original intention—to write a history of Te Kooti. Indeed, for a while it replaced it. We came to see that oral history concerning the more remote past (the mid- and late nineteenth century), rather than that of people's living experiences, is much more difficult to recover. In the dialogues with the women we obtained insights about their own lives in their own communities, and as Maori women; but the narratives they told about Te Kooti were of a different quality or kind. First, they were more structured. They belonged to their communities, as well as to particular families, and they were mostly myth-narratives, or what are sometimes called 'chronicles of the impossible'. They are the kind of myth-histories which have proved fertile for the novelist Gabriel García Márquez, who draws on the continuing oral world of the northern Andes of Colombia. Orality there has generated contemporary guardian figures from seventeenth-century ancestors such as Juan Tama de Estrella of Páez, who, like Maori taniwha, lives in water and re-appears in political crises like La Violencia in the 1950s.[9] In the regional stories in Aotearoa, Te Kooti appears as the magical protector of a number of tribal groups and their land, as he rides his great white horse, which is sometimes called Pokaiwhenua (Travel Across the Land) and at other times Te Ia (The Crest of the Wave).[10] As we were told these stories, they seemed to be portions of a system of knowledge or autonomous memory worlds. They were local stories, varied and similar at the same time. They contained 'miraculous' content, and thereby cut through the restrictions imposed upon the narrators' own lives by entangling laws and bureaucratic structures of authority. They were, essentially, stories of freedom; and they are still being told (and reworked) as I write in 1998. In the late 1970s and early 1980s, when I was first hearing these stories, there was by then no-one alive who had known Te Kooti personally. I was, moreover, being told about a man who was, in essence, elusive in his own lifetime. After his escape from Chatham Island, he was never captured in war, and his body was hidden and contested from the moment of his death in 1893. He is quintessentially the stuff of which myth-narratives are born.

As recently as seven years ago, I was still uncertain whether the third book, Te Kooti's life, could or indeed should be written. Some certainly said that it should not because Te Kooti is considered to be more than mortal by some sections of the Ringatu. There were also several claimants to owning his history. Te Kooti had been sheltered by a number of tribes when he was in permanent exile during and after the wars of the mid nineteenth century. In addition, there are several distinct branches of the Ringatu faith today. All these claims added to the volatility of this history within the Maori world.

But the book just grew. It grew out of listening to the 'other' discourse—the families' oral narratives. It grew by a kind of inevitability. If there was one single occasion to which I could attribute its origin, it was the day, back in 1978, when I was sitting in the sun on Rua's marae at Matahi—a most appropriate name, as it turned out, for it means 'to open your eyes wide' (there, to the beauty of the place)—and talking with Mau Rua, Rua's son. Mau narrated a story of Te Kooti's gun—how Te Kooti, the warrior in all written literature, turned the barrel down to the ground, prophesying: 'War won't reach New Zealand. It is a holy land.'[11] Soon, Ned Brown (Heni's husband) was to tell the same story, but located in his tribal region. In Ned's version it was a sword, and Te Kooti plunged it into the ground, saying: 'There'll be no more wars by the Maori people with the Europeans; the last will be with me. This is a promise from God to us.'[12]

These narratives told of a man of peace who was unknown in the European histories. I became aware, too, of the recurrence of crucial stories. In this clustering, Te Kooti is seen as laying down the path of lasting peace, te maungarongo. Te Maungarongo was one of the names which Rua's followers later took for themselves. The oral narrative explained why, for they were Te Kooti's successors in time and heritage. Their commitment to peace explained, in turn, Tuhoe's refusal to volunteer in World War I; that refusal, in part, underlay the mounting of the armed police expedition to Maungapohatu. But this was a history, and an explanation of history, which was unknown outside these particular regions of the Maori world.

In October 1995, the biography of Te Kooti was launched in a whakamanawa (blessing) ceremony at Te Wainui, the marae that belongs to the Haahi Ringatu. I took the book back to Boy Biddle, the 81-year-old secretary of the church, and a gathering of elders whom he had summoned. Te Maaka's sister, Ema, was present, as daughter of the former Poutikanga. The occasion was intended, on my part, as a mark of recognition for the source of the knowledge with which I had been entrusted. The hau, the spirit within the gift and the generative force of life, was being returned to its home. It was a statement of the ties that bind—the fact that the book owes its existence to the support of certain crucial elders and two men in particular. They are the late Sir Monita Delamere, son of the former Poutikanga, and Boy Biddle, who died in 1996. In the early 1980s, both men had given me access to papers belonging to their fathers. In so doing they had, independently, taken a decision that it was now appropriate to talk about the 'founder' (as they call Te Kooti) in his historical context. But, in turn, it was equally important, as Reuben Riki, the former assistant secretary to the Poverty Bay branch of the faith, had stressed, that the sharing of his knowledge had to have purpose for him and for his 'next of kin to come'.[13] That was the responsibility which grew with the book.

The narratives, records and explanations in the private Maori manuscript books were different to the European sources concerning the same events. First, I entered the world of song. Te Kooti composed (or adapted) over 90 songs for particular occasions, and he had the song texts written down by one of his three secretaries. Probably the most famous of all these songs is 'Pinepine Te Kura' (Tiny Precious

Child), which is an adaptation of an old oriori (usually translated as lullaby, which these songs are not intended to be). Oriori are composed and sung to children (sometimes an unborn child) to teach them their history; they are passionate songs intended to awaken the child as to who they are. Te Kooti composed his song for 1 January 1888. It anticipated the manner in which he would be prevented, by a travesty of justice, from returning home to Poverty Bay. These events were to lead to his rearrest in 1889 and subsequent Supreme Court trial. He sang of his betrayal by his own people in Poverty Bay, some of whom were continuing to threaten his life. Yet his theme and the song celebrated the 'new company of travellers' ('te tira hou')—the children of faith and peace ('Nō te rongo pai nō te rangi-marie')—who were setting forth in his stead to open the great painted meeting house, Rongopai, built in Te Kooti's honour in 1887, but which he would now never see.[14] Te Kooti sang of the fount of law, which stood *above* the Queen's authority. This was the primal source of justice, from which, as he expressed it in the song, both Taane (the Maori ancestor of humankind) and Rawiri (David), King of Israel, drew their generative fire-sticks for this world. Thus, he was depicting a shared fount for two coexisting systems of knowledge within Aotearoa, and a vision for a coequal and a more just future. This song is still sung on marae, partly because it remembers a recent history of manipulation of law, and partly because it reaches far beyond that recent history. It is a song in search of an equity of mana.

The song's essential theme—Te Kooti's search for reconciliation and proper bases for justice—was reinforced by a conversation that I had in 1981 with an elder from Whakatohea, Paroa (Jack) Kurei. Jack recalled:

> wherever Te Kooti went—wherever he step foot from one area to another—he's singing. And one song he had—this concerns the whole of New Zealand, this song—'Nei ka uru ahau i te ture ai matua mō te pani mō te rawa kore'—I shall join the law to make it a parent for the poor people, for the orphans, for those without.[15]

This story conveyed the essential image of Te Kooti as he journeyed from marae to marae, once he was (ostensibly) free to travel after his pardon of 1883. He travelled with songs, sayings and warnings for each and every place he visited. These were the local stories that I was hearing, and they are retained particularly in the eastern Bay of Plenty, the Urewera and, to a more limited degree, on the eastern Coromandel coast. This 'other' history had coexisted alongside the received history that had been produced and perpetuated by almost every newspaper article written from the 1860s to the 1980s: the stereotyped portrayal of Te Kooti as warrior and rebel. This 'dominant' history determined the understanding possessed by most Pakeha families, although, I would add, not by all. I had, therefore, entered into another contested domain—rewriting received history.

Received histories are the authoritative histories of a particular society. They are based on the constructions of the dominant society and its polity; in New Zealand, they have emerged out of a relatively recent colonialist past and a scale of values that were once thought to be inclusive but which were in actuality blind to others' experiences. All received histories about two cultures which share the same physical space will explode the moment the perceptions of the colonised are given equal weighting. Sir Keith Sinclair first probed the colonial engendering of the nineteenth-century New Zealand wars; Alan Ward queried the façade of justice and the legend of social amalgamation in New Zealand; and a decade ago James Belich, in a further exploration of the New Zealand wars, unlocked the myths of empire.[16]

The next step, it seemed to me, was to expose different historical experiences and consciousness within New Zealand. This is not to write a history of Maori land grievances. Rather, it is to display different memories, and the different ways of remembering and recording the past. What I tried to do was not to reinterpret—to find a new narrative—but to enable the 'other' history to be heard by juxtaposing the narratives; not to appropriate, but to allow an equality of perceptions. This method renders both the Maori and the European histories and historiographies visible. It shows not only how they had been constructed, but why they had been constructed. It hopefully means we are able to understand the differences, rather than merely decry their inadequacies—although the greatest inadequacy of European-authored histories in New Zealand has been their ignorance of sources other than those created by the colonists.

The Maori oral narratives all portray Te Kooti as protector of tribal lands; thus there are the many stories about the diamond he placed, or concealed, in a secret place, a lake perhaps, or sometimes covered over with his shawl on the sacred mountain of the people.

The story of Te Kooti's diamond is told for Maungapohatu, Tuhoe's sacred mountain; for Paparatu, belonging to Rongowhakaata; and for Whakapunake, which guards Ngati Kohatu's land. Not coincidentally, they are all mountains where Te Kooti took his shelter during the fighting between 1868 and 1872. Paparatu was where the first military encounter had occurred, after the prisoners' escape from Chatham Island in 1868. Reuben Riki told the story this way:

> They say the diamond came from India, on the *Rifleman* itself [the ship captured by the prisoners]. That's one story. The second story is—it refers again to the bible. One of those gems that used to go about, travel, with other people. They say this location of the diamond—if it's a diamond—some say it appears at night. People that go out opossum hunting, they could see this luminous light coming up from one area, only one area, at night. This one, here, it's at Pāparatū . . . This one here, it is a diamond. He [Te Kooti] came here with a purpose—as the story goes—that he came here to hide all the wealth. If they were to find the wealth of this country, they will ruin this country. He says, 'It's better to be hidden'. But there is a day coming. Some one, or somebody, will [be] bound to find this and there will be plenty for all.[17]

The stories are about the protection of the mana whenua, the authority and wealth of the people and their land. The details vary because they are regional stories; but Te Kooti, the Wanderer, the man without a turangawaewae (resting place), the man who could never go home, is always the central, guardian figure. They are moral stories. They construct meaning; they have purposes and messages. Essentially, they are statements about future changes in power relations. They are stories anticipating the internal decolonisation of New Zealand. By being remembered and transmitted, and also by being constantly reworked by the narrators, they continue to assert Maori autonomy. They are not fairy tales for children; nor do they simply resolve, symbolically, what had seemed unable to be worked out. They anchor the present and the future in a remembered history. As they anchor, so they shape memory. The narratives are woven in context; and that context was, and is, a continued quest for freedom. They find meanings in the past that escape lineality of time and a finite sequence of events.[18] Some contend that the narratives and predictions—especially those of Te Kooti's which emphasise working through the law to change the law,[19] in order to recover an internal autonomy in a complementary relationship with the Crown—were starting to be fulfilled in the last decade of the twentieth century, under the reactivated principles of the Treaty of Waitangi.

Similarly, the songs are reworked for and from specific historical moments. They are often songs of warning about the future. They, too, are sung in context, and are adapted for context. The songs, like the narratives, may be predictive in their style; they often tell of quests that are yet to be fulfilled. The quest-narratives and songs have, in turn, set other histories in motion; this is so because people live by them and act by them. History has been spun from the words: actions and decisions occur which are understood to be directly consequential of the predictions. Rua's entire history in the twentieth century stemmed from the predictions, even as his actions intersected daily with parliamentarians, government bureaucrats and police officers. Thus it is that Te Kooti (with others) has, as John Pocock commented, 'sung into existence' new histories.[20] Only the followers of the prophet leaders have reached for the inner meanings of the predictive stories or sayings. But they have interpreted scenes, including those not of their own making, through these words; they choose to act by the construed meanings, and they have thereby engendered new, living and significant histories. Such histories may take the form of pilgrimages. In 1906 Rua took 80 elders—a chosen number, which accorded with an earlier prediction by Te Kooti[21]—from Tuhoe and Ngati Awa to Gisborne, Te Kooti's place of birth, intending to meet King Edward VII; similarly, in 1979, a group of Ringatu elders ritually journeyed to Chatham Island, Te Kooti's place of imprisonment. These events were conscious enactments of cycles of renewal or rebirth, although the particular forms in which the ideas may be expressed will vary widely.

As soon as one removes the state, its agents and its institutions as the central framework for writing about Maori colonial and postcolonial experiences, the autonomy of the Maori world emerges, whether one reads Maori manuscript records or listens to their oral narratives. Instead of assuming that a gradual submersion within or under the settlers' polity took place during the nineteenth century, followed by abortive struggles, ebbing and flowing, in the search to find adequate representation or vehicles for decision-making, a completely new understanding springs into life. It was, after all, that skilled leader of Ngati Maniapoto (from the uplands of the Waikato), Rewi Maniapoto, whose intervention brought the protracted wars to an end, in 1872. It was not the military men, who had manifestly failed to find Te Kooti. It was Rewi's karanga (summons) which found him—he who could not be found—and Rewi set the terms of Te Kooti's sanctuary with Ngati Maniapoto, too. It was also Rewi who insisted on his pardon ten years later. Similarly, it was an independent Maori woman, Te Paea, famous as a mediator in her world but unknown outside it, who in 1870 nego-tiated the neutrality of Ngati Kahungunu of coastal Hawke's Bay, pulling one major contingent out from the government network of alliances. Te Kooti's history intersects with all these crucial, inde-pendent Maori leaders. These autonomous Maori decision-makers populate the later period of peace equally visibly, and they exist far beyond the end of the nineteenth century. Certainly the state and European society impacted upon their lives, but their decisions and their actions—and their analysis of what mattered—was, and remains, independent. The decisions are based in a shared sense of community, which reaches across the factionalism and across the rivalries of mana and lineage.

By displaying the sources on which I drew—by making them transparent—I hoped to reveal their biases, their purposes and their hopes. Through juxtaposition, the visible limitations of settler accounts—their stereotypes and their silences—are exposed. By the use of concentric narratives, drawing on very different sources, the intellectual frameworks of the nineteenth-century Maori world become much more visible. In the biography of Te Kooti, I moved the European actors into the wings of the theatre, because their presence in this particular history was well known, whereas the autonomous actions of Maori were not. Perhaps it will still be said that I have situated Maori in a constructed history that is not theirs. If that is so, the next strides will probably be taken by Maori histor-ians. Some, many, perhaps even most of the questions they will ask will be different; but the unexpected answer will still occur. The relationship between questioner and answerer may also be different, but they will still rest essentially on people's trust.

A long time ago I wrote a biography of a 'bad' missionary, Rev. Thomas Kendall, the initiator of the first published Maori grammar.[22] That biography's purpose was to probe a question posed in a histor-ian's poem, Keith Sinclair's 'Memorial to a Missionary'.[23] Sinclair asked, 'Instructed to speak of God with emphasis/On sin . . . what in that dreaming hour . . . did he learn from the south?' I wanted then to know whether Kendall had indeed crossed the beach (to borrow from another historian, Greg Dening).[24] Later, I wanted to know whether it was possible to find ways in which one could write histories which explained the silences and the absences, and which altered attitudes about the ownership of truth.

For these reasons, then, I will conclude with T.S. Eliot's words: 'in our end is our beginning.' I did not recognise the beginning when I first came across it, although now, looking back, it comes to mind: the missionary's terrified cry in 1822, 'All their notions are metaphysical and I have been so poisoned with the apparent sublimity of their ideas'.[25] Clearer beginnings came later: on the marae at Matahi; at Maungapohatu; and at Gisborne, with Te Kooti's kin. Each book of the unanticipated trilogy was launched where the spirit within the gift, the hau, originated: for Rua, at Matahi, where he is buried; for *Ngā Mōrehu*, with the women and their families, together; and, for Te Kooti, at Te Wainui in 1995, and later, in April 1997, when the paperback edition was published, at Gisborne, the home to which Te Kooti was never able to return. On this last occasion, in the whaikorero (formal speeches), Maori speakers freely and often with humour evoked the contested histories within the region and between themselves and their families. These are the histories held within the 'net of memory', living dynamically in the present.

The three books evolved out of dialogues, through time. Perhaps I could say the wairua (spirit) was there; and if this is so, it is a precious gift, which was briefly entrusted.

6

In the absence of vita as genre
The making of the Roy Kelly story

Basil Sansom

> He cannot give a sequential or, indeed, a fully coherent account
> of how or where he spent his formative years.[1]

This essay is the Producer's account of a production, my reflections
on the making of audio footage for the Roy Kelly story. My taping of
Roy Kelly was presumptuously intended to yield A LIFE, that of my
mentor, patron, friend and companion who was counted a Masterful
Man in the fringe camps of Darwin. The life—the whole life which,
as a construct, we distinguish as curriculum vitae and recognise in
autobiography, biography, obituary and so forth—is no natural or
eternal form. In the west, the life has a moment of origin and any
proper archaeology of the life would begin with St Augustine's
Confessions, written pro vita sua (that is, as a defence of one's own
life), and exhibiting curiously modern constructs and preoccupations.[2]
Not only does Augustine establish the confessional self with its

economy of secret and contained desire, he is also driven to produce text in order to secure that second order of immortality, which is achieved through the production of text itself. But what if we turn public artistic production into performance alone, as for example with the sand painting of the Desert Aborigines that is created for a ceremony only to be destroyed in its enactment, the painted body design washed off as ritual celebrants return to mundane activities? And what if we consider the pitted rock engravings of the Kimberley and Pilbara regions, where true authorship of pattern or design is denied to humans and assigned instead to Powers of the Dreaming?

I can attest that the story pro vita sua was no cultural familiar in those places in which I worked with Aboriginal people who sub-scribed to the old rules that governed performance.[3] Those who work either to elicit whole lives from Aboriginal people or work to assist Aboriginal storytellers who themselves now wish to realise whole life accountings do so, I contend, in the absence of vita as genre. My pro-position holds true unless there has been either a literary or a religious conversion: modern literary conventions require selves that have careers that may or may not collapse; religious conversion deals with the life progress of a soul that may or may not, given the Recording Angel's well-kept tally of sins and redemptive deeds, be damned.

But while Aboriginal conventions for rendering vita are absent, there remains narrative aplenty. Much of this is sacred story, but there has also been the space and the necessity for the rendering of the narrative of personal attestation. Narrators draw on their personal histories and knowledge to make facts that: (i) constitute narrow but definitive 'happenings' ('Time that dingo-dog bin die'); (ii) contribute to the characterisation of those sweeping 'times' of collective experience that, in our analyses, deserve to be distin-guished as historical periods or eras ('That horse and buggy time'); or, otherwise, (iii) either constitute situated selves or give character to admired or denigrated others.

Usually it is sets of stories made up of discrete accounts of 'times' that the re-makers bring to their thematic histories[4] or biographies. There is an alternative tactic. Get the tellers of story to change their ways. Subject narrators to imperative chronology. Teach them also to hold before themselves the ideal of completeness and the outcome could well be life story of a sort. A missionary job this one, persuad-ing narrators to put Aboriginal story behind them and enter instead along the way of St Augustine's tropes and recountings of a life's progress. A third lesson would be to supply narrators with Augustinian words with which to document not objective happenings, but the subjectivity of the inner life. ('And isn't this exactly what autobiographical writing is, the turning of oneself inside out so as to represent in narrative form one's internal subjectivity?'[5]) The Aboriginal world is one in which rules governing permitted discourse decree that stories rendered in public settings will be unconfessional. Arnold Krupat, after noting that 'the western notion of representing the whole of any one person's life . . . was . . . foreign to the [indigenous] cultures of the present-day United States', goes on to explain why: 'The high regard in which the modern West holds egocentric, autonomous individualism—the 'auto' part of 'autobiography'—found almost no parallel whatever in the communally oriented cultures of Native America.'[6] Generalised, the Krupat thesis is that 'communally orientated cultures' will not yield vita as genre.

ABORIGINES AND LIFE STORIES

Since the early 1970s there has been a surge in the publication of Aboriginal life stories and it is easier to view this as an active movement rather than characterise Aboriginal life story as an emergent genre that can be defined by stipulating its typical characteristics. In any case, (auto)biography is wavering and unstable as a genre because it is located uncertainly in history, belles lettres, fiction and semi-fiction, and we may add anthropology and hagiography to this list.[7]

To contextualise the Australian movement, I think it best to follow Richard Hoggart and Walter Ong[8] and envisage a worldwide historical continuum with orality at one end and the triumphant achievement of writerly competence by first or second generation inheritors of literacy at the other. Emergent indigenous writers and those emergent writers born as children into homes of un-literacy in societies dominated by literati are sited in particular space, a vantage from which they can come in their writing, to move back and forth between frames of their culture of primary orientation and the acquired frames and forms of the dominant literary culture. James Ruppert holds that, at the acme of self-conscious realisation of bicultural competence and mastery of literary craft, such authors assume two implied readers as they work, writing each sentence with both an indigenous audience and a western readership simultaneously in mind.[9] For their inventiveness, Gerard Vizenor refers to accomplished métis writers like himself as 'earthdivers', latter-day creation figures who 'dive like the otter and beaver and muskrat in search of earth' and who are 'both animal and trickster, both white and tribal, the uncertain creator in an urban metaphor based on a creation myth that preceded him in two world views and oral traditions'.[10] I have yet to discover an Australian Aboriginal author of literary life story who qualifies as 'earthdiver'.[11] The most popular of Aboriginal life stories, Sally Morgan's *My Place*,[12] combines several popular genre forms from success story (the fortunate life) through to detective story,[13] but there is none of the earthdiver's supple to-ing and fro-ing between literary genres and traditional forms of orality.

In the majority of instances, published Aboriginal life stories are works mediated by second parties in which personal narratives once orally given are rendered into prose. First order mediation is either translation or 'Englishing'; then there is arrangement and editing; but, most often, there is appropriation distinguished by the telltale authorial urge to have the reported life make sense as a whole and this is inescapably part of the western literary heritage. This temptation to transform, 'to do the best one can' for an original perceived as 'raggedly given', has been irresistible where the made-over lives of Aborigines are concerned. In the balancing of the bio- against the -graph in 'biography', it is usually the -graph (with its transfer of authorship and authority from original subject to latter-day reporter) that wins out.

In 1960, Joseph Cassagrande rallied a set of well-established anthropologists, challenging them to write for a change about some human individual rather than the normative tribesperson or the socially conforming peasant. His twenty recruits were to provide brief biographical 'portraits' of those particular men or women who had been their 'chief informants' during fieldwork. Writing as editor and with reference to all the essays in his collection, Cassagrande remarked the trend of common enterprise: 'The authors' aim has been to reveal a unique personality, to delineate the individual as a credible human being seen against the background of his own locale and culture and show him in the context of his social roles rather than to simply chronicle a life.'[14]

As well as asking for lives that were more than mere lives, Cassagrande also noted in all the contributions 'a recurrent theme of personal tragedy, muted in some sketches and reaching the proportions of a kind of cosmic doom in others'.[15] For example, in one of the most appealing essays, W.E.H. Stanner's account of Durmugam, a

Nangiomeri man of Northern Australia, his biography stretches on into the later years of this one-time warrior's life. Durmugam is depicted as failing to brook the predations of young men who would seize one or other of his three wives and would prefer to take the youngest of them who is joined to Durmugam in a marriage of May to December; his 'tragedy' is that, despite his reduced aptness with a spear, he must still issue a pretentious challenge to his world and strive to keep three women to himself. The hubris of Durmugam finds a dramaturgic counterpart in the nemesis of another fine essay in the same volume, Victor Turner's life of a Ndembu man of rural Zambia, 'Muchona the Hornet'. It is structured around the life-diminishing fact that Muchona has by unreasonable and unreasoning Powers been struck in the groin. Captive to lurking literary doctrines instilled during their own schooling, these two anthropologists similarly cause their respective protagonists to obey received literary canons to the extent that two tribesmen—one African, the other Aboriginal—must play out lives that their biographers have brought into congruence with the dramaturgy of the ancient Greeks. Even today, Pat Caplan observes, authors who render up lives of indigenous subjects still often present the lives they write as lives of the protagonist, the 'little heroine' or the 'little hero'.[16]

Exempt from ills of appropriation is the conjoint work issued by Stephen Muecke (linguist and anthropologist) in partnership with Paddy Roe, an Aboriginal man of the West Kimberley.[17] Roe's stories have been published as text with minimalist second-party mediation, Muecke declaredly attempting to act always as 'informed scribe' rather than 'back[ing] up this work with any . . . ethnographic description of the region, language or traditional society as a whole'.[18] But there are problems for ethnography when such exposed and naked texts are taken from other cultures. Some of these can be solved, though, if the true interpreter acts also more thoroughly as guide, haunting each text with commentary sufficiently detailed to suggest and describe the forms that would govern a culturally canonical reading. Caplan defines an ideal for this, the mediated biography: 'to write a seamed narrative in which the ethnographer sews the seams and is seen to do so, but in which the people who are its sources—their voices and the occasions on which they speak—are made explicit.'[19]

This account of Roy Kelly and me is about the origination of personal narrative and those orders of things that give relative status to each speaker and ethnographic definition to all acts of speaking. In their original settings, these things are often implicit and do not stand proud in the recorded text of a speaker's utterance. Unless they are provided as pre-text and context, much of a speaker's meanings will be lost despite a text's authentic mediation.

INTRODUCING ROY KELLY

Roy Kelly is the chief inhabitant of my book *The Camp at Wallaby Cross: A Study of Aboriginal Fringe Dwellers in Darwin.*[20] And well does he deserve to stride through its pages. He was the mentor who brought me to an appreciation of things Aboriginal, working all the time to see also that I did not get into trouble. As it happens, Roy appears in my book not as Roy Kelly but as Tommy Atkins. Back in the mid-1970s, I gave all fringe dwellers and associates the assurance that, while I wanted to know everything about them, I would give no identities away when I put things into print. The act of gratuitously naming people in a book robs them (and their descendants) of degrees of freedom in the business of making and remaking their own pasts.

In 1988 when I returned to Darwin, a now elderly Roy Kelly announced that he would like in future to be himself in all the things written about him. There were two reasons. He had become frail, too weak to travel over rough roads in a four-wheel drive. Death impended and Roy wanted to be remembered. He regretted that he featured as chief protagonist in *The Camp at Wallaby Cross* bearing a name that was not his own. But, more profoundly, the running of Aboriginal land claims after the enabling legislation of 1976[21] had imbued Roy with a new sense of the uses of history. My book is useless as a source of detail in the lands claims process precisely because I name no-one and even give fictitious names to places. Land claims demand history, which is to say they require the named person, the dated event and the designated place. To write actual persons and places out of ethnography is to deny a history of association between country and those who actually use it.

In this account of the making of the Roy Kelly tapes, then, I have given Roy back his true 'whitefella name'.[22] With others, I keep to my old compact.

STORY FOR NO REASON

I asked Roy Kelly for life story. From the outset, he told me that I was after something 'funny', which is to say a kind of thing he did not know about and didn't understand. And why choose him? In answer to the question, I said he was a man of parts—prominent, a leader, a 'Boss'. And ol Luke (recently deceased) had given us the proper term to use for the kind of man who is a leader, an exemplar and a local hero too. 'That's a Masterful Man, Roy, that you are.' Using ol Luke's label, we went on to discuss what I proposed. Our project, to craft a story that would justly be *The life of a masterful man.*

'Alright', said Roy, 'so you askin for that story, THAT STORY FOR NO REASON'. In this, Roy does not deny me reason. Concerned not at all with my desire, Roy denies reason to the asked-for story as story. For Roy, stories are given character by the purpose that they serve. For him and his brothers and sisters, stories are *stories for.* The story is signed and signalled by its vectored and purposive pointing towards the goal that is its reason. So, 'that humbug story for policeman'[23] is its own sort or kind, its purpose being to turn accusatory police away by serving them up with 'all that humbug and gammon', a pack of plausibly implausible lies. 'This job', said Roy, 'gonna be very different'.

I was neither eliciting a ceremony story, nor a travelling story, nor a Dreaming story, nor a story about this 'time' or that. I did not ask Roy to give any one a character. I was not asking for any one of the kinds of story people render as appropriate story in the ordinary way. Our project is to be life story and both of us adopt that word. New and different thing! The terms for production of life story will have to be negotiated between Roy, me and the tape recorder. And what sort of 'life' will come out of the taping?

ROY KELLY'S MOB

News of the life story project has got abroad. And, indeed, the initial negotiations have been witnessed—'Story for no reason . . . why me?' and so on.

In this camp at Wallaby Cross, Roy is in charge of a section. It's 1975. Roy is white-haired yet athletic and he is ostentatiously active. Roy will chop and split wood impressively for show. When trucks are to be loaded, he'll lift one or two of the heaviest ports or swags before standing back to let mere others drudge. With weight-lifting followed by abstention, Roy makes two points: he's still strong, and he's decidedly the Boss. With regard to another department of exertion and excess, his prowess is capsuled in a nickname. Roy is called 'Tom Cat' when he decides to go philandering. Domestically, Roy's prowess is expressed by the fact that he can often keep two wives. He is also a man surrounded by dependent women who are not his wives. Most of these women call him 'Daddy' where 'Daddy' signals instant relationship to be described thus: this man has a degree of authority over me and I exist under his protection but my relationship with this man is not a sexual relationship for I disclaim status as wife or girlfriend and will do nothing to make his wives jealous. 'Daddy' puts an incest taboo in place. Dads do not sleep with those who call them 'Dad'. But these are not Roy's daughters, not even in some sense of extended kinship.[24]

The women about Roy are older women, all beyond child-bearing, all with eventful marital histories of widowhood and/or divorces. Most have husbands with them. Without exception, the husbands are physically or mentally damaged, once hailed by titles derived from their work in the rural industries of the Darwin hinter-land (such as Drover, Station Man, Buffalo Shooter, Croc Shooter, Cookie, and Driving Man) but now human wrecks. Their debility makes them cash rich (since they get a pension) but also robs them of the strength to guard and keep their cash unless helped to do so. All are in need of domestic care. These men make marriages with robust, older women, some of whom are pensioners too; then each couple (doddery husband partnered by a forceful wife) must contract into camping association with some Masterful Man who, helped by muscled aides, will grant place, space and, above all, the guarantee of safety—daylight and night-time immunity from attack, robbery, insult, battery and the bludger's nagging attrition of one's holdings. The demand is for round-the-clock protection. Ideally, old people should, as declining parents, be looked after by grown-up children and by sons-in-law. Those about Roy have either been forsaken by living children or they own no acknowledged 'kids'.[25]

Roy Kelly 'bin look after that whole mob' to establish himself as 'properly Daddy' right in the middle of a pool of cash. Protectors truly earn those financial rewards they manage to extract. Masterful Men: 'All the time gotta watchin' for that mob', the mob of those contracted to their care. Roy's fringe camp is a drinking camp where any adult can sometimes drink too much, become 'silly drunk' and be prone to accident or to the gratuitous mouthing of insults that gets drunk, weak people into fights. Masterful Men work full-time to police regimes of drinking.

Unless he found a deputy, Roy had to be constantly on the scene.

It thus came about that life story as project was mooted with every-body listening. This was to be paid work and all the women in the Roy Kelly mob wanted to tell and earn. Nor could they see any reason for the singling out of Roy. 'Get out that tape Basil; every-body gonna have a go.' And so I got a set of unsolicited but insistently proffered tapings.

HIJACK

In a camp of comings and goings, I'd not met Lottie before, but it was she who thrust herself forward to grab up the recorder and announce her claim: 'Me first!' With project hijacked and Lottie holding the microphone, I set things going by leading when one should never, never lead. And I led with a true whitefella question.

Basil: Where were you born?

Lottie: Daly River.

Basil: You Marrannungu then?

Lottie: No, Brinken. Daly River. Growing up. My brother Roy Kelly and my sister Nell Kelly.

Basil: All the time [on the Daly River]?

Lottie: We bin coming longa Batchelor. We bin losim mother there longa Rum Jungle. Mother died there . . .[26] [some mur-murs of dissent are heard]. No . . . died longa TOWN [de-fiant, the word 'town' is uttered as loud challenge to any who would gainsay her].

Basil: When did you get married? Big or small?

Lottie: I WAS BIG ENOUGH.

Basil: Yeah. [This is a most neutral, quiet and deflecting 'yeah'.]

Lottie: This [points at Roy]. I grew him up Roy Kelly and this Nell Kelly. They my little daughter and my son. His own mother . . . You knew there was a war and bombing, hey?[27]

Basil: Yeah.

Lottie: Well, Roy Kelly and Nell Kelly here, I have to get from brother [in Darwin]. Who that brother agin? Who that ol man, father bla [belonging to] him? C'mon, who that olfella? [There are no answers and Lottie's submission ends.]

It's a rather nasty bit of text, this conversation between two unknowns that survives on tape to be transcribed after a lapse of

25 years. Basil has all the appearance of a Government man. Like Government men before him, he acts straightaway as one who has licence to pry. 'Where were you born?' Six months into fieldwork, I had learnt the futility of asking 'When?' That is, in Government terms, I knew not to ask for Lottie's d.o.b. To pin down time, one needs to submit to the forms of a local, 'punctuate' calendar that tells time by events and ask not '*When?*' but: '*What time* youfella bin puttim up this house?' And the answer comes: 'Time that Aunty Daisy bin visitin longa we for court.' This was a famous time for Aunty Daisy was summonsed to come up to Darwin from the Daly River to answer a police charge and, as things turned out, she contested the charge and 'beat' that court. On the afternoon after the hearing Aunty Daisy came back to camp in triumph to announce that she was released from the charge and there was no fine to pay for her alleged offence of swearing at Bill Grey, a local sergeant of police.

'Time Aunty Daisy bin beat that court' becomes a moment in collective memory; other things are calibrated to this celebrated and remembered day, and now, by the cross-referencing of a famous with an ordinary happening, you are given *what time* in regard to the putting up (not building) of that thin-skinned iron and timber house. If you have never heard about Aunty Daisy and her doings there is a problem. A speaker with patience would have to sacrifice precision[28] and, turning to gross calibrations, tell time by referring to the range of those big events all people of the region share: 'After that cyclone Tracey comin up.'

And my question about the time of Lottie's marriage? My 'When?' is followed at once with category words for the answer— 'Big or small?' So, use your tongue to tick a box. Lottie then uses her tongue indeed. 'I was big enough.' This is pub talk. It is given in the wide-eyed challenging mode[29] that belongs to sparring between white man and Aboriginal woman at the bar, who both take licence to talk sex and talk as if the casual sexual encounter is a possibility. 'I was big enough [then]' all the way through to: 'And now, reckon you got big enough for me?' Lottie is then very rude about Roy. 'This . . .', she says, pointing with no respect. Lottie reduces the Masterful Man. Then she continues to assert her claims of adoption and mothering: on the banks of the Daly, she reared up Roy Kelly and his big sister too.

Lottie was up to something. Had she won approval for her ploy, she would have been given answers when she called for the name of

Roy's father. Somebody would have sung out the name of the Chief Administrator, that of a disliked shopkeeper, a Boss Drover or a sergeant of police. There could even be a vying, making Roy first the offspring of bureaucracy, then countering by proposing the retailer as forebear. Pretended contention would end when those present finally agreed to settle on one fictive name rather than the other. As things happened, Lottie's story of Darwin and wartime and domesticity on the Daly was to be exploded. Some man, previously unheard and heretofore no presence on the tape, quietly drops the telling word, putting an end to the long silence that was leaving Lottie without a name: 'Captain Cook him father really.' The tape registers no laughter; Lottie's audience must in all politeness have been bursting with contained amusement. For them, Captain Cook who took possession of Australia for the Crown has been made to stand for the bringing of all that is bad about government— massacre, hangings, floggings, the penal system—to Australia.

A minimal form for presenting a gammoning story goes like this: (i) for those in the know, a ludicrous proposal (I reared the Kelly kids up); (ii) elaboration of proposal (detail to supply an air of verisimilitude to an, as yet, uncorroborated story); (iii) ratification by group agreement (in this case, calling for the name of the alleged father in Darwin and thereby attempting to gain affirmation that the named person did indeed hand over children into Lottie's care. The supply of an agreed name would indicate that qualified listeners assented also in the story). Lottie had asked for more than a name. She called for complicity and this was refused her. In the end, only its proposer was to be party to this gammoning lay.

While I cannot supply Lottie's d.o.b., everyone in camp knew that Lottie was a good deal younger than Roy. She was much, much younger than Nell, Roy's older sister. What Lottie proposed had the structure of transposition that belongs to the images on those inky, old Dutch woodblock prints—The Ass Leads its Master, The Knight is Ridden by the Churl, Wife Chastises Husband, Rooster Dines on the Man.[30] 'The child brings up its elders.' In one way or another, the gammoning lay is an essay in absurdity. The natural response to the anonymous bureaucrat who pries and impertinently asks questions is to reply with gammon and to ask for one's gammoning to be agreed in, affirmed by present company who then become party to the ploy. But Lottie miscued. I was not the anonymous other. I had been part of the mob for months. Lottie had applied for a place in camp while husbandless and away 'on holiday', released from the controlling influences of a home place on the banks of the Daly River. Roy saw trouble in her undedicated sexuality, in her boldness of body and in her glibness with the gammoning word. Maybe a husband would come chasing up after her. Roy sent her away in a taxi. 'Too cheeky', he told us.

DECLARING THE SITUATED SELF

With Lottie departed, the women who belonged honestly to Roy's mob could make personal attestations, some long, some short, but all crafted to the same end. I consider one of their stories to show how these are to be counted as *stories for*—stories, that is, of a socially essential kind.

Edna gave her minimal assertion thus:

Edna: Roy Kelly bin looking after me after my husband bin finish. [Roy Kelly has looked after me ever since I became a widow when my original husband died.]

Basil: And Andrew Little [is] your husband now?

Edna: Yes.

Basil: What's wrong with Andrew?

Edna: His leg. Can't get up but . . . Can get up for pension! He was a Stockman. Long time.

Basil: What station?

Edna: Barry Helms' . . . Timber he bin cuttin [at] one station . . . [Then] working at Pannadoo. And I finish now.

Basil: Only two station?

Edna: Yes. Look that [grey] hair, what you bin do? You gettin [to be] that olfella right presently!

Edna makes a ringing main assertion and then she wants to rest her case. She declares her dependency on 'Daddy', the vital thing to be asserted. I respond not with questions, but with prompts. Tell us that Andrew is your husband, tell us he's afflicted, say how he used to be sound and a long-time worker. And Edna's last flourish is a confirmation of her familiarity with me.

I assisted in administering the 1976 Australian census to people of the Darwin fringe camps and had difficulty in the business of eliciting any personal facts which respondents thought I knew already. 'You got all that, Basil, just put it down.' No charade of providing the already provided. I had been driving Edna and Andrew to the clinic for weeks past, hence that essential minimum and the play concerning hair.

The primary statement that Edna volunteered accounts for her presence at Wallaby Cross, declares her widowhood and proclaims her 'Daddy' relationship with Roy Kelly. This is the information that is needed to establish Edna as situated self. And the situated self-attestation is a standard form of *story for*. Camping affiliation, camping aegis and present marital state are three basics. Then one may see advantage in giving more. (Edna's emphasis on widowhood rather than on marriage to poor Andrew is an indication of how easily she would give that Andrew away.)

The situated self-attestation indicates grounds from which the speaker will proceed in potential association with the person or persons addressed. Further, the situated self-attestation is an artefact of a world of movement and can be given to previous acquaintances as an updating: 'Camping la Wallaby Cross longa Roy Kelly; me singlefella now.' So, Edna establishes her present state, defining with shrewd economy a situated self with reference to her widowhood and her dependence on Roy Kelly. The past enters the present in standard form as a *story for*. And the form for this kind of story is the string of assertions that define one's current status and condition. The string is presented before witnesses and it rehearses the facts in terms of which one's relationships with all those present are structured. (In the ordinary course, someone would soon pipe up to remark Edna's unremarked marriage to her neglected Andrew.) There is no detail to enliven these accountings because conduct in camp and mob is based on a rule that forbids 'tellin all that detail for no reason'. Telling detail opens up issues that have been duly settled. The opening of troubles from the past makes telling detail a sort of loose talking that leads instantly to fights, and these may rapidly escalate from fisticuffs to bottle fight to 'fighting kad (by means of) knife'. To ask 'Why you givin all that detail?' encodes the basic question 'Why are you thus inciting people to violence?'

AVOIDING DETAILS: THE THREE STICK STORY

My answer to presentations of the situated self so insistently given and often with mention of a broken marriage is to ask questions in an attempt to improve my comprehension of divorce as a formally recognised event. How to divorce? The answer to this question was indicated in one woman's declarations. Divorce is by displacement of the erstwhile spouse by a new one: 'He bin divorce me, he bin havim nother girl.' 'But', I ask, 'is there a difference at law? What's the difference in the law if you take somebody else? At law, is a first marriage better than a subsequent marriage?'

Roy Kelly starts an essay on divorce and marriage according to the law. We begin with The Suitor's Approach:

> Roy: Youngfella comin up la camp. 'Hi olman,' he said, 'all this girl bin married?' 'He not married too much.' 'Alright.' 'Son,' him reckon, 'son, can have my daughter now. Can have my daughter, be married'. Like that. 'I want you to get me flagin.' 'I really happy bring flagin. How often?' 'Every day. Every morning, every afternoon, all the time.' Grog Marriage, that what they callim.
>
> Basil: And what's a bush marriage?
>
> Roy: Bush Marriage they reckon . . . promise marriage, that different agin.
>
> Basil: So, bush marriage, promise marriage, grog marriage and kangaroo marriage?
>
> Roy: Tell you some day. I'D RATHER MAKE A PLACE.

Roy has just tried and tired of a mode of exposition celebrated in an essay in which Stanner deals with 'Durmugam's three-stick model of kinship'.[31] At the start of Roy's story, there's one stick to stand for the suitor, one stick for the oldfella guardian of girls and one stick for the unmarried girls ('themfella alabat'). Once the grog marriage has been ratified, a pair of sticks is located on Roy's sand patch to stand for husband and wife while the third stick stands for the olfella exacting his unending dues in flagons of port. Three stick stories can be given thus in an envisioning of hypothetical situation after situation. And because three stick stories deal only in typicalities and only with the unnamed and always pronominal actor, three-stick stories do not directly and scandalously impugn any known person. By telling three-stick stories, one avoids mention of instances and tells no detail. The price is that one loses all history and tells everything about nobody. Roy cannot go on in camp in front of Edna, Nell, Derry and the rest. Nor does he want endlessly to move sticks about in order to put visualisations of the alliances and oppositions of hypothetical protagonists at the centre of discussion. Life story requires detail; in camp, the giving of all detail is monitored and the ownership of detail will be subject to contention. Unimpeded supply of detail, the provision of an unratified and individual story, requires the finding and making of a place apart. In that place there will be no audience avid to check representations and determined to allow no exhumation of the instigating past.

JET'S ROAR AND ADZE-SCRAPE

Two sorts of eruptive background noise annoy the transcriber of the six Roy Kelly tapes. Roy discovered the place apart for taping in thick bush. This bush was on the airport perimeter right under the approach to the main runway. Each time we sought privacy, we sat down near a crater made by a Japanese bomb (a near miss) and I'd fossick to go home with pieces of shrapnel for souvenirs. When the big jets flew over, we usually paused the tape until they'd landed. Yet Roy would often render up some cryptic remark just as the engines of the landing plane screamed in reverse-thrust to their crescendo. The second kind of noise is insistent, that of a craftsman working wood, a chopping and a scraping and those breathed plosives of effort the ardent whittler vents. All the while that he filled tapes, Roy carved and carved and carved.

Each time we set out to record, Roy ostentatiously took tools and wood from camp and when we returned he'd have some improved artefact for campers to admire. The first day out, he made notched spearheads of the kind called 'man killers' and he smoothed a spear shaft too. On the days that followed, he gave himself to the making and perfecting of a pair of resonant boomerangs that are not designed for throwing but are made instead to clap together and give the beat when the songs of secret men's ceremony are sung. While in camp, Roy could spend long afternoons and evenings talking or telling with his hands idle or occupied only with a beer can. On our car trips, he would simply ride and talk.

One can divine why, as our sessions were to go on, Roy settled for the ceremonial boomerang as best object to be fashioned. Such boomerangs are made by someone whose participation in and with Dreaming Powers is part of the carving and smoothing of the object itself. Out there, next to 'that Jappanee bomb hole', Roy had found the means to reverse the priorities of our mission. Our expeditions ended up as a business of making sacred boomerangs during which some experiential storytelling was yielded to the tape recorder on the side. Our goings out were thus normalised. And this was achieved by giving them sacred purpose. My instruction was done under sign of a Dreaming. And campers would all suspect that I had been given pertinent Dreaming Story and had come to some appreciation of Dreaming Powers as, all the while, I watched and witnessed a dedicated boomerang come into its realisation according to ordained pattern, raw wood into sharp-edged clap stick, before my very eyes.

There is more. Roy put confidentiality into the performance. I was to be given his story just as men go bush to give, receive and discuss the things of the secret life. Roy did not want me to carry round what he gave me to be used as gossip. Okay to publish and put in a book, not details to be retold at large—and especially not to be mentioned in the mixed company of the home camp. The taping, note here, was given as men's talk, not only man to man but in the mode of men talking apart from women and talking, therefore, about the problems women (those sexual others) are fated always to cause them. Finally, there is a promise implicit in the confiding ambience of each one-to-one session: No humbug.

DEAFNESS, DIVORCE AND DEATH

Our first time out was the day not of boomerangs but spears. Most of the time we talked 'dead body' and tried to plan the future. Ol Luke had recently died and his burial at the cemetery had been an unsatisfactory and messy affair. In arranging the rite of secondary disposal when the last clothes and intimate possessions of the dead are burnt and the ashes buried, we would need to redeem a botched funeral. Mabel, ol Luke's widow, held the things that would be burned. Any ceremony would be carried out only at her behest. She might even take the ceremony away from us and nominate a Ceremony Man other than Roy to 'burn rag' and put the dead man down.

Were we straight with regard to cause of death? If we weren't sure of the identity of the person who had caused ol Luke to die, we might have to send an item of the dead man's clothing to the oracle at Kununurra. Located in a cave, this southern oracle can point to the identity of killers after smelling the body smell of the murdered victim.[32] Consulting the oracle costs a lot. Nor did Roy favour having the 'rag' of clothing passed down along the track from hand to hand, eventually to have a verdict relayed back up said track from mouth to mouth. 'Should be, we drive all the way down there', he said. This extravagant proposal apart, we sensibly explored ways and means for staging a good ceremony once we had persuaded Mabel to let us do the job and not surrender ceremony to some other mob.

At afternoon's end (about six jets had landed), Roy said something special. 'Divorce business. You see, you really know you got that divorce WHEN YOU CAN'T HEAR, WHEN YOU CAN'T HEAR AND THEY GOT DEAD BODY.' Despite an afternoon spent talking dead body, I did not understand at once. Roy had to explain at length. If the news is brought to camp that a certain person has died and in that camp there is a person who once was a spouse of the deceased, divorce is complete and final only if the one-time spouse 'cannot hear' the news. If divorce has become truly absolute, one will in no way be moved to attend the ceremony of secondary disposal or otherwise to participate in the mourning for an erstwhile spouse.

At ceremonies of putting down, those who in life were closely associated with the deceased are smoked to rid them of any lingering body influence the dead person may have left behind. They are made 'free'.[33] On Roy's accounting, those who cannot hear the invitation to ceremony are already and wholly 'free'. There's an ellipsis here. The ex-wife or ex-husband who does not respond to news of obsequies that are to be held for an erstwhile spouse is said by others to be 'deaf' to the invitation to participate in the ceremony of putting down. No need to. For such a survivor, there is nothing of the past relationship that is not already all finished up and cleared. Then the deafness that others impute to one is taken to the self. Divorce is absolute when you, in and of yourself, can't hear.[34] 'THAT', said Roy, 'THATTA LIFE STORY THING!'

The rest of the Roy Kelly tapes are topically divided into segments. The segments are topical/episodic. Roy draws on experience and tells how things once happened (episode) culminatingly to reveal a 'life story thing' (topos). His episodic tellings are *stories for*. As with 'Deadbody Business' retailed above, each telling subserves the enunciation of life story thing. Under the banner of life story, Roy supplies a sort of wisdom literature. He has discovered in one of the cultural forms for inter-generational transmission of value a way to deal with my request for life story. He gives me what he may well in confidence have given those grandchildren he never was to have. Let me provide some episodic labels. Roy told of: Jungle Time,

Escape from Prison, Sly Grogging, Cloth and Dancing, Love Knot, Hair Belt, and on and on. Roy ends the parade of episodes with what we have recently learnt to call 'The Stolen Generations'. The topos of Roy's 'Stolen Generations' is: You whitefellas will never put an end to your grabbing confiscation of our kids.

Our taping of life story ends with alienation. I am reverted to my racial type, and Roy and I resume our public lives together for nine months more. We will do no confidential life story again until I return to Darwin in 1988.[35] Roy's 'Stolen Generations' episode finishes with attribution of shared responsibility to me:

> Roy: They grabbit baby. Some kid here, he was a half caste kid. My little niece that, that half caste baby. YOU'VE GOT ONE, in hospital now. Gubmin will take him.
> Basil: Well, there's something wrong with that kid. They've got him there because there's something wrong with his stomach. They say he eat tucker but doesn't get fat. [The medical diagnosis was the classic 'Failure to thrive'.]
> Roy: THEY [are going to] DO IT LIKE THAT AGIN!

This time, the culminating message of Roy's story sets him radically apart from me. I take on the character of whites at large, and the confiscating 'Gubmin' (clearly, Captain Cook's 'Gubmin') is my 'Gubmin' and not that government that afflicts us all. Did I not two days ago transport Katie with her baby to the hospital?

Life story sessions cease. Roy's final verity ('They do it like that agin') not only disturbs my relationship with him, it also plummets the local hero who I own as friend and mentor into a privately borne grieving for a long succession of lost kids whose names or kinship he had put on tape. Roy withdraws, retreating into a silence that lasts for days. He projects his sadness through the camp. Oh, so quiet this time and so sorry.

IMPERATIVE CHRONOLOGY

When anthropologist Kingsley Palmer set up a man called Clancy McKenna for the interviews that would provide the stuff of life story, the biographer and his subject sat down in the sand of a creek bed in the Pilbara. Palmer explains that, as a preliminary to all else, he worked to bring McKenna to the discipline of chronological

116

renderings, to convert him to sequence and the calendar. It seems he succeeded.[36] But an uncompromised Roy Kelly refused chronology.

Here's a passage in which the anthropologist tries to force sequence into Roy Kelly's resistant being. In his telling of a story, Roy has just returned from Maningrida to which distant and inaccessible place he had been exiled for twelve months after a magistrate found him guilty both of drinking and supplying grog. Dates can be provided here from outside sources. Maningrida was established by government in 1957;[37] the prohibition of alcohol to Aborigines was ended in 1964. And so Roy's stretch of exile to East Arnhem Land for drinking crimes must have been spent there between 1957 and 1964. Basil is impelled to bring the Maningrida episode to temporality, to search for sequence and so bring proper chronological ordering and therefore meaning to the progress of a life. Roy all the time cannot either concede or conceive the sense of a progression that is grounded in abstract chronology.

> Basil: But Roy, when were you working down near that hospital; when were you working with Mrs Evans? Was that before [your stint on] Upping Downs Station or after? [LONG PAUSE].
>
> Roy: Before Upping Downs I think.
>
> Basil: Straightaway when you bin come back from Maningrida then?
>
> Roy: Which one that Mrs Evans?
>
> Basil: Remember you bin tell me, that big house near that . . . behind the hospital there. You said you did garden work there and that Mrs Evans was cooking in the kitchen. And you reared up, I dunno, maybe two, three kids. One was Noggin.
>
> Roy: Before that I think [A VERY LONG PAUSE]. That's from Adelaide River this time. You know we get [enemy] action there [Darwin]. After the war, everything bin settle down. We bin go back to Berrimah.
>
> Basil: Ah, you worker for Forestry then! [Another intrusion of information taken from a separately framed accounting; note the anthropologist's satisfaction.]

The time marker that put an end to Roy's work on the sweeping lawns of the big house was the evacuation of Darwin 'due to enemy action' and Roy's compulsory removal to Adelaide River where one of the larger Army camps for Aborigines was sited. I hear for the first time that Roy was, in fact, incarcerated during that 'Army Time'. He was required to work building airstrips. He has no stories for me from 'Army Time' (neither now as he records 'life story' nor at any other time), just one further remark: 'good rations.'

The passage cited above begins with me charging Roy with information I once got from him in the form of travelling story as we moved about town on a day when our journey took us past the big house. I make travelling story intersect with 'Maningrida Grog Story' which has, for its 'life story thing', the theme of triumph out of infliction. At Maningrida Roy 'caught' a new language; he made a marriage that gave him significant in-laws who still came up by plane to town; and he learnt a new song cycle that informed a series of eastern ceremonies. Roy was exiled into empowerment. When I arrest him to ask for sequencing, Roy is taken aback by the intrusion of Mrs Evans into his storyline. Who is this Mrs Evans anyhow?

There are two things we may note about life story as vita. One is sequence, the second is our notion of gaps which derives from sequence, but adds to it the ideal of completeness. Roy's experience of Army Time is a gap. Then there was that time when Roy served for three years as Police Tracker. I found a record of this service in government archives and I taxed Roy with my finding. He turned away saying: 'Never Tracker really, I jus been do that little bit to spell ol Rolley.' But the records show Roy doing more than relief work for a short time just to please a countryman. In 1975, the stint of police tracker work, done in youth, is for Roy a required gap. It's a time without story, consigned with good reason to the backward abyss of deliberately relegated experience. Things beyond recall are not unremembered, but are rather things deliberately to be put away. About disremembering, Roy told me: 'That [unwanted] time, you gotta lose im', and 'gotta' is personal imperative. This brings me to discussion of my epigraph, Stanner's reflection on his subject, Durmugam.

For Durmugam, those 'formative years' have been relegated—he has made of them a gap, a period unpunctuated with story. As for 'coherence' and sequential renderings, Durmugam is a distant relative of Roy Kelly's. Their kinship with one another and the rest of their countrymen and women extends to abrogation of chronology. There is a reason. The present generates need for stories and stories are always pointed selections to be given in that order which, in a speaker's judgement, serves present topicality and present purpose best.

THE CONSTRUCTION OF 'LIFE STORY THING'

What Roy Kelly called 'life story thing' is a sort of story to be located within an Aboriginal epistemology, and is not to be taken as a westerner's 'for instance' since it is not representative of some concept or trend of thought. Rather, life story thing is instantiation. Sometimes, life story thing can transfer a proposition stored in what Alfred Schutz would recognise as a cultural 'stock of knowledge' to that which Michael Polyani establishes as 'personal knowledge'.[38] This, in local terms, would be to transfer an item from 'What them-fella (specified) all sayin' to 'This thing/business I got myself'. In terms of our everyday speech, such a shift is a shift from the command of well-accredited hearsay to personal attestation of experience of a primary event.

Sometimes and rarely, life story thing is attestation of a wholly original discovery of storied truth, and attestors like Roy Kelly have a talent for discovery of such truths. Always, life story thing is subtended by story—either a received and sourced story or a story drawn directly from life experience. Received stories are presented as accredited hearsay and so are drawn from a second order of life experience, the experience of receiving the story. Stories drawn directly from a person's own experience of active life, have, sui generis, the greater value.

In providing first-hand stories of life experience rather than in the telling of received stories, the teller of story takes on the role of primary source. As remarked above, stories drawn from original life experience can either present new truths or may confirm proposi-tions that belong to the general stock of knowledge but, even when given in the confirming rather than the originating mode, stories of true experience colour the theme addressed with particular verity. Neither character nor circumstance is lost in the affirmation and reporting of any generality of cultural supposition.

In sum, Roy Kelly appended the label 'life story thing' to an order of culturally conformed story which is delivered in two modes: to announce, attest and propose a personally discovered and novel truth or, more often, to confirm and communicate a culturally familiar proposition, the truth and value of which has been recon-firmed in the retailed adventures of the speaker. In the first instance, the listener is challenged to embrace novelty. In the second, there is a comfortable reassertion and reconfirmation of that which cultur-ally and previously has been given as something generally known.

Hence 'life story thing' is the very stuff of inter-generational transmission of value, communicating either new and personally
discovered truths or, for the most part, passing on instantiated
cultural wisdom by integrating culturally given propositions with
the life experience of the speaker. 'These things I have, in my doings,
found to be things you really can believe.' 'Life story thing' is gnosis.
It puts the 'really can' into 'believe'.

EPIPHANIES

All this noted, there remain issues as yet undiscussed and these
derive from the fact that my reporting has been the reporting of an
anthropology of return. I use 'return' in a double sense. There is,
first, my return to old tape recordings; then there is also my return-
ings over years to the site of original fieldwork. The self that revisits
old data is a transformed self. The self of true return visits is
changed and, furthermore, is a self that visits a scene modified by its
recent history and the subjective changes within those who still are
living and remain in place. My argument is that the anthropology of
return can yield orders of perception impossible to experience the
first time round.

First fieldwork is done with openness. After a little while, one
comes to acquire a linguistic pattern for asking for things that is just
as provisional as one's notion (pro tem) of the local conventions that
govern the conduct of marriage and divorce. Learning proceeds as a
day-by-day overturning of provisional models and one plays the
wholly inept to slightly inept incomer right until the end of first
fieldwork, the conclusion of which, in the classic model, is with-
drawal. The next steps are the making sense of fieldnotes in
academic seclusion. Then one consolidates and 'writes up' one's
vision. My own vision out of first Australian fieldwork was made
public as *The Camp at Wallaby Cross*. And I contend that the
writing up of fieldwork is the condition for experience of an anthropology of return. In writing up, there is a commitment to a form of
modelling. Any revisiting that precedes the essential writing up is
just an extension of first fieldwork because the fieldworker is still
working in the open, provisional and free-wheeling mode.

The sine qua non of return is that the investigator has taken time
out to produce something that, in part or whole, can be challenged
by the re-envisioning confrontation that calls for reconstitution,

overturn, or an expansion beyond previously set bounds into territory not known about before. Such consolidation is the prerequisite if one is to pursue epiphany and constitute a theory of the experience of epiphany as grounds for identifying the moment, and the means, for acquisition of significant personal knowledge. For me, epiphany signals those moments of ultimate reference in which some particular perception or happening sweeps old envisionings aside and there is a replacement of fondly or complacently held assumptions that were basis for the conduct of one's being in this or that regard.

In *The Logic of Sense* Gilles Deleuze poses and answers a question: 'But where do doctrines come from, if not from wounds and vital aphorisms which, with their charge of exemplary provocation, are so many speculative anecdotes?'[39] It is such a moment of wounding when Roy Kelly discovers the kidnapping: 'They grabbit baby' through to 'They do it like that agin'. The year 1975 was supposed to be located in propitious times. Citizenship has been granted to Aborigines; the era of prohibition and sly grogging has ended; Aboriginal people now get pension and welfare benefits on the same scales and bases as whites; the Aboriginal Lands Commissioner has made his rounds, interviewed Roy Kelly among others, and signalled the coming of Aboriginal land rights; the old Department of Aboriginal Affairs is shredding files as it abdicates; and there is a 'new Gubmin' called the Aboriginal Development Foundation. Roy's wound is in the discovery that in all the change there's been no change. So, he grieves for lost children past and the coming loss of children yet to be snatched away. For a while and in his woundedness he wants no truck with anyone, emerging from seclusion when he has taken this latest most wounding epiphany into his being. After each wounding one needs to recover a reconstituted self and thereby 'become the offspring of one's events'.[40]

At the beginning of this project, my memory of the Roy Kelly tapes made Roy a recounter of the stratagems and disasters by which a Masterful Man had acquired his cunning. Returning to the tapes and with benefit also of return visits to Darwin, I have just now come to know what Roy Kelly had been about all the time: what I have called his 'wisdom literature' is about the development not of a grounded philosophy of life but of an aesthetic of response by which to live. My own woundedness is that I can never tell and share with him the fact that I have so belatedly tumbled to the nature of those things that all the time he spoke from because epiphanies had woundingly emplaced them at the very centre of his being.

LAST WORD

I have been prodigal with Roy Kelly's words and teachings. Back in 1975, Roy did not want the stories he called 'life story thing' to be retailed to his countrymen at large. These were stories to be vouchsafed to the chosen confidant in a place apart. But Roy said that I could take his private stories and put them in a book. By 1988 Roy had become more appreciative of the force of media through growing Aboriginal use of tape recordings, videos, photographs and newspapers (Roy had himself long used the advertising columns to call people to ceremony). He now wanted personal records to be created and he wanted them to survive. In his wallet and in his treasure box, Roy kept photographs of dead countrymen, which, in earlier days under the old conventions, he would certainly have destroyed one by one whenever a depicted person died. He would also listen to the taped song or ceremony in which performers now dead had played their parts. Together with countrymen, Roy was working to establish new ways in which to ensure the preservation and the transmission of knowledge. With the acceptance of the post-mortem survival of the photograph, and with the further acceptance that taped voices can independently survive and pass beyond the control of the communities in which they have their origin, comes the perception of the continuity of the self, a perception of selfhood and a public continuity of the person made instantiate by means that are amply provided in an age of mechanical reproduction. Among the 'new generations' of Roy's countrymen, there is now and emergently a selfhood that finds expression in recognition of vita.

7

Autobiography and testimonial discourse in Myles Lalor's 'oral history'

Jeremy Beckett

One of the criticisms levelled against anthropology is that western-trained researchers impose their own reality on their subjects. I would argue, nevertheless, that a challenging—and to me redeeming—feature of anthropological fieldwork is the way it subverts the researcher's preconceptions and, in greater or lesser degree, remakes the project in its own image. Our subjects are not inert, and have a way of setting their own terms, even making demands that send us off doing things we never intended to do. Right at the beginning of my career, I found myself being required by one of my best Aboriginal informants, named George Dutton, to take down the details of his career as bush worker and ritual leader. His story formed the basis of the first article I published. Many years later, in 1987, a much younger friend of this man, also Aboriginal, named Myles Lalor, proposed that I should do what he called his 'oral history'.

I had a tape recorder at hand and we started straightaway. He recorded some four hours of reminiscences the same evening, and another three a week later. He then went back to Broken Hill, the

New South Wales town where his family lived, and made further recordings, some with his daughter as audience, some on his own. He died about twelve months later, aged 62, leaving me to edit some 70 000 words of transcription, without benefit of his advice or wishes. I have just finished this task, for better or worse.[1]

Myles' story might be called an autobiography, but it includes political content of a kind that some critics have called testimonial. In Australia, as in other places, the 'voice' of an indigenous person is in a sense political, whatever the content. Correspondingly, the kind of framing and interpretation that is required to make the text accessible outside a specialist audience—which I think Myles would have wanted—is likely to incur the reproach of distorting if not appropriating his voice and, in particular, his Aboriginality. As is the way with identity politics, various critics, indigenous but also non-indigenous, have appointed themselves the guardians of what one might call an 'alternative' cultural capital.

In the latter part of the twentieth century a structural opposition between the settler majority and the Aboriginal minority in Australia became part of a global discourse of indigeneity, under the aegis of the United Nations and other international governmental and non-governmental bodies. There are two strands to this discourse, which I might designate as colonial victimisation and cultural authenticity. The former, deriving its legitimacy from the anti-colonial struggles of the post-World War II period, represents the oppression of, and discrimination against, indigenous peoples within nation-states as a latter-day colonialism. Although, in its earlier phase, this discourse was dominated by the non-indigenous civil rights advocates, it now gives priority to the previously unheard indigenous voice, 'the voice of the voiceless'. The latter stresses cultural difference not just from some dominant national culture, but from modernity in general. Thus, indigenous peoples claim and are credited with special qualities such as spirituality, care for the environment and non-acquisitiveness, which many in the west think of themselves as having lost. In this global formulation, the various indigenous groups are interchangeable, and yet, paradoxically, it is their particularities that are required for authentication. These particularities are cultural capital, to be deployed by nation-states, international media, and the various indigenous mobilisations. Representation of the indigenous is, then, critical, and control over it, including the 'native voice', is contested.

There has been a heightened interest in the writings and

transcribed oral depositions of indigenous people among both scholars and concerned readers in recent years, and I shall look at some of them before coming on to Myles' story. A remarkable feature about these writings is that in a great many if not most instances the editors, interlocutors and facilitators who have been instrumental in the diffusion of the indigenous voice have been non-indigenous; for the most part, the readership has not been indigenous either. At the same time, there has been an increasing awareness of the political position of such cultural mediators; some critics have questioned whether, good intentions notwithstanding, their interventions have compromised the authenticity of the indigenous voice, even appropriated it.

Some of this anxiety stems from a preoccupation with the difference between indigenous and non-indigenous to the point of disregarding the common ground that makes communication possible. There is also some tendency to regard indigenous subjects as ingenuous, rather than having their own agenda and being capable of effecting their own reverse appropriations when the occasion arises.[2] But, either way, an awareness of the conditions under which an utterance, particularly an extended utterance such as an 'oral history', is produced is essential to an understanding of what is being said. It is also necessary to have an awareness of how this utterance stands in relation to communication within the indigenous and non-indigenous domains and, since extended narratives are unusual in either, how these come to be articulated.

The life course narratives of western people who are not writers, or perhaps even literate, have long been the concern of social historians and sociologists. Correspondingly, indigenous life histories have been the preserve of anthropologists and ethno-historians; recently, however, they have come within the purview of what is called Comparative Literature. In the United States, Native American work has received its share of attention, particularly from Arnold Krupat and Hertha Dawn Wong.[3] For Krupat, Native American autobiographies are:

interesting both for the model of the self and the model of the text they propose, the first of these more nearly collective, the second more nearly dialogic than what has been typical of Euramerican autobiography . . . the self most typically is not constituted by the achievement of a distinctive, special voice that separates it from

125

others but, rather by the achievement of a particular placement in relation to the many voices without which it could not exist.[4]

Viewed as a 'textual representation of a situated encounter between two persons (or three if we include the frequent presence of an interpreter or translator) and two cultures, Indian autobiographies are quite literally dialogic', he argues further.[5] I am left uncertain as to whether the collective nature of the Native American self derives from Krupat's reading of the autobiographies, or his assumptions about Indian society as the milieu in which Native Americans achieve a sense of self; either way I am left with a sense of prescription—this is how their autobiographies ought to be. However, the suggestion poses some interesting questions that I shall take up again later on.

Latin Americanists have formed some rather similar notions, but in a context of more fundamental, and at times violent, conflicts between indigenous and non-indigenous. Some of their thinking has formed around what has come to be called testimonial discourse. These writers, also exponents of Comparative Literature rather than anthropology, have addressed the kind of problems I have outlined and have posed some interesting questions—most recently in a collection of essays entitled *The Real Thing*[6]—that I shall try to follow up with the Australian case, and Myles' autobiography in particular.

The Latin Americanists have designated testimonial discourse a genre 'marginal to literature'. First coming into currency in Cuba in the 1960s with the publication of the autobiography of the runaway slave Esteban Montejo,[7] its most celebrated example is the autobiography of the Guatemalan activist and Nobel Prize winner, *I, Rigoberta Menchú: An Indian Woman in Guatemala* or, in its more eloquent Spanish title, 'I am called Rigoberta Menchú, and this is how my consciousness was born',[8] produced in collaboration with a Venezuelan anthropologist, Elisabeth Burgos-Debray, and first published in Spanish in 1983.[9] I should add that there are others, which some consider better, and of late some awkward questions have been raised about this book.

Since a number of scholars are active in the field, there are also many definitions, but let me start with George Yúdice, who was among the first. He begins by asserting that 'testimonio' has contributed to the demise of the intellectual/artist as 'spokesperson for the voiceless'. By contrast, the *testimonialista* speaks, addressing a specific interlocutor in the first instance. But while the story is personal and told in the first person, the story is shared with the community to which the speaker belongs, without the speaker speaking *for* that community, thus performing an act of 'identity formation that is simultaneously personal and collective'. Yúdice continues: 'testimonial writing may be defined as an authentic narrative told by a witness who is moved to narrate by the urgency of a situation.' It is:

> first and foremost an act, a tactic by means of which people engage in the process of self-constitution and survival. It is a way of using narrative discourse whose function is not wholly pragmatic . . . but just as significantly aesthetic (in so far as the subjects of testimonial discourse rework their identity through the aesthetic), though that aesthetic does not usually correspond to the definitions of the literary as legitimised by dominant professional, educational and publishing institutions.

Testimonio has also to be free of the master discourses, and the testimonialist has to be in dialogue with a politically committed or empathetic transcriber/editor, who does not unduly control what is said through leading questions or doctoring the text.[10]

The term 'authentic', to which several of his colleagues object, alerts us to the dependence of all this on recognition by non-indigenous and in many cases non-Latin American scholars. It seems to me that Yúdice and some of his colleagues are at risk of conjuring up an 'unspoiled Indian'—what Alcida Ramos (in a somewhat different context) has called the Hyperreal Indian—who doesn't talk to mining companies or communist ideologues, and doesn't get mixed up with the wrong kind of non-indigenous interlocutor.[11] Even speaking Spanish (or whichever is the language of the dominant group) is compromising.

Here, of course, is the contradictory element in testimonio, for in most of the instances that have come under scholarly attention it is delivered not to the testimonialist's own people, but across a cultural, including linguistic, divide, apparently driven by some urgent situation to seek a sympathetic listener who will in turn provide access to a wider audience. Menchú, for example, told her story to a Venezuelan anthropologist in Paris who, according to Kay Warren, did not know Guatemala well and spent only a short time with her.[12]

Oddly, although a good deal is said about the editor/interlocutors and their variable but generally suspect influence on the testimonio that eventually appears in print, almost nothing is said about the readership, which may include indigenous intellectuals but is mainly non-indigenous. What should be said is that the readership is of crucial importance, given the political incapacity of most indigenous peoples to not only raise the consciousness of their own people but also to appeal to non-indigenous sympathisers. This appeal may be directed to a national or a transnational constituency, such as an indigenous rights organisation or a church network—whoever is in a position to exert pressure. Over the last 30 years, applied or anticipated outside pressure has been a major factor in the politics of indigeneity, and indigenous mobilisations have been increasingly directed towards making their grievances news, preferably television news, as in the case of the recent Zapatista uprising in Chiapas, Mexico.[13] Up to a point it seems to work; it is hard to say how far in most cases, though the Menchú autobiography won her the Nobel Prize and her cause a lot of international attention, which may have assisted the move from military to civilian government in Guatemala.

The point is, however, that unlike the stereotypical anthropologist's informant who is induced to provide information, the testimonialist wants urgently to get a message across to some audience. (I would add that this situation is not as unusual in ethnography as its critics seem to think.) This brings into focus the question of how the testimonialist stands in relation to some wider collectivity. For Yúdice, as we have seen, the message witnesses an experience that is both personal and collective.[14] And, as I noted earlier, Krupat has more generally argued that Native Americans (along with most of the world's peoples) tend to construct themselves as persons, which is to say as a bounded entity invested with specific patterns of social behaviour, normative powers and restraints, rather than as individuals who have interiorised consciences, feelings, goals, motivations and aspirations.[15] The testimonialist, however, is often displaced, in Paris, Mexico City or, in Myles' case, Sydney. And, as Santiago Colás has remarked, he or she is not identical to other members of the community, at least in the sense of having chosen to speak.[16] How this has come about is one of the questions that need to be asked. Is it simply a question of being in the right place at the right time, or of having a catalytic experience, or of possessing an unusual capacity for telling a story?

It is not altogether surprising that scholars trained in literature should focus upon the testimonial voice, even though they are at pains to distinguish it from the authorial voice of western literature, since they regard the autobiography as 'the quintessential form in which the so-called centred subject has been constructed in the West'.[17] Situating the testimonial voice in some kind of *gemeinschaft*, which is opposed to the West's *gesellschaft*, becomes critical if they are not to fall back into conventional literary analysis. Even so, Thomas Luckman's characterisation of biography, including autobiography, seems applicable to testimonio, at least to the extent that it integrates 'short term into long-term temporal sequences' which are '*individual* rather than social', and are 'tailored to fit an individual lifetime rather than institutional times'.[18] This then raises the question of how the testimonio came to take this form: either the narrative form was already to hand, or it was articulated in dialogue with an interlocutor, though not necessarily in a form imposed by the latter. What is certain is that such extended narratives do not just come naturally. Raymond Williams, discussing nineteenth-century British working-class writing, remarked: 'Very few if any of us could write at all if certain forms were not available. And then we may be lucky, we may find forms which correspond to our experience.' In this case they wrote autobiographies '[b]ecause the form coming down through the religious tradition was of a witness confessing the story of his life, or there was the defence speech at a trial when a man tells the judge who he is and what he had done'.[19]

The testimonialist may not have to make the transition from the oral to the written, but he or she still has to integrate short-term into long-term temporal sequences, a practice that may well be a departure from everyday discourse, or which makes explicit what is normally left implicit. If the form for a long-term sequence is not readily to hand, probably it is the interviewer that provides it, through questions and in editing the text, perhaps obscuring this intervention in the final version, as Miguel Barnet seems to have done with the autobiography of Esteban Montejo.[20] But it may rather be the unusual situation—a tape recorder rolling, an interested listener, and an uninterrupted period of time in which to talk—that induces the speaker to expand an already existing narrative form, or to bring off an impromptu bricolage. However, it has still to make sense, first to the listener, and, if the listener is to be the means of access to a wider audience, to others who may not have the local knowledge that the listener—an anthropologist, perhaps—does.

With rather more sensitivity to the hybrid nature of the situation, Colás has suggested: 'The resistance value of the testimonio as cultural practice and artefact, far from resting on the absolute identity between a people, their representative, the interlocutor, and the foreign sympathiser, seems rather to derive from the tension generated by the disjuncture between these different subjects.'[21] Colás sees Menchú's self-presentation accordingly:

> she both presents the appearance of being a 'genuine' Guatemalan Indian, and frustrates our expectations with regard to the proper contents of such an identity. She tricks us by being a Euro-North American Marxist and Feminist in Indian clothing. Not the stability of her identity, nor the fixed truth of her discourse, but the protean character of these . . . lends her work such 'dangerous' power.[22]

For Colás, the testimonialist may or may not intend this effect, although he seems to think that Menchú, moving in ever-widening circles outside her native culture, is aware of her 'protean' and 'hybrid' qualities. John Beverley similarly remarks on the 'performative transvestism' in 'her use of traditional Mayan women's dress as a cultural signifier to define her own identity and her allegiance to the community she is fighting for'.[23]

It seems to me that Colás is raising some interesting questions when he draws our attention to the tension generated by the disjuncture between 'a people, their representative, the interlocutor, and the foreign sympathiser'.[24] Warren has remarked on the complexity of the Maya experience of the military terror in Guatemala, and the different positions that various individuals found themselves in during this time,[25] and she implies that Menchú is obscuring important differences and diversities when she claims that 'My story is the story of all poor Guatemalans. My personal experience is the reality of a whole people'.[26] This indeed has been the reproach of anthropologist David Stoll in a recent book.[27] More generously, Richard Gott has suggested that Menchú was using her own story to provide a generalised account for a fairly ignorant non-Latin American audience.[28]

As I suggested in my introduction, however, the preoccupation with difference and disjunction tends to obscure the conjunctions which enable the testimonialist to work with interlocutor and to reach a non-indigenous audience, and still sustain some kind of recognition among at least sections of his or her own people. Without these conjunctions the testimonio is impossible, even though the speaker's rhetorical strategy may be to deny them. It seems to me that the tension to which Colás refers is also to be found in the space between conjunction and disjunction.

I have dwelt upon the Latin Americanist writing on testimonio because I have found it helpful to ponder the questions they ask as I try to come to terms with the Australian material, and Myles Lalor's oral history in particular. The last quarter of the twentieth century also saw a proliferation of indigenous biography and auto-biography in Australia and, on a smaller scale, similar kinds of commentaries, particularly on the part of Mudrooroo, who has written poetry and novels under the name Colin Johnson. Mudrooroo comments on the extent to which any kind of non-indigenous involvement distorts Aboriginal discourse, even if it is only self-censorship. One of the few books produced under an Aboriginal control of discourse is Bob Bropho's *Fringedweller*, which shows a mixture or ignoring of European genres, being both a polemic and an autobiography. Mudrooroo comments that it 'is not so much the story of Bob Bropho as of the people living on the fringe. Community is foremost, and the cover illustration is not the smiling face of the author, but a family pressed together into a collective whole'.[29]

Sally Morgan's autobiographical *My Place* has been by far the best-selling Aboriginal work, and perhaps on this account has provoked the only sustained debate.[30] This has centred on Morgan herself, with critical scrutiny focused mainly on the tension occurring between her and her kinfolk, and the Aboriginal community at large.[31] There is no question of translation or transcription, since Morgan was working in her first, indeed her only language, and she wrote the book herself. An editor worked on the manuscript but we do not know what changes were made and, in any case, this has not been made an issue. As for the readership, which has numbered in the hundreds of thousands in Australia and also in North America and Europe, it is overwhelmingly non-indigenous.

Morgan might almost have taken Menchú's subtitle in the sense that her book is about the birth of her Aboriginality. In this case, however, it is not military atrocities that form this consciousness, but a series of small incidents that arouse her curiosity about the indigenous origins that her family has tried to conceal from her. This need to know builds up to a state of urgency in herself, rather than in a collectivity. The stories that she eventually induces them to tell reveal the oppression that her mother and grandmother's generations suffered, and which, though abating by the time she was born, still cast a shadow over her childhood. 'Coming out' as Aboriginal in the 1970s was not the dangerous act that it could have been for her mother, 30 years before, and indeed for Morgan, the budding artist, it might be considered a smart career move.

In eliciting the stories of her grand-uncle, mother and grand-mother, which mediate the experience of being Aboriginal of earlier generations, Morgan herself is the interlocutor, privileged by being 'family', and thus able to press where outsiders might have felt diffident: the identity which she is discovering is, after all, her birthright. The accounts are in English and, although nearer to Aboriginal English than Morgan's own narrative, they probably needed editing but not translating. However, rather than standing on their own, they are incorporated into Morgan's own autobiographi-cal narrative, which, Bain Attwood suggests, takes the form of 'an inexorable movement towards the discovery of her real self'. He dubs this as a 'romantic view of an individual life', while in somewhat similar vein Eric Michaels refers to Morgan's 'Protestant self' and Mudrooroo claims it is 'an individualised story, and [that] the concerns of the Aboriginal community are of secondary impor-tance'.[32] But even if this is so, the life and the self are realised through and in relation to other people.

My Place is accessible to non-indigenous readers in the form of an autobiography but also a mystery story, though they are reminded that the characters are real people when the dark secret that would have been revealed in a novel is left as a suspicion. What also makes *My Place* so accessible to non-Aboriginal readers is that the young Morgan is very much like themselves. Although we know from the start that she is 'really Aboriginal', her realisation of it is delayed, and she takes us with her through the voyage of discovery, getting to know her mother and grandmother's past little by little, and in due course meeting other members of the family, until even-tually we go north to meet the 'real Aborigines'. Meanwhile the author, who is in so many respects 'like us', mediates these encoun-ters. She is also, through her own story and that of her Aboriginal kinfolk, quietly delegitimising her white antecedents. It comes as a literary surprise when Morgan declares her Aboriginality, leaving the reader as 'other'.[33] One can read this, and perhaps is intended to read it, as subverting the assimilationist scenario that ruled during her childhood, and is still the expectation of many non-indigenous Australians: this Aboriginal woman is still 'like us' in all sorts of ways, and yet declares her difference. However, she practises her

Aboriginality as a painter, which has proved the most acceptable aspect of indigeneity to the wider community.

What makes Morgan accessible and acceptable to non-indigenous readers, however, is almost bound to set up a tension between her and other Aboriginal readers. The fact that she and her mother were able to 'pass' as white, so that she had later to discover her Aboriginality, has not pleased those who, whatever their appearance, have always lived as Aboriginal.[34] This said, Michaels also perceived a tendency in her book to construct a pan-Aboriginality;[35] certainly kinship and spirituality are represented as transcending or transecting diversity, as is so often the case in Aboriginal writing.

Myles Lalor's 'oral history' sets up a different set of conjunctions and disjunctions among the subjects. There is as yet no readership, so I shall focus on the tension in Myles' story between him and myself as non-indigenous interlocutor, between him and the Aboriginal people who are, as you might say, his significant others, and between the two of us vis-à-vis the readership we anticipate.

Let me begin with the circumstances attending Myles' proposal that I should 'do his oral history'. I had known Myles for almost 30 years when he came to my house that evening. I had met him first in Wilcannia, a small township on the Darling River, where he lived with his wife and children, working as a truck driver, stockman and all-round labourer. From the late 1960s through the 1980s he spent long periods in Sydney, and from time to time he would drop round to my house. These were convivial occasions, but did not have much to do with my current research interests, so I did not write anything down. What, then, was different about this particular occasion, and wherein lay the urgency?

Myles was already suffering from the heart ailment that would kill him within the year, and it may be that he wanted to leave some lasting record of his life, but he never said anything of the kind. What he did mention was that he had just looked up his personal file in the records of the New South Wales Aborigines Protection Board that had control of people like himself during the early part of his life. At one stage he had been taken from his family and placed in the Kinchela Home for Aboriginal Boys. Myles had been in the home only from the ages of twelve to fourteen years and had absconded several times, but he had wanted to see what they said about him. When he arrived at my house he was still angry about what he had read, and he wondered what they had said about his mother, who had also been institutionalised, along with several of her siblings, years earlier. Since these reports of long dead officials were in writing, one can imagine that he might want to have his side of the story in equally permanent form. Talking to his daughter, he said: 'I feel like burning the bloody thing, but then I think, maybe a hundred years from now, someone will pick it up and wonder.'

But if it was his and his mother's reputation that he was immediately concerned about, he quickly widened the narrative to include the many other Aboriginal people who had similar experiences. The authorities made a practice of 'removing' Aboriginal children in those years; there were various pretexts, but underlying them was the view that Aboriginal children would have a better future if brought up away from the 'unsuitable' environment provided by their families and communities. In recent years historians have seen this as a strategy to disrupt the reproduction of Aboriginal culture and identity, and some have called it genocide. In his narrative Myles repeats the move from his own case to that of other Aborigines, with the difference that he represents his own experience as less damaging than theirs; thus he observes that, while he had only been in Kinchela for a short time, many of them had been taken as infants and sent out into the world not knowing where they came from or who their kinfolk were. The opening up of the archives was a response to people such as this, and the demand for restitution by those who have come to be called the stolen generations was already building up. Myles also perceived the removal of children as a tactic in a wider strategy of control, explaining how the police and officials could coerce Aboriginal women with the threat of taking away their children; he even claimed that his father, who had been killed in the war, had been recruited under the same duress. In his telling, this state practice becomes the quintessential assault on Aboriginal sociality.

Early on Myles states, 'I'm classified as Aboriginal wherever I go', but his Aboriginality resides in the first instance in his colour. Morgan tells how she discovers the Aboriginal descent that has been hidden from her; in the process her white antecedents are by one means or another delegitimised, leaving her finally with an immaculate Aboriginal pedigree. Myles tells a different story, describing how the hatred of colour, which was unconcealed in Australian national ideology in the years when he was growing up, corrupted relations among his Aboriginal kin. There is a paradoxical calculus to his pedigree: he remembers two great-grandfathers, both of whom were alive when he was a child. The one on his mother's side was white, 'an Englishman'; the one on his father's side was black. He mentions no Aboriginal antecedents on his mother's side, and no white antecedents on his father's side: they existed but they do not get mentioned. One can read this as an instance of the way race played out in Australian society in the 1930s: families who identified as white denied their Aboriginality. Thus, his father's family kept their Aboriginal grandparents hidden on the edge of town and disowned their son's child by an Aboriginal woman. For Myles kinship was not the bond that transcended difference among Aboriginal people but a travesty which he left behind him as soon as he could. His Aboriginality begins with his 'showing too much colour' and continues as he lives on the reserve, sees the police targeting the Aboriginal homes and, in due course, comes under the control of the Aborigines 'Persecution Board' as his mother had before him.

Of his father's mother, Myles recalls: 'You used to see the hurt on her face for me to sit on her verandah . . . and call her granny, but I only did it out of devilment.' As this passage reveals, when he talks about victimisation he also talks about the way he fought back. Similarly, his account of the brutality and poor teaching in the boys' home is also a story of the way in which he coped with them; in this way he distances himself a little from the others:

> I didn't spend a lot of time in Kinchela because I went walkabout from there a couple of times . . . I got up one morning just sunrise, I dressed and I walked through the bloody paddocks of corn so as no bastard would see me, right into the country, fourteen mile. I was off the road, walking rows of corn, and of course it wasn't hard to dodge the bastards from the home because they had a little yellow Bedford truck. You could see the bastard coming miles away. Plenty of time to squat down and let it go past. It took me until dark to get to Kempsey. There was a train standing there, so I jumped in the bloody train. I suppose I was lucky, no ticket or anything. There's an old woman there with a heap of bloody kids, heading to Sydney. The poor old conductor must've thought I was one of hers, because I got right through to bloody Sydney.

Here we have a characteristic feature of autobiography, as set down by Luckman: 'In addition to those elements of an individual life that are predetermined by a social structure and those that are simply contingent, there are those that are the result of his own actions—and *those* are guided by biographical schemes that were internalised by him.'[36]

Earlier I referred to the critics who characterised Morgan's autobiography as 'romantic' or 'Protestant'. Myles' story has the same quality: his survival depends on his own determination, not some community that stands behind him and helps him out.

In much of Myles' recordings with me, travel can be read as a metaphor for self-determination. His absconding from the boys' home is but the beginning. And when, after being brought back for the second time, the authorities go one better and send him 1000 kilometres away, to a place he has never heard of and people he does not know, he manages to get himself sent home, but then some years later makes his way back there of his own accord and eventually marries into the community. He moves beyond the territory normally traversed by Aboriginal men of his natal or adoptive communities, to find work and make friends, almost always Aboriginal, including lovers, whom he will in due course leave but not forget. Travelling is also knowledge in the sense that he can hold forth about the places that he has been, often in fine detail and always named. And with the places go the people, also named.

Once we get started, Myles knows what stories he wants to tell, scarcely stopping for me to change the tape. Now and again I ask a question, maybe just to clear up a confusion, sometimes to show him that I know what he is talking about, occasionally to raise a matter that I think may be interesting. But if I ask questions that he doesn't want to answer, he will say so, and once, when I have sent him off at a tangent, he abruptly stops and gets back onto the course he wants to follow, reminding me that I am the one who is going to have to straighten all this out.

Nevertheless, I am an interlocutor in a sense: as these stories are told to me we have eye contact, and he laughs a lot, though the laughter is often sardonic, and my laughter, also to be heard on the tape, indicates that he has left the space for me to join in. After so many years, we have done a lot of talking; he has also read some of the pieces I have written. So you might say the ground for this dialogue has been laid. In particular he knows about my work with a much older man, long since dead, who brought us together in the first place. 'Old George', as we always called him, had been initiated according to several Aboriginal rites, spoke a dozen languages, and had learned the mythological tracks over a vast area of country, including the Flinders Ranges and the Birdsville Track.[37] Myles also knew this country but in a secular way, as a truck driver and bush worker, and they spent a lot of time arguing about the various places. Myles has never been initiated, a practice that had ceased in his part of the country long before he was born, and he does not presume to talk about the mythology, even if he knows it.

When Myles talks to his daughter, some weeks after the sessions with me, he adopts a different, familial tone, referring to a trip they made to Uralla, the town where he was born: to them 'it's pretty little town', he teases, mimicking their voices; to him it's 'a bastard of a place'. Again, he is the one who holds the floor, though the daughter gets to ask a question occasionally, and despite the playfulness he intends to instruct—about the way life was for Aboriginal people when he was growing up and when she was a child. Some of the stories about the oppressiveness of the authorities he has already told me, but they loom larger in these recordings, whether because he has been brooding about them or because he has been holding back the tide of anger in the presence of someone who, though a friend, is still white. In the tapes he recorded on his own the witticisms, the play-fulness and laughter fall away. Some of what he says seems to be intended to gratify workers in the Aboriginal Medical Service, where he had worked some years earlier, but at other times the bitterness and brooding that underlie the earlier stories come to the surface. Although he has attacked the government's record throughout the recordings he did with me and his daughter, he only attacks white people as a group on the tapes he recorded alone: 'I still have a lot of things I want to do, but problems are stuck in front of me, not by the blacks but by the whites, who have the black chuck the problem up to me. It's left to the black to put that problem right. I'd notice that all the way through it's the white who's the expert, the black knows bloody nothing.'

How did Myles put together this long, sustained narrative? How, for a start, does it compare with everyday talk among his Aboriginal contemporaries in the town where he lived? What they would have recognised would have been the individual stories, or 'yarns' to use the local term; indeed, I recognised some of them myself, having heard them before. Yarning was a common pastime among Aboriginal people in the Far West of New South Wales, a way of passing the time in bush camps in the days before transistor radios, but also in town, before television reached the bush in the 1970s, and in gaol. The stories ranged from ephemeral gossip to crafted anecdotes with a punch line, typically a smart retort to some overbearing individual, that 'rhymed it well' and which might be repeated several times to savour its wit. Such stories might already be known to some of the listeners, but they didn't seem to mind the repetition.

Recalling Yúdice's reference to the aesthetic of testimonio, I should explain that Myles was a stylish raconteur, ornamenting his delivery with the swearwords that are standard in rural Aboriginal English, though he never used them to convey their literal meanings.[38] He took his time in the telling, savouring the details. Reported speech was a regular feature, with the characters rendered in different voices—sly, pompous, dumb, gossiping. There were well-turned phrases such as 'I was an occasional drinker, but I wasn't an occasional gambler'. In this art, he was perhaps better than most, but not quite out of the ordinary.

Our project was nevertheless out of the ordinary, if only for its length. Among Aboriginal people the competition between the speakers, particularly when there was alcohol flowing, meant that sooner or later someone else would want his turn and butt in. The situation of the recording session and the understanding that he had the floor to do his 'oral history' created the space in which to construct a more ambitious narrative. But this, of course, did not provide him with the framework for it.

When I was interlocutor Myles strung his yarns together in a sequence that was roughly chronological but also, because he was talking about travelling for much of the time, topographical.[39] Indeed, the itinerary may be said to determine the sequence, inasmuch as many of the incidents he describes could have happened at any time. At one point in his narrative, when he is still a long way off the Birdsville Track, which he had often talked about before, he pauses to promise that later on—that is, when his narrative lands him there—he will 'take me through all that country where old George travelled', and in due course he does, telling it in a kind of counterpoint, rather as the two of them used to argue about their conflicting memories, 'like he was talking yesterday and I was talking today'.

I don't think his narrative would have taken this form if he had not been telling it to someone who knew George Dutton. With his daughter, who was only a child when the old man died, there is less about country, but the chronology remains: his early childhood, hard times in Uralla during the Depression, the oppressiveness of the authorities. He went over some of the ground he had covered with me, though with further details which had perhaps come to mind after we had talked about them.

It is Myles' past that is being recorded here, whether for me, or the family, or the world at large, and one can read his 'oral history' as autobiography, in the modern sense. There is a dwelling on childhood—something that Krupat says is uncharacteristic of Native American autobiography—and some sense of personal development flowing from certain key events. For example, at one point he speculates that he was drawn to old men such as George because he had lost his father early in life. The recurring 'Protestant' theme of self-reliance can also be read as the lesson he learned early in life, through his rejection in his own birthplace and lack of family support. Throughout a lifetime of displacement and disconnection, his own sense of self is the primary source of continuity.

Displacement in one way or another, as I suggested earlier, is the experience of many if not most testimonialists. It is also a common experience for Aboriginal people. Morgan calls her autobiography *My Place*, although it is her grandmother, mother and grand-uncle who were physically displaced; Myles was likewise displaced, in the first instance by his relatives and the authorities, but later by his own choice. For such people, the stereotypical *gemeinschaft* of Krupat and Yúdice's formulation is not an option. Displacement and a need to constitute the self in a new way, and with conscious deliberation, problematise the relationship with any collectivity, at least to the extent of having to make explicit what might otherwise be left implicit. This may go some way towards explaining why testimonial narratives so often take the autobiographical form.

Myles' narrative consists of a dialectic between himself as subject and the Aboriginal world with which he identifies and is identified with. This is because this world is his own articulation. In identifying as Aboriginal, his credentials are his appearance. This is critical for a travelling man such as himself, for, as he tells it, when he goes beyond the places where he and his name are known he can get some kind of recognition from the local Aborigines, though there may be some who do not want to know him. By the same token, he has to expect rejection from many of the whites, though he does not avoid them on this account, developing the front to come to terms with them when the occasion arises. Some figure in his stories: employers, some of whom were 'all right', doctors in the medical service who will talk to you on an equal footing, as well as the police and the welfare board officials. It is Aboriginal sociality he wants to remember, however, naming the individuals whom he has known during his travels and the places where they live. The names of the people, and his rehearsing in fine detail where exactly their houses were situated, and often what they said on a particular occasion, even mimicking their voices, stand for the 'community' that Mudrooroo perceives on the cover of Bropho's book.

Frederic Jameson, discussing the Third World testimonial novel, heralds the dispelling of the 'authorship' of the old centred-subject-private-property type, and the instituting of 'some new collective space between named subjects and individual human beings'. 'Anonymity here means not the loss of personal identity, of the proper name, but the multiplication of those things; not the faceless sociological average or sample or least common denominator, but the association of one individual with a host of other concrete individuals.'[40] But it is Myles' life course rather than a pre-existing community that articulates this world of names: in this life he has travelled far and wide so that the people who live in one place may not know those who live in another place he talks about, and with his death this world falls apart, unless it has been recorded in some lasting form, which is what he seemed to want to do in his oral history.

Myles is prepared to generalise, beyond his own experience and that of the people he knows, about the experience of being Aboriginal in settler Australia. But, despite a strong sense of the opposition between black and white, and a sceptical commitment to various Aboriginal causes and organisations, he stops short of political rhetoric. He has a bitter disquisition on 'the white man's morals', but does not articulate the nature of Aboriginal difference. On the contrary, there is a sense of the plurality of the Aboriginal world.

In contrast to most Aboriginal writers, including Morgan, Myles makes little of traditional knowledge. He refers to such matters when he is talking about his times with 'the old people', but it is as an outsider who is puzzled and amused, not as an heir to this knowledge. He mentions them, he says, because he knows I am interested. Even with his great friend George Dutton, he admits there were times when they were just not on the same wavelength. It is not just the difference in age. Myles can imagine some of the stories the old man tells about the past, like his people's forced removal from Tibooburra to the Brewarrina settlement in 1936, and the subsequent flight of him and his family, travelling by night to avoid the authorities. But, he says, Wilcannia township, where they both lived, 'just didn't exist as far as George was concerned'. 'But if you go the opposite way (back towards Tibooburra) every hill existed. And when you get talking to him, you get beat then, because he's talking about something that was bloody vital when he was a young fellow, but you can't see it the way he's seeing it.' The nexus of people, place and myth has disintegrated and, separated from one another, they have changed. In his history, Myles rearticulates the nexus in a secular sense, but he knows that it won't last out there in the real world. Again, unlike Morgan and many other Aboriginal writers, he does not deploy the trope of spirituality, although at one point he says he could tell such stories (and had in fact done so, the first time I met him).

As for the disjunction between him and me, this is not so much stated as implied in the subject matter. I would gloss it in terms of race, in a relatively unmediated form, but also of class, as implied in the stories he tells of a life as an Aboriginal man who has been a stockman and truck driver and much beside. As a middle-class white academic I have never experienced such things, but I know something about them if only because he has told me on earlier occasions, and I did once have a hair-raising ride with him in the Ivanhoe to Wilcannia mail car, of which he reminds me. But the conjunction between us resides finally in the fact that I have known some of the people he is talking about. This, of course, is not going to be the case with other readers, for whom as editor I have had to make the history accessible.

Myles Lalor's oral history does not as yet have a readership. It has been my job to find him one, bearing in mind the strictures placed upon non-indigenous editors and interlocutors, particularly those who may be presumed to have their own academic and ideological agendas. For the most part his meaning is clear and, as I have suggested, his narrative is sufficiently connected for him to speak for himself. I have had to take the risk of tidying up the false starts, the sentences that go awry, the repetitions; otherwise, reading will become wearisome. I have also provided some factual background for the reader who does not know what kind of a place Uralla is, or how the mallee camp in Wilcannia came about, or what the government policy on Aborigines was during the years when Myles was growing up. But these passages will be marked as mine, and the purist is free to skip them if they seem intrusive. What I cannot eliminate is the part

I played in Myles' discourse, through being his audience and interlocutor during the first rounds of recording, and because of the
memories we shared. On his visits Myles often arrived with gifts—
Aboriginal gifts such as wild meat or emu eggs—and once he made
johnny cakes on the electric stove; in a way his oral history was also
an Aboriginal gift.

8

Taha Maori in the *DNZB*
A Pakeha view

W.H. Oliver

The terms of this title may need some introduction for readers who are not New Zealanders and, possibly, for a number who are. *DNZB* is the abbreviation for *The Dictionary of New Zealand Biography* and is used here to indicate both the publication itself and the agency (a section of the Department of Internal Affairs) which produced it, in a bilingual series of volumes beginning in 1990 and completed, at least for the time being, last year.

Taha Maori is, on the face of it, a simple term, but a small story may show that nothing which prompts bicultural considerations remains simple for long in New Zealand. In 1985 the *DNZB* placed an advertisement in the major newspapers for a new editorial appointee. Innocently, we described the position as 'Assistant Editor (Maori)'. One paper refused to publish it on the grounds that such terminology would be found objectionable by the Race Relations Commissioner. The advertisement was withdrawn and replaced with one identical in all respects except that it sought to fill a position entitled 'Assistant Editor (Taha Maori)' with a person equipped to

143

work on 'the Maori side' of the project. In the event, a Maori was appointed and others followed, one as a translator a little later and a few to research positions. But in the end taha Maori work was finally discharged by: a Pakeha General Editor with considerable competence in Maori language and long experience in Maori history; two Maori heading a team of Maori translators and consultants; a Pakeha scholar with rare skills in Maori language, history and archival material; the Victoria University Maori Studies Department and Te Taura Whiri I Te Reo Maori (the Maori Language Commission) as language consultants; and two Maori advisory bodies. Further, what might, not quite properly, be called 'the Pakeha side' was also involved in the Maori program, in the editing, research and preparation for publication of the essays on Maori subjects in their (for by far the greater part) original English language form.

The further term in the title, 'a Pakeha view', indicates my standpoint; it is a highly personal Pakeha view. The greater part of this account is limited to events and developments in which I participated or closely observed as General Editor from 1983 to 1990. The following decade, thanks in good measure to the lessons learned in this earlier period, would be the subject of a much more orderly tale, but it is not one that I am qualified to write.

I had (and have) few claims to be considered bicultural. Andrew Sharp makes a useful distinction between two ways of 'being bicultural'.[1] On the one hand there are those who have chosen to be (in the case of some Pakeha) or cannot avoid being (in the case of many Maori) fully bicultural through a deep familiarity with both cultures. On the other there are those who, for their own good reasons, do not choose that course but learn enough to show respect for those belonging to the other culture; such people are normally Pakeha, for competence in the other culture at an appropriate level is less an option than a necessity for most Maori. When I took up the position of editor I would not even have qualified according to Sharp's second definition. I had made one vain attempt to learn a little of the language, had had a few Maori students, and had chaired a university department that taught a good deal of Maori history in the contexts of New Zealand and 'race relations' history. While I learned quite a bit in the next few years, it remains the case that my main contribution to the *DNZB*'s taha Maori was in raising the money so that others could do the work. But even with such a meagre background I did not doubt for a minute that the published outcome should be as bicultural as the circumstances would permit.

It is difficult not to be, if in no more than a rudimentary and even in a discriminatory way, a little 'bicultural' in New Zealand.

The great silence which Henry Reynolds explores and has done so much to dispel,[2] and which went far to eliminate Aborigines from the historical memory of twentieth-century 'white' Australians, has never fallen upon New Zealand. Few Pakeha children in the first half of the twentieth century would have grown up with historical memories in which Maori did not figure[3] (though they were not the memories Maori had of themselves, even if Maori participation in such bodies as the Polynesian Society had helped to shape the Pakeha memory).[4] The deployment of Maori items to express a generalised sense of antipodean identity was considerable and has not abated; indeed, it has become a flood of what might be called 'cosmetic decolonisation'. That the Maori side of the *DNZB* may be simply (or, more truly, complexly) part of that flood is a possibility which should hang like a question mark over this essay.

The first *Dictionary of New Zealand Biography* was published in 1940, the year of New Zealand's centenary, edited (and in fact written) by Guy H. Scholefield, who was assisted by Apirana Ngata, a prominent Maori leader.[5] Whatever may be said about the quality and scope of the Maori entries in this publication—and there is not much that could not also be said about the Pakeha entries—they are both numerous and prominent. Scholefield had an intimate acquaintance with the early years of colonisation and a traditionalist intention of giving prominence to soldiers, politicians and other (usually male) leaders. On both counts Maori scored well and there are quite a large number of them in his two thick volumes—around eight per cent. Some of the longer essays are devoted to Maori heroes and villains, as well as to political and tribal notables. His selection is certainly slanted towards the regions of early contact and conflict; the archival record makes some such bias hard to avoid, but one has the impression that it did not occur to Scholefield to try to do so.

The task before the new *DNZB* was to ensure a more balanced as well as a more numerous representation of Maori, and to do this through the advice (and the requirements) of Maori who could speak with some authority, especially for their own tribal groups. That goal was by no means completely achieved; nor was it approached (insofar as it was) in an entirely harmonious manner. Probably both the incompleteness and the disharmony were unavoidable; no activity that brings Maori and Pakeha together will be without the stresses and conflicts inherent in their past and endemic in their present. This was inevitably the case when the meeting place was an activity of the state designed to celebrate 150 years of—no-one was quite sure what—in 1990.[6]

That this was an enterprise set up by the ancient enemy, 'the Crown', was a stumbling block for some. For others it was a once-in-a-lifetime chance that should not be rejected. Whatever 1990 stood for, and the lack of definition was both intrinsic in the event and a piece of good luck, it was at least an occasion which produced enough money to support a major scholarly activity; and many Maori leaders, with a long history of fastening upon whatever openings the settler state, intentionally or not, makes available, accepted the thrust of this argument.

Some, Pakeha as well as Maori, suspected that an enterprise conducted within a state department by public servants would be subject to intolerable political pressures upon editorial integrity, but with one benign exception (to be noted below) this was not the case. In another respect, however, some limitations could not be avoided in an enterprise created and funded to produce a substantial work of reference. Traditionally biographical dictionaries have been set up to serve some kind of nation-building function, most transparently in those former colonies which achieved independence in the twentieth century and sought to assert their self-awareness. Although, of course, we knew that we were among the more distant offspring of Leslie Stephen and the British *Dictionary of National Biography*, we also knew that we were a younger sibling of the *Australian Dictionary of Biography* and the *Dictionary of Canadian Biography*, two patently nationalistic enterprises and, as well, models of historical scholarship. However advantageously difficult it was to read our political masters' minds, it was clear enough that they wanted something monumental, celebratory and—at least plausibly—germane to 'national identity'. The outcome, the product, had to be recognisable as a member of the 'national biography' club.

Even so, the project design proposed an outcome considerably more varied than an assemblage of nation-building 'greats', for the most part male, European, and distinguished in such pursuits as politics, war, commerce and science. The greats were to be required to keep company with others less prominent in their time, but whose eminence would (it was hoped) be apparent once attention was paid to considerations of gender, social status, region and ethnicity. This last, wider than taha Maori, nevertheless accorded Maori an eminent place, one that in the realm of language was to approach parity. (This

146

is the 'benign exception' noted above: publication in Maori. It was firmly proposed by Brian McLay, Deputy-Secretary of Internal Affairs, and as firmly insisted upon by Claudia Orange, appointed Assistant Editor early in 1984.)

Responsibility for this outcome was placed upon a single individual, contracted to the government and accountable to a head of department. The official expectations were focused upon him—and, when I was succeeded by Claudia Orange in 1990, upon her. From time to time both Maori and Pakeha participants found the exercise of this power unwelcome. Maori, probably, found it especially so, coming from a Pakeha in some obscure way embodying 'the Crown' and, from their perspective, ignorant and without authority. Although such conflicts were not common, they are instructive and one or two will be recounted below.

When we examined other biographical dictionaries, especially our Australian and Canadian elder contemporaries, we found that the great silence had fallen over both, especially over their earlier volumes. There were plenty of reasons why this should have been so: the smallness of the indigenous populations, their diversity in language, their distance (at that time) from the centres of settler population, perhaps the lack (relative to New Zealand) of an indigenous intelligentsia, and their (as seen by the colonisers) lack of connection with 'nation-building' for, after all, they were the nations which the new nations had pushed aside.[7] In New Zealand, however, indigenous people have always been emphatically present, reasonably accessible and distinctly 'audible', more than ever so in the 1980s. Three factors made for a degree of accessibility. First, Maori had become a single written language in the 1830s and this had substantially eliminated the not very great tribal and regional variations. Second, there was a Maori elite, of scholars, politicians, officials and people of mana, to whom one could go. And some, at least, of the Pakeha who went to them were already of standing and commanded some respect in Maori circles.

If one wished to make it seem orderly, one would say that there was a great deal of trial and error in the *DNZB*'s early efforts on 'the Maori side'. Less charitably, one would have to say that there was for a while near-total chaos, from which, just in time, a sufficient order emerged, in good measure thanks to Claudia Orange's energetic intervention early in 1990. There were, however, three powerful and wonderfully talented people who provided an element of solidity and a thread of continuity through the early chaos: Tipene O'Regan of

Ngai Tahu, academic, politician and storyteller; William Parker of Ngati Porou, scholar, orator and linguist; and John Rangihau of Tuhoe, a leader of such eminence as to be unclassifiable. Te Rangihau gave the project the immense benefit of his endorsement; Parker the blessing of his regular presence in the office, a deeply informing experience for those, like the present writer, who needed it; and O'Regan his persistence in moving matters forward both as a consultant and as chairman on the Maori Working Party. The whole process may be examined in terms of structures, participation, goals, research, selection, authorship and translation.

SETTING UP THE STRUCTURES

Here it is much easier to describe the outcome than the way in which it came about. In the end, and in time to publish the first Maori volume in 1990, there was a fairly tidy structure consisting of a Policy Committee with strong Maori representation, a Maori Working Party, a Maori Editorial Committee, a panel of translators, a consultancy with the Maori Studies Department at Victoria University (later with the Maori Language Commission) to supervise translation, a group of specialists in language and history on the staff and also a sizeable share of the unit's research and editorial capacity.

In November 1984, the first 'Maori meeting' was held, chaired by Te Rangihau and attended by Wellington residents with a 'reasonable' tribal spread. It considered plans for consultation, the appointment of an Assistant Editor (Maori), and the formation of a Maori Editorial Committee. At its next meeting, in February 1985, the Policy Committee formally constituted a 'Maori Advisory Editorial Committee' as a sub-committee, with Te Rangihau as chairman and Neville Baker (at that time Deputy-Secretary of the Department of Maori Affairs) as his deputy. That body, known as the Maori Advisory Committee, did not meet again until October 1985; a good deal of the interim was taken up with the search for an Assistant Editor, ideally a person who would combine academic qualifications, bilingual capacity, administrative and/or editorial experience and acceptability in Maoridom.[8] The Advisory Committee was supplemented from time to time by a more numerous meeting of 'the Maori network', but the distinction between the two was not sharp, nor was the membership of either fixed—people who happened to be in Wellington often showed up. Towards the end of 1986 it was proposed to the Policy Committee that a smaller working group, drawn from the Advisory Committee, should be set up. So, from the beginning of 1987, the program was accelerated by the efforts of a smaller (but still fluctuating) Maori Working Party under the chairmanship of Tipene O'Regan. It was a 'working' group in deed as well as in name; it contributed in a major way to the activities described in the following sections, and to the eventual outcome, the publication of the first volume of *Ngā Tāngata Taumata Rau* in 1990.[9]

This bald account does less than justice to the character of these bodies. The task was formidable, both to do it at all and to do it on time, and the opening and closing of meetings with prayer often seemed much more than simply culturally appropriate. And, in spite of the seriousness, indeed at times the desperateness, of the situation, these meetings were filled with high humour and hilarity, with the monolingual editor often feeling obliged to demand a translation of the joke. Meetings were, in fact, bilingual—the editor was not the only one in need of an English translation.

INVITING PARTICIPATION

Not just on the Maori side but with the Pakeha side quite as much, the *DNZB* had to make itself known, gain acceptance, enlist support and secure participation. Indeed, the problems inhibiting this campaign were common to both sides: suspicion of a government activity (but more acute among Maori because of their suspicion of 'the Crown'); a concern for the repute of an ancestor (again more acute for Maori because of the special characteristics of mana); and an occasional anxiety as to the destination of the 'profits'. In spite of these qualifications, however, there was enough shared experience to unify the two sides of the program.[10]

The campaign to make the project known among Maori and to secure their participation began early in 1984, under the guidance of Te Rangihau, a founding member of the *DNZB* Policy Committee. At first it was directed at prominent individuals in tertiary institutions and government departments, and in the two major national organisations, the Maori Women's Welfare League and the New Zealand Maori Council. Te Rangihau (together with Claudia Orange) addressed the annual conference of the League, and (with the present writer) a meeting of the Council. Trust boards, district councils and welfare league branches were contacted.

The initial thrust was towards the ideal that was at that time coming to be identified as 'partnership' and (with the exception of the final authority of the editor) towards parallel structures based, on the Maori side, on the tribe. (At one point, to the dismay of some of them, the *DNZB*'s regional working parties were asked to keep off the Maori patch.) Thus, the initial proposals to the Policy Committee emphasised that work should be on a tribal basis, through tribal nominees and trust boards, that tribal archives should be built up with *DNZB* assistance as a koha (gift) in return for cooperation, that essays might well be written by groups of tribal members, and that while 'Europeans might also write tribal biographies . . . this would have to be carefully negotiated'. It was also considered that Maori cooperation would be 'strictly limited' if the goal was merely translation from English.[11]

Many of these ideal goals, like those noted in the next section, did not survive the cold breath of reality. One of the problems with the notion of 'a tribal basis'—only a 'problem' when Pakeha are interacting 'politically' with Maori—is that 'tribal' indicates groups which vary from the large to the very small and from the well-organised to the (for such purposes) entirely unorganised; further, there is no fixed notion of what constitutes a 'tribe' nor any agreement as to how many, at any given point of time, there are. In effect, the *DNZB* directed its attention to the larger and more readily recognisable tribal entities, and did so with at least some success.

These efforts were accelerated with the appointment of Miria Simpson as Assistant Editor in 1985. She undertook a series of visits to tribal and regional centres and had covered most of the North Island by the middle of the following year. This included going on one occasion to the annual Coronation hui (meeting) of Te Arikinui, Dame Te Atairangikaahu, on the Kingitanga marae (community space) at Turangawaewae, joining the party which took the mate (death) of Ruka Broughton (a member of the advisory committee) to the marae. Such occasions were not explicitly directed towards securing active participation; the purpose, in Miria Simpson's oft-repeated phrase, was 'to see and be seen'. And, by the end of 1986, she was able to report: 'I can say that there is a glimmer of light at the end of the tunnel.'[12] By this time lists of prospective subjects were being drawn up, some of them nominated by tribal leaders, and before long the first trickle of essays began—alas for high hopes, in English. But other demands came to dominate the time and attention of both the Working Party and *DNZB* staff: subject lists, an in-house research base, the commissioning of writers, and the translation of essays.

SETTING THE GOALS

Inevitably, perhaps, some idealistic goals were quite rapidly translated into more attainable objectives. The first to go was the notion that a separate volume should be devoted to Maori biography in the centuries before the arrival of Cook. The idea of a traditional volume surfaced a few times at Policy Committee meetings in 1984—as late as November of that year it was still 'firmly proposed'—and passed away. The projected series began with Volume I (1769–1870). Time and money were at a premium, and the effort to do some kind of justice to Maori in the first century of written record would absorb enough of both. But even had time and resources been more plentiful it is unlikely that the project would have access to highly tapu (protected or sacrosanct) traditional information unless it was under Maori control, and perhaps not even then. Further, it was known that a comparable proposal for a Maori tribal history carried through by tribal representatives had foundered as recently as 1980.[13] The stories of earlier times remain hidden away in learned (and at times not so learned) publications,[14] in public and tribal archives, and in the memories of 'the old people'.

The other major non-achievement was the disappointment of the hope that the essays should be written by Maori in Maori and then translated into English. In the event, only a small handful were; the rest were written in English and translated by language experts. In 1984, the year of hope, it was reported that 'a straight translation job would not constitute a publication that could truly be called Maori'. But when the notable scholar Ruka Broughton was consulted early in that year, he reported that 'there were very few Maoris [sic] with both the academic ability and the language capacity to compose in Maori'.[15] Around the same time, and for the same reasons, the proposals that essays be put together by groups of tribal informants and that tribal elders be recorded on tape, disappear from the record.

This goal, of Maori life stories written in Maori by Maori drawing upon traditional sources, remains an ideal for the future; at one point it was suggested (by the present writer) that when the

bicentenary arrived, in 2040, a distinct Maori biographical dictionary, organised and produced by Maori, might have become a
possibility.[16] In the meantime, it was assumed that we should get on
with what we could do, publicising the project, enlisting support,
defining principles, and selecting subjects and authors. Maori
writing ceased to be seen as a point of departure and became an
objective to be attained through an elaborate translation process.

This publicity led to a degree of acceptance among many Maori.
There were exceptions: a leader who forbad a younger tribal
member to write on an ancestor, because the project was a government one and the government was treating Maori unfairly in the
matter of public broadcasting; and a renowned traditional scholar
who persuaded a major trust board to withhold cooperation
because, much earlier, traditional material he had supplied had been
broadcast on public radio without his authorisation. (In the event,
milder counsels prevailed, and the latter participated as a joint
author of an important essay.) But, as the following sections will
show, there were more serious limits to the extent and to the efficacy
of participation.

DOING RESEARCH

From early on, both as a supplement to contributed essays and as
a fall-back position should they not be sufficiently numerous and,
in addition, to ensure a complete tribal/regional coverage, the
Dictionary began to list names of people who would have to be
included (known in the unit as 'dead certs') and to compile basic
information files upon a range of potential subjects. There was
nothing of a 'special treatment' kind in all this; from the outset a
sizeable biographical database had been created for general selection purposes and extensive files built up for all those selected for
entry. The DNZB intended to be in a position to impose a rigorous
check upon all entries, Maori, Pakeha and 'other'.[17] The core of this
information base was provided by Claudia Orange and Angela
Ballara, who made available biographical material from their own
research resources. Thus, the DNZB was in a position both to
prompt tribal memories with names and data, and to fill the gaps.
The crucial importance of these Maori subject files became more
apparent when it was realised that a sizeable proportion of essays
would need to be written 'in the office'.

By September 1987, one and a half members of staff were employed on Maori research and more than 400 Maori names and related data had been entered on computer. The greater part of the 'target lists' of names which were taken up and reviewed by the Maori Working Party were from this database. Where the lists revealed gaps in tribal and regional coverage, staff members were designated to fill them.[18] As the 1990 deadline approached more staff were assigned to this research. That publication, both in English and Maori, was managed in that year is due in no small measure to their efforts and to the effectiveness of the research program within which they worked.

SELECTING THE SUBJECTS

The nomination and selection of subjects for dictionary essays turned out to be the activity in which Maori consultants, advisers and helpers were most effective. Tribal representatives knew pretty clearly those of their own whom they wanted to see in the publication. Although there were times when an editor could hardly resist envying his predecessor, Scholefield, who consulted only one Maori advisor, this degree of participation, while more arduous, was also more rewarding.[19] There were three major decisions facing the *DNZB*: how many Maori entries there should be; how they should be distributed among tribes and regions; and, most critically, who they should be.

There was a good deal of discussion about the number of Maori subjects and the proportion they should bear to the total number in the English volume. From the outset, *DNZB* ideas on representation had taken the latter into account; it was considered that population data should be heeded, though not slavishly followed, in establishing a degree of equity between variously defined groups, including Maori. However, for the period of the first volume, 1769–1869, this approach met insuperable problems. There were no Maori censuses of any kind until the 1850s, and none of even marginal reliability until the 1870s, and while the Maori population was, of course, preponderant, before the 1840s estimates varied widely from less than 100 000 to over 500 000.[20] Although the late Keith Sinclair, a member of the Policy Committee, is on record as stating that the proportions of the first volume should reflect the pre-1840 population, no one took this view seriously.[21]

The dual process of selecting subjects and nominating writers went on in tandem. In September 1986 it was decided to draw up an initial 'target list' of obvious subjects. By the end of the year nominations were coming in, some prompted by Miria Simpson's tours in the two preceding years. By the beginning of 1987 a preliminary list of 140 people had been drawn up, derived from a much larger list of possibles. There had been a marked input from some twelve tribal or regional groups. In the same year a series of 'target lists' were taken to the Working Party for discussion, amendment, addition and, in the form in which they survived, endorsement. At the same time, the Working Party suggested writers to be commissioned. Sizeable additions to the list were made as a result of direct negotiations with four major tribal groups: Waikato/Tainui, Tuhoe, Ngati Porou and Ngai Tahu.

In an effort to achieve some kind of balance, it was decided to try to get somewhere in the vicinity of 150 to 200 Maori people in a volume with a total number of about 600—this figure could be described as an educated guess. At the end of 1987 the prospective target stood at 160; by mid 1988 it had risen to 205. By the time of publication it had fallen back to 161. The difficulty of finding writers for all the subjects it was hoped to place made a contribution to this decline. In the end some 27 per cent of subjects in the first volume were Maori; in the following four volumes, reflecting the decline of the Maori and the increase of the settler populations, the proportion fell to around thirteen to fourteen per cent. Over the eventual five volumes it stands at sixteen per cent, serendipitously close to the current Maori share of the New Zealand population. Whether or not these proportions reflect a rough kind of bicultural justice is a question left to the reader.

The tribal/regional distribution was—or at least it was hoped it would prove to be—as fair as time, participation and the archival deposit would permit. Although some effort was devoted to securing an equitable distribution based on tribal population numbers,[22] the eventual list could not help but reflect two contingent factors: the generation of a skewed archival record by the regional incidence of Maori–settler interaction, and the superior capacity of some tribal organisations to respond to the opportunity to 'place' their people. Clearly, the outcome was a good deal less than perfect. But many of those who did find their way into print were those whom tribal groups had nominated, and most had been endorsed by Maori advisers and consultants.

WRITING THE ENTRIES

The *DNZB*'s dual approach—commissioning writers and yet storing data to provide a check upon them—testifies to its clear intention not to depart very far from the conventional canons governing works of reference. This caution applied to the whole operation, to Pakeha as well as to Maori participation. But, of course, on the Maori side it ran a greater risk of cultural dissonance, though not one wholly unknown on the Pakeha side—a good deal of Pakeha storytelling failed to survive the editorial process. Still, much attention was paid, by *DNZB* staff and by the Maori Working Party, to the question of what the essays should be like and whether, in the context of this kind of book, there was room for a distinctive Maori character. The answer was a qualified 'yes'—qualified by the structural limits of a western literary genre.[23]

It was perhaps a rash and an unreal ambition, but an effort was made to identify the kind of entry which 'would be expressed in a way acceptable to Maoris [sic] as well as satisfactory to the *DNZB*'. Towards the end of 1985 the Working Party adopted a set of 'essential elements' for Maori biographies. The essays should express 'the identity of the person in terms of descent and relationships; of tribal membership and affiliations; and of place, landmarks and region'. The statement went on to note that while there no doubt were 'European conventions corresponding to these expectations' the stress placed upon them would be greater in a Maori essay.

Inevitably, consideration of the right kind of essay led to a search for the right kind of writer. A draft paper prepared for an early 1987 meeting of the Working Party defined an 'ideal' writer as one familiar with both traditional and documentary material, competent in both languages and willing to air divergent viewpoints. The paper actually considered by the Working Party opted for less than this; it proposed that writers should be 'either recognised specialists, or capable people willing to have a go, or writers on contract, or *DNZB* staff, selected for their competence and for their readiness to observe Dictionary guidelines'. But the idea of a 'distinctively Maori character' was maintained, 'especially in the Maori language versions'. At the same meeting the authorship problem presented by subjects important to a number of tribes was discussed. Te Kooti Arikirangi was a leading example; there was to be consultation with Ringatu church leaders, which led to the commissioning of Judith Binney.[24]

By early 1987 the Working Party and *DNZB* staff were rather more concerned with identifying prospective writers, whether Maori or Pakeha (but certainly Maori when there was a good prospect), than with describing the ideal essay, though in mid year, after a discussion of a handful of 'pilot essays', it identified as many as 18 biographical items which, ideally, should be covered in an essay. Commissioning began when, in March of that year, the Working Party proposed writers for the first 60-strong 'target list'; it continued to do this with succeeding lists.

By May 1987 the first ominous signs appeared. Twenty-three of those invited had not responded and of the 20 who had, five were members of the Working Party and two were on the *DNZB* staff. Later in the year, a commissioning list was drawn up of 133 subjects for whom authors had either been invited or, it was hoped, could be found through tribal group commissions, as well as individual commissions. Of those as many as 46—over a third—do not appear in Volume I; a few were held over to the next volume, and many find at least a place in the nominal index because they were mentioned in other essays.[25]

In the end, the in-house share of writing had to be expanded greatly. Of the 160 essays on Maori subjects in the first general volume, about half were written by *DNZB* staff. In many instances, however, these essays incorporated items contributed by family or tribal sources, especially stories that would not otherwise have been available. Some of them were written with close tribal cooperation. Of the rest, a number were written by descendants of the subject, and some significant groups of essays were written under tribal auspices by both Maori and Pakeha writers, especially those relating to Waikato/Tainui, Ngati Tuwharetoa, Tuhoe, Ngati Porou, Rangitane and Ngai Tahu.

TRANSLATION AND LANGUAGE ISSUES

Even the meagre knowledge of Maori which arises from a failed attempt to learn a little of it is enough to make it obvious that the problems of translation between two fundamentally unlike languages are much more formidable than they would have been with the *DNZB*'s bilingual contemporary, the *Dictionary of Canadian Biography*. No-one engaged upon the English to Maori translation program was prepared to tolerate a simple word-by-word translation, one in which the vocabulary would be Maori but not the basic structure. The exercise became one in which the English essay was dismantled into its component thought-items and rebuilt from the ground up in Maori. As a report of March 1990 put it: 'we are venturing into new territory where we regularly encounter . . . unexpected problems.'[26]

Once the essays were available for translation, and this did not occur until August 1988, a team of contract translators was recruited.[27] They worked under the administrative supervision of Tairongo Amoamo, himself a translator, while Miria Simpson began to prepare the essays for publication. By mid-1989 it had become clear that the program was well behind schedule. The contract translation team was expanded to fifteen, two translators were added to the staff, and Angela Ballara, already a part-time staff member, became a full-time copy editor. In addition, contracts were entered into with the New Zealand Translation Centre, the Maori Language Commission and the Victoria University Maori Studies Department; the latter, through Hirini Moko Mead and Pou Temara, monitored the whole output for the first volume. This program was directed by Claudia Orange (by this time Associate Editor). As well as being highly labour intensive, the program was extremely expensive; the skills required by it were (and remain) in short supply on a sellers' market.

A couple of the 'unexpected problems' encountered on the way to publication are worth exploring. The Dictionary became enmeshed in linguistic problems inherent in the Maori language's 150 years of coexistence with English. The translators minimised the use of transliteration, preferring to adapt old words to new uses. It was decided to use the macron to indicate vowel length, thereby displeasing the remnant who persisted in doubling the vowel for this purpose (as well as some opposed to any such phonetic device). And the Dictionary became, quite inadvertently, embroiled in a controversy over the hyphenation of complex Maori words. The retired Auckland Professor of Maori, Bruce Biggs, was pursuing a private agenda in favour of the system of hyphenation designed by his colleague, Pat Hohepa, to clarify the meaning of multisyllabic words—often place names which in themselves told the story of the naming. This meaning was obscured, it was argued, by running all the syllables together. He proposed to the *DNZB* that it convene a meeting of Maori and Pakeha language specialists to hear him read a paper. During the following discussion a Pakeha specialist, not a *DNZB* staff member, was rash enough to use the word 'standardisation', one likely to offend the more emphatic tribalists in the gathering. One such, the formidable Ngati Porou leader, Api Mahuika, reminded the meeting as a whole and Biggs in particular that his taiaha (long club) still hung over his mantelpiece, and that he would defend the traditional place names of his people.[28] In the event, the Dictionary did employ hyphens in many personal names of six or more syllables.

Both the order of an individual's names within an entry heading, and the overall order of names within the volume, provided matter for discussion and, at least once, for sharp controversy. Nineteenth-century Maori had been in the process of shifting towards a first name and surname convention, as a result of names taken in baptism or under other European influence; further traditional names were sometimes added in the course of a lifetime.[29] Many Pakeha have grown up knowing that there was a great mid-nineteenth-century leader called Wiremu Tamihana; they may have known that this was a transliteration of the name taken at baptism, William Thompson. Probably they did not know that his inherited name was Te Waharoa and his acquired traditional name was Tarapipipi. How should he be named for listing purposes? Given the flux of the situation being dealt with, no hard and fast rule could be applied. In general, the Dictionary gave priority to the traditional name. Thus, the published volume lists 'Te Waharoa, Wiremu Tāmihana Tarapīpipi', a form which minimises while it continues to reflect the pressure placed upon tradition by western conventions.

The same pressures were reflected in a controversy over the organisation of the first Maori language volume. The English language volume was clearly going to put all names, of whatever racial origination, into a single alphabetical order. The proposal that the Maori volume should do things differently—that names should be clustered according to tribal affiliation—occasioned sharp conflict. Alphabetisation, it was argued, was a 'western' convention and should not be allowed to shape the Maori volume. Other Maori opinion was less dogmatic: the alphabet was certainly western but, for that matter, so was the very idea of a reference book. Further, this was to be the first in a series of volumes, and as time went on cross-tribal marriages made tribal affiliation multiple and difficult— and also politically hazardous—to prioritise. And even if tribal organisation had been attempted, the alphabet would still have had its say unless, of course, within tribal divisions the entries had been set out in a purely random manner.

There are now five volumes of *Ngā Tāngata Taumata Rau*; the most recent, launched at the end of 2000, takes the series into the second half of the twentieth century. While a 'Maori history of New Zealand' is being planned and will be produced under Maori auspices, these volumes, for all the limitations of collective biography, will in the meantime meet something of the need for such a work. It is a 'history' in the language of the people whose life stories it recounts. (A further characteristic is instructive; while the authors' names were appended to the English versions, this was not done with the Maori versions, on the grounds that these texts were the product of a team effort and not just of the original author.)

The question remains: how was this series received? The short answer is that it is very difficult to say. The amount of publishing in the Maori language is quite small (though it is growing) and, outside the categories of fairly elementary readers for schools and 'how to learn' books, very slight. That in itself suggests that the market for expensive works in sophisticated classical Maori is not great. Certainly that market did not prove to be a major one, once the éclat surrounding the first volume had passed. Of that volume, 1700 copies were sold in the first year, but after ten years the total had risen to only 2267. The second volume, published in 1994, sold 875 copies in the first year; sales rose to 1090 by the end of 1999, while the third volume (1996) began with 281 sales in the first year and rose to 436 by the end of 1999. For the fourth volume (1998) 329 were sold in the first year and no more than nineteen since then. Not surprisingly, print runs declined in the light of these figures, from 2678 for the first volume to 2096, 1493 and 742 for the later volumes.[30]

It is not easy to identify the market for these books. They were all quite expensive; many were institutional sales, including some 400 of the first volume purchased by the NZ Lottery Grants Board for distribution to secondary schools. The decline of the use of the Maori language and its limited recovery (chiefly as a spoken tongue among young people through immersion schooling), the extent to which Maori society remains responsive to the spoken rather than the written word, the 'high culture' level of language aimed at by the Dictionary's translators, the distance at which many Maori, whether in remote rural areas or in outlying suburbs, live from the kind of bookshops likely to take a punt on such expensive volumes, would quite severely limit the market. Perhaps it would be instructive to note a story told of Oxford University Press. An erudite (and probably unique) grammar of the Coptic language was published in the later eighteenth century. As was then the custom with learned books, the printed sheets were stored in the attic and brought down for binding as orders arrived. The last sheets were brought down well into the twentieth century. Copies of *Ngā Tāngata Taumata Rau* are all bound, but they are there, waiting for the orders to come in. This is publishing as an act of faith, *sub speciae aeternitatis*.[31]

9

Maori land law and the Treaty claims process

Andrew Erueti and Alan Ward

In recent decades much of the historical research and debate about settler–indigenous relations in New Zealand has arisen from Maori claims to the Waitangi Tribunal. This tribunal was established by the *Treaty of Waitangi Act 1975* as a forum where Maori could bring claims for any future actions by the Crown which breached the principles of the Treaty of Waitangi and prejudicially affected them; and under the *Treaty of Waitangi Amendment Act 1985* it has had jurisdiction to hear claims for injuries dating from 1840, when the Crown assumed sovereignty and negotiated the Treaty. There are now over 850 claims before the Tribunal, from every district of New Zealand, and the nation's colonial history is being radically revised. So, too, is Maori customary law. In this chapter, we begin by considering how historical evidence is being researched and structured in the claims process.

The claims process has had the effect of pitting Maori claimants not only against the Crown but also against each other. Maori groups never were wholly discrete entities sitting within tidy land boundaries, but complex clusters of lineages connected by intermarriage and political alliance, and with intersecting and overlapping rights to land. While favouring the male line, Maori descent principles were ambilineal; individuals could activate rights derived through either parent and four grandparents. The main levels of social groupings—whanau (extended families), hapu (groups of closely related families) and iwi (a number of hapu also linked by common ancestry and common purposes)—reflected the dynamics of demographic change, politics, migration and war. Some hapu and iwi grew in numbers and strength as others weakened and declined. Leadership, or chieftainship, reflected an ideological preference for the first-born, those in the most direct lines of descent from the ancestor gods and hence possessed of an intrinsic mana (authority ultimately spiritual in origin). But among these senior or tuakana lines especially, particular individuals revealed superior mana through successful leadership in war and peace. Such people secured the recognition and allegiance not only of their closest kin but also of hapu more distantly related.

This dynamism commonly meant that, while various hapu and iwi were dominant in their core areas of residence, several groups had intersecting interests in the same general territory—claims of right of greater or lesser strength and validity, reflecting the history of waves of migration into the area, the actual usage of resources by gardening, fishing and hunting, and the waxing and waning mana of various chiefs. Maori leaders and their kin constantly had to adjust competing claims and accommodate demographic change. Often this could be achieved peacefully, according to widely accepted norms and processes. Sometimes it could not and tribes fought. The durability of the peace that followed reflected the extent of bloodshed, the transfers of goods offered in compensation, and the marriages made to bind former adversaries in new alliances.

British officials interrupted these dynamic processes in 1840 in two main ways: first, they tried to determine which Maori leaders and groups 'owned land' and were entitled under custom to 'sell' it, permanently, either to the Crown or to settlers; second, they declared that, because of the Crown's assumption of sovereignty, warfare was now illegal, and future acquisitions of land rights by force were invalid. Both of these strategies affected Maori attitudes towards land and both resulted in the generation of a body of records which are primary sources for historians today who are seeking to determine what Maori customary land law actually was, and how well (or how badly) the Crown construed it.

There had been a welter of transactions between private settlers and Maori in the decades prior to the assumption of British sovereignty, with entrepreneurs claiming, often on the flimsiest evidence, to have purchased the entirety of the South Island and most of the North Island. Among the more serious claimants was the New Zealand Company founded by Edward Gibbon Wakefield, whose agents claimed to have purchased some 20 million acres on either side of Cook Strait. Indeed, the activities of the Company, and speculators based in Sydney, were largely responsible for the British government's decision to establish the Crown's sovereignty in New Zealand and set up a Land Claims Commission to investigate all pre-1840 purchases.

Between 1840 and 1865 the Crown, for the most part, asserted a monopoly over the right to purchase Maori land, and the Land Purchase Commissioners (led by Chief Land Purchase Commissioner Donald McLean) had the responsibility of determining who, according to Maori law, had the authority to make transactions in land. They signed agreements with the chiefs, which they regarded as deeds of purchase, for the whole of the South Island and Stewart Island, the southern North Island and most of greater Auckland. The policies of the officials were vacillating and expedient. Governor Grey and McLean generally tried to deal with prominent chiefs first (such as the Ngati Toa chiefs in the Cook Strait region), assert that a purchase had been effected, and then make subsidiary payments to other resident chiefs who adduced claims. Where the leadership of a district was complex, however, or the senior chiefs were opposed to land-selling, the officials tried to work through the lesser chiefs and outflank the resisters. As with the Company purchases, the complexities of rights were not usually pursued in detail; rather, the senior chiefs who received payments were left to deal with the various rightowners by distributing the payments as they thought fit.

In 1859–60 Governor Gore Browne, McLean and other officials made a disastrously wrong interpretation of Maori land law in respect of their attempted purchase of the Pekapeka block at Waitara in Taranaki. They attempted to push through a purchase from one of the principal rightowners in the block, the Te Atiawa chief known as Teira, against the veto of Wiremu Kingi Te Rangitake, a chief of at least equal rank as Teira and undoubtedly of greater authority in the tribe. Te Atiawa resisted the governor's use of British troops to force through the survey. They were joined by many fighters from the central North Island tribes, including supporters of the Kingitanga, the movement among the Tainui tribes to establish a Maori monarchy whose principal purpose was to resist further land sales. The resulting wars lasted for ten years, and led to the confiscation of large areas occupied by invading British troops.

The disastrous Waitara purchase discredited the Land Purchase Department and the Crown monopoly of dealings in Maori customary land. Under the *Native Lands Act 1862* and its successors a Native Land Court was established in which the Maori owners of land rights under customary law sought to establish their often competing claims before Pakeha (settler) judges and Maori assessors. Those deemed by the court to be owners of the land received a Crown-granted title in lieu of their customary title—a title by which those named by the court as owners could severally alienate their shares to the Crown or directly to settlers. All other customary rights were extinguished in respect of land that passed through the court, although the court maintained a considerably distorted form of customary succession rules where the recipients of Crown grants died intestate.

The decisions handed down by Chief Judge Fenton and his colleagues from 1866, awarding title to one or more groups and declining to include others, formed precedent judgments. By the end of the nineteenth century, when most customary land had passed through the court, a quasi-codification of Maori land law had been developed, and was subsequently to appear in textbooks such as Norman Smith's *Maori Land Law*, published in 1960. The origins of customary rights in land were said to derive from three main roots or take: unbroken succession from the first occupants of the land (take tupuna), conquest (take raupatu) and gift (take tuku), in each case followed by ongoing occupation of the land (ahi ka, keeping domestic fires burning on the land). Statements by several of the early judges tended to emphasise conquest as the most important factor—the ability to hold the land against all challengers. But many situations had elements of all take—competing claims of right of greater or lesser strength and longevity. The judges often simplified this complexity and made rulings that recognised some groups as exclusive owners of the land and others as having no rights equivalent to ownership.

Very commonly, however, the judges were unable to decide between the competing claims of various hapu and sent them out of the court to come to some agreement, which the court then ratified. While, to a degree, this enabled Maori to work out the priorities and proportions of their respective interests (which were translated into arithmetical shares in the titles), the arrangements reflected prevailing power as much as principle. Some of the claimants were strong, forceful leaders, knowledgeable in the new ways of doing things; some were heavily backed by the intending Pakeha purchasers for the costs of surveys and court fees; others were heavily indebted to Pakeha who advanced them money in the hope or expectation that their faction would win in court. A small army of interpreters, 'native agents' and lawyers made a living out of the process. In short the outcomes, whether of formal judgments or out-of-court agreements, were not derived from wholly customary situations and principles, though they approximated to them to a greater or lesser extent. Moreover, many Maori claimants quickly 'learnt the ropes' of how to tailor their claims to secure the judges' nod. They were culturally obliged to advance the interests of their groups in any case; sometimes more blatant self-interest got superimposed upon that as well.

The minute books of the Native (later Maori) Land Court constitute much the largest body of written records of Maori land tenure, namely, the direct testimony of thousands of Maori men and women. It is relied upon heavily by claimants before the Waitangi Tribunal today, who are seeking to establish the interests they held in the land before it was alienated to the settlers. But, as we shall see, the findings of the Native Land Court, and the evidence presented to it, though enormously valuable, have to be treated with caution. As with all evidence, it is necessary to have regard to the contexts and circumstances in which it was created, and the particular interests and purposes of the witnesses.[1]

Alongside the Native Land Court's attempt to codify the complexity and fluidity of Maori land rights and translate it into a system of ownership of discrete territories, the Crown's administrative processes and early anthropology were also busily identifying the main tribes and giving them tidy boundaries. Official records began giving lists of tribes, which, though they varied between about 30 and 50, attempted to identify the larger social aggregation, the iwi. The hapu, the smaller but more fundamental building blocks of Maori society, were increasingly omitted. The devastating demographic impact of diseases new to Maori also caused hapu to decline and merge with others. In the twentieth century the officially sponsored tribal committees or trust boards that administered remaining lands were at the iwi level or even larger. Mid twentieth century textbooks (some still being used in schools and universities) printed maps of tribes, each neatly bounded by thick black lines, purporting to define tribal boundaries. In fact, even tribes such as the Tuhoe of the central North Island, who had occupied stable heartlands for many centuries, overlapped with other large tribal aggregations at the outer reaches of their domain. In areas which had seen several waves of migration pass through—some very recently—the intersecting interests and inter-hapu relationships were extremely complex, and attempts to map tribal boundaries tidily were misleading.

By the second half of the twentieth century, however, many Maori had come to accept the simplified accounts of land tenure and tribal boundaries as custom. (Their experience, after all, had largely been shaped by encounters with the Maori Land Court and the large tribal trust boards.) And, much later, the early hearings of claims by the Waitangi Tribunal did not seriously shake accepted orthodoxies about tribal rights; the research and findings focused on the grievances against the Crown and did not require a close exploration of relative tribal interests. In the Ngai Tahu claim for example—the first great historical claim heard under the 1985 amendment—it was convenient for all concerned to pursue the claim against the Crown as expeditiously as possible, under the aegis of the Ngai Tahu Trust Board. However, the question of intersecting customary rights could not be ignored for much longer. When the Ngai Tahu leaders deposed their claim on the Tuahiwi marae north of Christchurch in October 1987, speakers on behalf of Rangitane and other tribes located in the north of the South Island lodged a cross-claim, asserting that the northern boundary of the Ngai Tahu territory was not as far north as the Ngai Tahu alleged, or at least that sections of the northern tribes had lived—indeed, still lived—within the territory claimed by Ngai Tahu as being under their mana.

The Tribunal's jurisdiction was not considered to extend to disputes between Maori groups; it was concerned with claims by Maori against the Crown, and that is still the formal position in law. In 1987 the recourse open to the disputing claimants (and the Tribunal) was to refer the dispute to the Maori Appellate Court, a body created in 1894 to hear appeals from the Native Land Court and to determine disputed boundaries. Thus, the Appellate Court heard the claim of Rangitane and others and ruled that Ngai Tahu, in the inter-tribal fighting of the late 1830s, had indeed established control—and hence their boundary—at the line they still claimed in 1987; other tribes did not have rights equivalent to 'ownership' below that boundary. The Privy Council, the final court of appeal, did not overturn this decision. The proceedings, however, aroused considerable concern among Maori observers, and the Appellate Court itself recognised that there might be individuals of either con-tending party living in the territory of the other. The concept of sharp tribal boundaries analogous to those of European states began to be recognised as ill-fitting to the complexity of Maori custom. Furthermore, as the Ngai Tahu claim was heard during 1988 and 1989, it became increasingly difficult to maintain the view that the Ngai Tahu iwi had subsumed all hapu in the region—deriving from several waves of migration—within some kind of corporate entity. At marae in south Canterbury and the West Coast in particular, the identity of specific hapu was asserted, and with it their distinct interests in lands and waters.

The Treaty claims process, in fact, virtually invites Maori to emphasise the competitive, rather than the cooperative, aspects of their culture. Consequently, in the North Island and in the northern South Island, the long-established trust board structure began to be challenged. Claims initially brought before the Tribunal by a trust board or by a runanganui (great council) representing a wide area, several iwi and many hapu, began to be overtaken by claims brought on a hapu or even a whanau basis. In short, the customary Maori social structure, cloaked for a hundred years by Pakeha-derived administrative processes, once more broke through. Claims multiplied rapidly and, as historical research disclosed more and more hapu names within any given area, still more claims were lodged. Expectations held in the mid-1980s—that the historical claims could be dealt with through a relatively small number of large claims, and a scattering of relatively minor claims at family level—were being overtaken by the prospect of hundreds of claims, largely at hapu level and largely in competition with one another. This was a prospect that threatened to bog the whole process down, leading to endless research and litigation and to a serious slowing of compensation to tribes injured by colonial spoliation.

Several steps were taken to meet the situation, notably under the aegis of Edward Taihakurei Durie, appointed Chief Judge of the

Maori Land Court in 1981 and ex officio Chairperson of the Waitangi Tribunal. Legislatively, a section (s.30 (1) (b)) was added to *Te Ture Whenua Maori, 1993* (the revised *Maori Land Act*), giving the Land Court authority to determine who are the 'most appropriate representatives of any class or group of Maori affected by the negotiations, consultations, allocation or other matter'. This clearly gets away from the concept of determining 'boundaries' between intersecting groups where this is inappropriate. It has been used in a number of cases but with mixed success.

Other initiatives, probably more far-reaching, were taken by Chief Judge Durie. First, in 1993 he instituted new, root-and-branch inquiries into Maori customary law, especially as it related to land rights, in order to get behind the quasi-codified law developed and applied by the Maori Land Court since 1865, and identify more authentic Maori principles and practices. He hoped that such inquiries, among other things, would assist Maori leaders and groups to come to terms with one another in the modern claims process, rather than pursue adversarial and mutually exclusive positions such as the Land Court had fostered in its task of finding discrete groups of owners holding exclusive rights to defined blocks of land.[2] Second, Judge Durie developed within the Tribunal a 'case-book method', whereby New Zealand was divided into about 40 'claim areas' and all Maori groups claiming customary interests in those areas were required to research and present their case-books to the Tribunal before it began formal hearings of claims against the Crown for breaches of the Treaty in each area. By this means the Tribunal hoped to gain a comprehensive picture of all Maori groups holding interests in a given area, and the nature of their interests, including their relations with one another. This was expected not only to provide a swifter and more economical approach to the researching and hearing of claims (for many claims within a given area could be heard at the same time) but to lead to fairer outcomes, in the sense that the nature and strength of the various groups' interests could be ascertained as well as the extent to which each had been affected by the actions of the Crown. From the mid-1990s the Tribunal began to work its way systematically through the various claim areas, and expects research and hearings of all of them to be completed within the first decade of this century.

The actual *settlement* of the historical claims is another matter. That rests upon negotiation between the various claimants and the Crown, via the Minister in Charge of Treaty Negotiations and the Office of Treaty Settlements. Direct negotiation between Maori claimants and the Crown can take place without the necessity for a prior hearing and report by the Tribunal. Indeed, the first big land claims settlement took place on that basis in 1994, with the Tainui confederation in respect of the vast confiscations in the Waikato district in the 1860s. But that was a situation in which the grievance had already been well established by a commission of inquiry in the 1920s, and the Kingitanga (Maori King Movement) had long represented Tainui in respect of it. Where the issues are less clear, and the inter-tribal relationships more complex, the Crown is skating on thin ice in attempting to negotiate settlements without the benefit of thorough prior research and a public hearing by the Tribunal.[3]

These, then, are the circumstances that have led in the last decade to a huge escalation of research into the customary rights of Maori tribes and the impact upon them of the Crown's actions since 1840. Several hundred reports have been deposed before the Tribunal dealing with these matters but they vary greatly in quality. This is, in part, a product of certain weaknesses in New Zealand's scholarly tradition. For the best part of a century a great deal of effort in anthropology and Maori Studies went into reconstructing 'classical' Maori society, along fairly static structural-functional lines. Comparatively little detailed attention was paid to change since European discovery—to the diverse responses of Maori communities to contact, colonisation and the land grab. This situation changed markedly in the 1980s and 1990s, with the work of Pat Hohepa and Jeffrey Sissons,[4] Anne Salmond, Judith Binney and Angela Ballara,[5] which drew on the skills of several disciplines and sources in Maori and English. However, these are very recent works and they are mostly by Pakeha scholars. Furthermore, most Pakeha historians working on Maori–Pakeha relations do not know Maori and so have little access to the considerable Maori-language source material that is available.[6] Conversely, New Zealand universities have produced very few Maori with research degrees in history— historians who are trained and comfortable in the critical use of sources, and accustomed to tracing complex changes between the contact period and the late twentieth century. In short, there were very few researchers with bicultural skills ready to meet the burgeoning demands of Treaty-related research.

The Treaty claims process itself tends to foster particular kinds of evidence and argument. The procedures of the Waitangi Tribunal are those of a commission of inquiry. Although much less formal than those of the courts, they are essentially adversarial in that the Crown does contest many of the claims. Maori claimants have to adduce evidence to establish their claims on the balance of probabilities. The Tribunal, and parties before it, are aware that the Crown might call for a judicial review of a Tribunal report, especially in respect of Crown forest lands and lands formerly held by State-Owned Enterprises—lands over which the Tribunal is authorised to make binding orders for their return to Maori (as distinct from simply leaving them for possible inclusion in settlements negotiated between the Crown and claimants). Because of the importance of the issues and the value of the settlements, claimants and Crown almost invariably engage counsel, who formally call witnesses to present historical and other evidence, and develop opening and closing submissions based upon that evidence.

In the Ngai Tahu claims of 1987–89 the practice was developed of hearing Maori elders present their arguments and assertions, largely based on traditions passed by word of mouth, but of not subjecting them to detailed cross-examination. This practice, adopted largely out of respect for the elders, allows communities to express their long-held grievances and deep feelings but it tends to limit opportunity for the oral tradition to be fully explored and tested, including the elders' understandings both of their particular group's experience and of their connections and common interests with other groups.

The Tribunal, understandably, tends to follow the usual judicial preference for evidence generated closest to the events under discussion, and to evidence given by direct participants in those events if possible. Moreover, such evidence exists, for example in the form of many statements by Ngai Tahu leaders who participated in the transactions of the 1840s and 1850s, which were recorded in considerable detail by government officials at the time and by various courts or commissions of inquiry investigating the transactions subsequently. For most of New Zealand a great deal of evidence about the actions of Crown agents can indeed often be found in archives of the former Native Land Purchase Department or of the Department of Lands and Survey, unpublished proceedings of committees of inquiry, judicial proceedings (reported and unreported), parliamentary papers, collections of private papers and a host of other obscure sources.

Yet unearthing such evidence, and explicating it in the light of the contexts in which it was given, requires professional skills. This has meant that evidence based on the documentary record has been presented mainly by highly qualified academic historians, usually Pakeha, experienced in searching out the mass of archival material available, and shaping argument and rebuttal. These scholars produce lengthy and detailed reports on each main aspect of the claim and are subject to cross-examination by counsel and questioning from the Tribunal. In the Ngai Tahu hearings, by the time the academic protagonists of the claimants, the Crown and the Tribunal had produced their submissions and counter-submissions and their rebuttals and defences, the claims against the Crown had been sifted very finely. Most were substantiated; some were rejected. The Crown's historical breaches of Treaty principles are, in fact, widespread (though often cloaked by specious assumptions of Maori consent), so that the sifting of claims through the researches and interpretations of professional historians usually wins the claimants far more points than it loses. For this reason many Maori claimants have tended to accept—indeed welcome—the role of professional historians.

On the other hand, there is a strong desire on the part of claimants not only to control the research but also to do much of it themselves. This is partly because of the strong resurgence and rediscovery of identity, at iwi, hapu and whanau level, and the shrugging off of colonial subordination more generally; Maori have wanted to 'own their research', not have it done for them by Pakeha contract historians. Furthermore, because iwi and hapu in a given area are largely in competition with one another, as well as challenging the Crown, they have wanted to keep their knowledge to themselves, until the day it has to be formally deposed before the Tribunal. There are powerful traditional reasons for this. Knowledge of the internal dynamics of groups is usually obtainable *only* from the claimants themselves; it is insiders' knowledge, and precious knowledge, usually given out only to researchers whom the families concerned know well and trust to safeguard their reputation. Moreover, the ability to name particular places on the land, accurately and in great detail, is strong proof of association with that land. Such knowledge is not to be bandied about in public so that it becomes common knowledge; indeed, when they do come to present their evidence, some groups ask the Tribunal to allow them to give it *in camera*.

Funding has generally been available for hapu to compile at least one research report, either through Legal Aid (on the recommendation of the Tribunal) or through the Crown Forestry Rental Trust (CFRT), a statutory trust, part of whose income may be used to establish whether forested land was alienated in breach of Treaty

171

principles and from whom. Throughout the 1990s scores of Maori groups, large and small, enthusiastically pursued their claims, largely with CFRT funding, which in total ran into some $20 million. Despite its unique insights and its value to the communities undertaking the work, however, such claimant research tended to have major weaknesses.

First, descriptions of Crown actions were often given at a very general level, and contained inaccuracies which the Crown's own researchers and law officers were readily able to challenge or rebut. Where some of the customary rightowners had participated, to some extent, in the early land transactions, early claimant research, however heartfelt, did not always establish clearly that the Crown had breached Treaty principles. To do this it is necessary to show that the Crown had either: purchased from the wrong people (or from only a few of the right people); used various forms of pressure or manipulation; exceeded the agreed boundaries; failed to make promised reserves, negotiate in good faith, or accord Maori the reasonable protection that the Treaty promised; or otherwise acquired the land without full and free consent. This required not just a long-standing sense among Maori that they had somehow been fleeced. (As noted earlier, they commonly *were* manipulated and fleeced; professional historians had been showing this since the 1970s; a 'National Overview' of Treaty claims commissioned by the Tribunal in 1996–98 showed it again and in more detail; and the government acknowledged it to be so in January 1999, not only in respect of the land confiscations of the 1860s but also with regard to the Crown purchases of 1840–65 and the era of Native Land Court purchases after 1865.) Unless the Crown was to settle Treaty claims by means of some blanket compensation payment to all Maori, there had to be a degree of detailed demonstration that this has indeed been so in respect of each particular claimant group. Therein lies the difficulty for claimants, and the need to employ skilled historians. By the mid-1990s there was increasing reliance on professional researchers, notably the 20 or more employed by the Tribunal itself, about eight engaged by the CFRT, and about 30 more (many of them academic historians) retained on contract by either body or by claimant groups. For its part the Crown also began to employ more historians, and the discussion about claims became increasingly thorough.

Second, because claimant groups were in competition with one another, they tended to work in isolation with little cross-

checking of data between them. Consequently, groups who cus-
tomarily had intersecting interests in the same land often belatedly
challenged each other in the Tribunal, and cloaked, rather than
disclosed, their common ground. An important instance of this
occurred in 1995–96, when the Ngati Makino hapu, who believed
they were the sole owner group of the Rotoehu forest lands, were
suddenly faced by a cross-claim from Ngati Pikiao for the same
land. Chief Judge Durie, chairing the panel of Tribunal members
that heard the claim, told both groups to go away and research
their customary relationship more carefully. He warned them that
a true understanding of customary law would very likely reveal a
variety of intersecting interests rather than the exclusive ownership
of discrete territories that had emerged as the erroneous model
during colonisation. Moreover, he suggested, Maori hapu had
traditionally gathered strength by not only identifying their
whanau and hapu, and the villages, lands and waters they specifically occupied and controlled, but also their common ground with
other groups—in terms of whakapapa linkages, marriage ties,
shared histories in migration and warfare, and common use of
resources such as forests and fisheries. Isolation, he emphasised,
was a very vulnerable state in Maori society, both at the individual
and the group level, and attempts to rely upon exclusivity of rights
could leave one quite friendless.

The outcome of such attempts to promote cooperation between
hapu and iwi has in fact been mixed. In some districts, after years
of difficult negotiation, clusters of closely related hapu are prepared
to consider joint negotiation and settlement with the Crown, but
many claims are still pursued by each hapu independently. It is
unrealistic to expect otherwise. Most claimant leaders tacitly
acknowledge that they will have to cooperate and even compromise
with their opposite numbers from other hapu in the claim area. But
some hapu—even adjacent hapu—have been injured by Crown
actions much more severely than others and these tend to want to
demonstrate this first, and maximise their own claims, before
entering into 'global' settlements on an iwi-wide or district-wide
basis. One consequence of this aspiration is that independent
'manawhenua' reports, setting out customary rights deemed tantamount to ownership of land and waters, continue to be compiled for
individual hapu and iwi. However, in order to understand the customary *relationships* between the various claimant groups, and the
nature and relative strength of their land rights, the Tribunal has

begun to commission overview reports, in which a highly qualified historian takes up the various 'manawhenua' reports, assesses them, and adds his or her independent views of the evidence. This necessarily involves some prior understanding of the principles upon which rights in custom were validly held.

Yet, the substantiation of who held what customary rights (and hence which groups were injured by Crown actions and to what degree) is difficult. This is because, as stated earlier, knowledge of customary law principles and procedures had become distorted or blurred during colonisation, and so it is necessary to review—and to some extent rediscover—them before sound decisions can be made by the Tribunal and the courts or by the Crown in direct negotiations to settle claims. The most obvious sources for such review and rediscovery are the oral traditions held in the memory of Maori elders, and their understandings of what constitutes a legitimate claim of right. Sound insights from this source are becoming scarce, however, because of the passing of many elders in rural communities and the urbanisation of the younger generations. This is why it is important to make the best use possible of the oral testimony of earlier generations, such as those recorded in the minutes of the Land Claims Commissioners of the 1840s and the Native Land Court. Such early statements provide the understandings that those who presented them had at the time, and this affords them a particular kind of authority. The earlier the statements are made and recorded the better, if one is seeking to get behind the distorting effects of the land transactions and the land court processes themselves.

The search for the relative strength of various groups' interests, and the search for the principles for determining that question, go hand in hand, then. In short, it is likely to be through the detailed sifting of the evidence before the Tribunal, in claim after claim, that the truth about Maori customary law will emerge. Without this detailed original research, general projects on Maori law are likely to remain the prisoner of received interpretations. In this spirit, the second part of this chapter will attempt to show, from a brief summary of claims in two regions (Whanganui and Wellington), how documentary historical evidence can be used to disclose Maori participants' understandings of their customary tenure, but also how difficult it is to interpret their statements without a good understanding of the meanings and values of Maori culture.

174

WHANGANUI

In 1877 the Whanganui Native Land Court investigated competing claims to ownership of Mangaporau, a 16 062 acre land block located between the Waitotara and Whanganui rivers.[7] The central figures were the Ngati Pourua, which had its principal settlements on the middle reaches of the Waitotara river, and Ngati Hau, with its main settlements to the east of the Waitotara river on the middle reaches of the Whanganui river. After hearing two days of testimony, the court declared Ngati Hau to be the owner of the land. However, the court evidence discloses that neither Ngati Pourua nor Ngati Hau could be said to own Mangaporau in the common law sense of owning virtually all rights in the land to the exclusion of others. Rather, certain members of both tribes owned rights in the land that intersected and overlapped on the ground.

Both tribes had managed to avoid the large-scale conquest and dispossession that occurred in other areas of the lower North Island, notably Port Nicholson (Wellington Harbour), in the early decades of the nineteenth century. Before the Native Land Court they were, therefore, able to show their connection with the land by speaking of many generations of occupation. Claimants traced their ancestry back to the peoples who first settled upon the land, and, in Ngati Pourua's case, even further back to illustrate where their ancestors came from and how they came to settle on the land. Yet, tracing descent from the original occupants alone—showing take tupuna— was insufficient. Claimants also needed to show ahi ka, that is, that their ancestors' line had continued to occupy the land down to their time; if these ancestors moved and settled elsewhere, their connection with the land began to grow cold so that over time their fires were extinguished. Therefore, after reciting genealogies, claimants tended to turn to discussing evidence of occupation by more recent ancestors (parents and grandparents) and by the claimants themselves. Most commonly cited were the proper names and location of important resources on the land—eel weirs, rat runs, bird-trapping trees, fruit trees, potato and kumara cultivations—and pa (fortified settlements), kainga (village or hamlet), waahi tapu (spiritual areas) and urupa (burial places). Also, reference could be made to significant events on the land such as battles with neighbouring groups, chiefly marriages, and the places where hakari (feasts), supplied by food taken from the land, were held. (See also Ann Parsonson's chapter.)

In this case Hohepa Tawhitopou of Ngati Pourua advanced his tribe's ancestral claim by tracing his whakapapa back eighteen generations to the great ancestor Turi, said to have migrated to New Zealand from Hawaiki in East Polynesia. He related how Pourua (the great-great grandchild of Turi, and eponymous ancestor of Ngati Pourua) and her peoples left their settlements in the south on the Waitotara river, heading northeast to Mangaporau where a boundary was negotiated with the Ngati Hau river people, with Pourua's people using the western area and Ngati Hau using the eastern side. Tawhitopou, therefore, claimed the western area of Mangaporau, noting that while some of the descendants of Pourua had moved on, others had remained on the land down to his time. For his part, Paora Poutini of Ngati Hau traced his ancestral ties with the land to Tutehaiao, six generations before his time. Striking a match in court and letting it burn down to his nails before blowing it out, Poutini noted that all six ancestors named by him had lived on and eaten food from the land. He claimed the whole block for Ngati Hau, citing Upokonui—the southern border of Mangaporau—and not the west–east boundary mentioned by Tawhitopou as the boundary dividing the two tribes.

The court testimony discloses that Mangaporau was a considerable distance from both Ngati Pourua and Ngati Hau's main settlements and at the margins of each tribe's area of influence—roughly a day's walk—and that in the appropriate season individuals and small kin groups journeyed there to snare birds (pigeons, kakapo and kiwi). There had been small kainga on this land and modest cultivations providing temporary shelter and food for those hunting on the land, and these were tolerated by all parties since they were never used on a long-term basis; activities requiring more intensive labour and longer residence on the land were avoided, as this would be viewed by others as the assertion of a superior claim of right to the land.

This pattern fits with evidence of settlement patterns in other areas of New Zealand during this period: tribal communities expanded and contracted over the course of a year with people occupying main settlements during winter or times of war, but otherwise spreading out across the land to hunt and gather food, exploiting one resource before moving on to the next. Closer to the main settlements, rights were more concentrated and there would be larger cultivations—there were the numbers to tend to large gardens, and, in the event of attack, crops could be quickly uprooted and stored in secure pa. But these rights gradually diminished in number and strength as members of a community fanned out until they eventually overlapped and intersected with the rights of neighbouring communities.

The evidence given in the Native Land Court to support a claim of right can thus be placed on a continuum of varying degrees of right. At one end of the spectrum there were major settlements, urupa, and large gardens, all evidence of a relatively strong claim of right. At the other end were seasonal hunting and gathering activities at the margins of the tribal territory, the rights to which were exercised with caution. Claimants appearing before the Whanganui court were well aware of this, and in disputed areas such as Mangaporau some tend to exaggerate the size and number of settlements and cultivations on the land.

Genealogies cited in the court also revealed, it should be emphasised, that heavy intermarriage between the two tribes over successive generations had resulted in very close genealogical ties. This encouraged the granting of rights across tribal boundaries— without necessarily conferring with tribal leaders—from, by, and to individuals or small kin groups through out-group gifting and inheritance. Members of Ngati Hau were therefore able to hunt within Ngati Pourua's area of tribal influence and vice versa. Not all of Ngati Hau or Ngati Pourua had the right to enter the other's territory and exercise rights there, only those individuals or groups who had been specifically granted the rights. These intersecting interests meant that the boundary line between the two tribes was loosely defined. For Ngati Hau hunting on the block there may have been no more than an understanding that the further they ventured into the western area without permission, the greater the risk of a hostile encounter with Ngati Pourua.

There was, in fact, a history of violence on the land spanning several generations with deaths on both sides. According to Ngati Hau witnesses, this had ended in the recent death of a member of Ngati Pourua and their subsequent expulsion from the land. It was suggested, then, that Ngati Hau had a greater claim of right to the land because of this final 'victory' over Ngati Pourua. This is the concept of take raupatu, a claim of right based on conquest. This was not one of the principal take advanced by Ngati Hau in support of their claim. Rather, this take emerged during the course of the court hearing as if to reinforce the original take. However, take raupatu was widely considered to be a less secure form of right, because recent conquerors were capable of being displaced by the conquered peoples if the latter returned to seek utu (satisfaction) for their defeat. It therefore needed to be backed up by evidence of sustained occupation of the land. In this case there is no evidence of Ngati Hau handing Ngati Pourua a serious defeat or holding the land to the exclusion of Ngati Pourua. The killings spoken of by Ngati Hau were episodic and appear to have been the result of skirmishes on the land over resources. Neither group had the military might to hold the land to the exclusion of the other. Both tribes may have been able to muster a fighting group to attack their neighbour but they would have been unable to sustain such a military presence on Mangaporau for long periods of time. Their people and permanent settlements were elsewhere.

The court, however, as we have already noted, ruled that Ngati Hau were generally recognised as Mangaporau's owners, and that upokonui was the southern boundary separating the two tribes. By way of conclusion here, two points can be made. First, the evidence presented to the court suggests that neither Ngati Hau nor Ngati Pourua could be said to have owned Mangaporau exclusively; instead, according to Maori custom, members of both groups owned rights on the land. Second, whakapapa was the principal means by which Ngati Hau and Ngati Pourua ordered and prioritised rights at the margins of their tribal territories, and close kinship ties enabled the out-group granting of rights through gifting and inheritance, thus creating a network of intersecting and cross-cutting rights across vaguely drawn tribal boundaries. The court's search for an exclusive owner undermined the importance of these customary principles and in doing so brought down a decision that was neither justified nor just.

WELLINGTON

Between 1842 and 1843 Commissioner William Spain, investigating the NZ Company purchases on either side of Cook Strait, soon became aware of the complexity of customary ownership. Various tribes had occupied and mingled in the area for hundreds of years: the very earliest Maori migrants, known as Ngai Tara, subsequently intermingled with Rangitane, Ngati Ira and Ngati Kahungunu. But in the 1820s and 1830s these tribes were conquered by new waves of migrants, led by Te Rauparaha and other chiefs of Ngati Toa (of

Kawhia district), in close association with kinsmen and allies from north Taranaki—Ngati Tama, Ngati Mutunga and Te Atiawa—as well as Ngati Rangatahi of the upper Whanganui river and sections of other hapu from that area. The newcomers almost completely displaced the earlier tribes around Port Nicholson and the Hutt Valley, but relations between the recent arrivals themselves were also complex, and changing rapidly even as the Company ships sailed into the region and the Company negotiators began to attempt purchases of land.

The pattern of evidence for the Wellington or Port Nicholson purchase (about 200 000 acres) therefore contrasts sharply with that in the Whanganui example. Ngati Kahungunu, Rangitane and Muaupoko could traditionally claim an identification with the land going back many generations. But so complete had been their conquest and expulsion by the Kawhia and Taranaki tribes that few if any were present in the area in 1839 and none appeared before Spain's commission. Conversely, the recent invaders did not (could not) claim on the basis of intermarriage with the previous tangata whenua (the people of the land). Most of the evidence given to Commissioner Spain and later to the Land Court embodies claims based on conquest of the land from the previous occupants or upon occupation of land found vacant. Indeed, much of the land was forest-covered in the 1820s and various chiefs from among the recent invaders spoke of clearing portions of it and building settlements.

However, there were also tensions and periodic clashes among the recent invaders. The Ngati Mutunga tribe and many of the Ngati Tama left the Wellington area for the Chatham Islands in 1835. Te Atiawa witnesses therefore gave evidence to Spain that Ngati Mutunga leaders had previously invited them to occupy portions of land near their villages, and in 1835 offered them the areas they were vacating. Much of that land was taken up by particular hapu of Te Atiawa returning from rather futile warfare with Ngati Kahungunu in the Wairarapa district; among the Te Atiawa hapu there was some rivalry, with particular chiefs claiming mana or authority over each kainga, but in general they had clashed with Te Rauparaha over the support his section of Ngati Toa had recently given to their rivals, Ngati Raukawa, particularly in a battle at Kuititanga (opposite the Ngati Toa stronghold of Kapiti Island) in 1839. Consequently, although the Ngati Toa chiefs strongly asserted that their mana still ran over the whole of the Cook Strait region, Te Atiawa declined to recognise it; instead they told Spain that they were 'taking' various lands from Te Rauparaha, namely the lands they occupied. On the other hand, those Ngati Tama still in the Wellington district had recently made a fresh rapport with Ngati Toa in resisting British occupation of the Hutt Valley, and, possibly because of this political relationship, Ngati Tama chiefs giving evidence to Spain still affirmed that Ngati Toa were the conquerors of the district and that they had received their land from Ngati Toa.[8]

The Waitangi Tribunal assessing the claims in the Wellington district thus had before it some difficult issues of customary law to resolve. The facts of actual occupation and use of land are not too difficult to discern. Maori witnesses were very precise about who cultivated which portions of land and who built houses and dwelt in them; and they distinguished these carefully from hunting, fishing and gathering rights that were often shared by more than one tribe in the same area. But the weighting of very recent conquest and occupation, as against long-standing occupation, constitutes a problem. The fact of conquest and the balance of tribal power as at 1840 provides one answer. But conquests could be challenged and reversed, especially if the newcomers had not acquired the added legitimacy of intermarriage with the previous occupants. Yet the evidence given to Spain suggests that, even if they came as usurpers and did not intermarry with the previous occupants, the newcomers began to acquire rights to the land from the time they cleared it, planted and harvested crops, had children born and buried their dead there. However, had this process gone far enough in 1840 to wholly displace the rights of previous occupants, ejected only a decade previously? Perhaps it had, especially as there were no groups of the first occupants left in the Wellington district to keep their fires alight.

The other large issue raised by the Wellington example is the question of 'mana' claims, in particular the rights of people such as the great Ngati Toa war chiefs to share in authority over land, even though Ngati Toa could not themselves occupy all of it. The evidence suggests that mana could not simply be claimed; it had also to be recognised. We have noted that Ngati Tama continued to recognise the mana of Ngati Toa from 1839 to 1842 but Te Atiawa did not. This suggests that the take upon which Maori based their claims to land were not absolutes—that tribal politics, and the making or unmaking of alliances, affected the take upon which chiefs based their claims to land.

Similarly, inter-tribal politics resulted in some aspects of whakapapa and some inter-tribal marriages being mentioned and others not. As in the Whanganui case, it can easily be overlooked that almost all the tribes in Port Nicholson were connected with one another, sometimes very closely, even though they did not mention this before Commissioner Spain. Although the chiefs and their hapu competed with each other within the Port Nicholson area, in another sense they shared it and from time to time made agreements about particular parts of it.

CONCLUSION

The matters we have discussed are not ones that the techniques of western scholarship alone can resolve. That scholarly tradition can uncover early documented statements by Maori participants, explicate the contexts in which they were created, and search these finely for indications of how Maori used the land and based their claims to it. The critical and sceptical approaches of western scholarship can also show how statements were shaped for particular purposes at particular times, reflecting the current politics of the protagonists and their need to win recognition from Land Claims Commissioners or Land Court judges; and why, therefore, statements cannot simply be plucked out of context and accorded an authority they do not all equally deserve. However, deciding precisely what value to place upon them requires something more still—a strong understanding of Maori culture, its meaning-systems and its dynamics—in order to appreciate what is being said (or perhaps what is not being said) by those who left their statements in the historical record. Although cultural anthropology and history can assist in this regard, those best placed to understand Maori culture are of course Maori themselves, notwithstanding that their culture will have undergone subtle changes since contact with the wider world. Thus, scholarly analysis of the earliest written records of the words of Maori leaders, and modern Maori cultural understandings of those words, can assist each other.

Both the examples we have discussed illustrate the problems involved in determining an exclusive owner in areas where the interests of adjacent groups meet on the ground. More importantly, the Whanganui evidence shows the key role whakapapa played in ordering these interests. Kinship relations were so closely intertwined with principles of customary tenure as to be practically fused with them in many cases. A search for these principles therefore

requires detailed knowledge of the genealogical ties and an understanding of the manner in which they were used, knowledge which
may go beyond that cited in particular cases before the courts, and
certainly beyond the grasp of many Native Land Court judges. It is
also suggested that, though it is often muted in the modern competition to display manawhenua, such knowledge may be crucially
important in mediating settlements of Treaty claims that encompass
more than one hapu or iwi in a given area.

This chapter, with its two contrasting examples, has also sought
to show the importance of cumulative overview analyses by and for
the Tribunal. No one single case or claim area will exemplify all
relevant principles, and the newly emerging expositions of Maori
customary law will, for some time, necessarily be incomplete. But as
each district is covered in detail, and more and more evidence is
disclosed and analysed, it will be possible to be more and more con-
fident of the fruits of the current re-examination of Maori land
tenure and land law.

10

'Learning about the truth' The stolen generations narrative[1]

Bain Attwood

During the last two decades in Australia, stories about indigenous children being separated from their parents or kin, once only told in Aboriginal communities and scarcely known beyond this domain, have become a historical narrative so widely disseminated that this history is now central to Australian historical consciousness. There is, I contend, nothing inevitable about this metamorphosis: this is not simply a case of 'the return of the repressed' or the oppressed, a necessary surfacing of a hitherto silenced or submerged history; instead, it might better be understood as a matter of 'narrative accrual' or 'narrative coalescence',[2] which has been enabled by a range of discourses during the last two decades or so. In this chapter I will critically evaluate what I will call 'the stolen generations narrative',[3] by considering who and what has been involved in the production of its stories; when and where it has been constructed; the reasons why it has been created; how it has been circulated; the ways in which it has changed over time; and the various outcomes of its telling.

183

The stolen generations narrative has assumed immense significance, not only for many Aboriginal people but also the non-Aboriginal Australians who have embraced it. As such, any analysis might readily be regarded as undermining its truth claims, especially in a context in which the narrative has been subjected to fierce and damaging political attacks by conservative political and legal players and commentators. However, I am of the opinion that a critique of the narrative might serve a number of useful cultural and political purposes—indeed, that such an interrogation is even more necessary in the wake of the assault upon it—and that the risks of *not* offering this outweigh those of presenting it. There are also other matters at stake in the controversy over the stolen generations, most importantly the nature of historical knowledge. In much of the telling of the stolen generations narrative, the attacks upon it, and the enormous debate that has followed, simplistic histories of colonialism in Australia have been advanced. This has severely limited the prospects for historical understanding among and between Aboriginal and non-Aboriginal Australians, and has undermined an opportunity for bringing about change.

For generations Aboriginal people have told stories about the removal of children of so-called 'mixed descent' from Aboriginal families and communities. For example, Margaret Tucker, who was forcibly removed from her mother on a New South Wales Aboriginal reserve, Moonahcullah, in 1917, recalled in the late 1930s:

> The people at Cummeroogunga [a nearby reserve] lived in constant fear of their children being sent away from them by the Board, and being placed in homes. Wholesale kidnapping (it was nothing less) occurred on the Mission only a few years ago [1919]. The Manager sent the aboriginal men away on a rabbiting expedition.
>
> No sooner had they left the station than carloads of police (who had been waiting) dashed in and seized all the children they could get their hands on. These children were bundled into the cars and taken away for the Board to dispose of. Many of them never saw their parents again.[4]

A couple of decades or so later Tucker's mother, Theresa Clements, gave her account of the removal of two of her daughters in a brief 'memoir':

One day some men came from the [New South Wales] Aborigines' Protection Board. They said they wanted to take my children away. I said, 'My children are well cared for'. They were said to be taking all the clever children to educate them. It was the most terrible thing that ever happened to me when they took my two daughters. They rounded up some of the girls from Cummera at the same time . . . I heard that a policeman at Cummeragunja resigned after the incident. He said that if taking children away from crying mothers was a policeman's job, he didn't want it.[5]

And in the 1980s one of Tucker's daughters, Mollie Dyer, told this story: 'My mother, Margaret Tucker, was one of the children that were taken from their parents under the old Aborigines Protection Board Act. When she was 13 she was taken to Cootamundra [Aboriginal Girls Home] for what they call an apprenticeship. After three months she was sent to work as a servant girl for a well-to-do family in Sydney.'[6]

In the telling of such stories over several decades some of the factual content has remained constant but the forms in which they have been told and their relative importance have varied enormously. Between the late 1930s and the late 1970s, the removal of children was, as far as we know, neither the subject of many stories told in Aboriginal communities nor central to their historical consciousness[7]—for example, in an Aboriginal history of Cummeragunja published in the 1950s there was no reference to the removal of children[8]—and it was certainly seldom a part of narratives heard by non-Aboriginal people. A number of reasons have been or can be canvassed for this.

In the course of reflecting upon the creation of the stolen generations narrative (which occurred in the early 1980s), Peter Read has suggested that one factor was a lack of historical knowledge among Aboriginal people: they were baffled as to why they or their children were removed, and did not know children were also removed from other families or communities, and so they failed to realise large numbers were removed. Had Aboriginal people understood it was a government policy, he implies, they would have realised children had also been taken from other communities and would have known they had been removed in very large numbers, and so this history *would* have been told. More recently, Aboriginal people have understood why and how so many of their children were removed, and so they have been able to gain an 'understanding of child separation as central to their history'.[9] Read's argument is undoubtedly logical and seems to be evidenced, for example, by Aboriginal testimony; for instance, after telling of her removal in her autobiography, Tucker recalls that she had 'often wondered how many other [Aboriginal] children were taken like that, just like animals'.[10] However, this is to overlook historical evidence that reveals Aboriginal people had a general sense of what government was seeking to do and why (though there seems little doubt they were unaware of the extent to which children were being removed).[11] For example, in New South Wales in the late 1920s the Australian Aborigines Progressive Association called for 'the family life of the aboriginal people [to] be held sacred and free from invasion and that the children be left in control of their parents', and attacked 'the raiding of homes of the people' and the '[tearing] away' of 'girls of tender age and years' to be 'put to service in an invironment [sic] as near to slavery as it is possible to find'.[12]

Read's hypothesis is suggestive in the sense that it implies that an explanation for the nature of stories about removal in the postwar decades might be found in a consideration of what happened or happens afterwards, in the disjunction between an occurrence and its representation. Three arguments can be advanced here: First, that the various practices of government—of which the removal of children was merely one—not only had the effect of undermining Aboriginal communities but also the forms of communal memory that were so fundamental to Aboriginal remembrance. (Remembrance at a later date, it can be argued, depended on the emergence of forms of community or Aboriginal consciousness that transcended earlier, more local constructions of kinship.) Second, the traumatic nature of removal would have made representation of it difficult: knowledge of the event would be repressed or only partially symbolised in stories (and this remained the case until such time as the emergence of a coherent and authoritative public narrative enabled a more adequate articulation of the experience).[13] Third, the masculinist political discourse of these decades placed an emphasis on civil rights and the like and paid little attention to matters such as the removal of children.[14]

Another explanation has been advanced via a consideration of the nature of Aboriginal historical experience and narration. During these postwar decades, it has been argued, Aboriginal people constructed their histories—or at least those told in the non-Aboriginal realm—in such a way that the emphasis seldom rested (or seemed to rest) upon their experience of oppression. This reticence has been noted by historians who recorded oral testimonies in the 1970s.[15] Heather Goodall, for example, has remarked that many Aboriginal people 'recalled active, complex lives only sometimes completely dominated by oppression', and that where 'they described such experiences at all they were as likely to brush them aside with "not too bad" or, if asked, to deny them altogether'.[16] This form of storytelling suggests a conscious strategy on the part of several generations of Aboriginal people; they had to come to terms with the racial structures that governed their lives, and minimising oppression by denying or forgetting events, or suppressing the feelings of loss and anger they provoked, was an important means of survival.[17]

A further explanation for the nature of stories of removal during these decades lies in the troubled relationship Aboriginal people had to the past in which these events had occurred. Read notes that many of those removed were reluctant to tell stories of being separated from their parents because '[t]hey believed that maybe their parents had not been able to care for them properly, or worse still, didn't want them, and felt this reflected badly on themselves or their families'.[18] What was true for the children was even truer for their kin. More generally, many Aboriginal people at this time were, according to Kevin Gilbert, 'deeply ashamed of what they know is the truth about their people'.[19] (There were also those children who could not rather than would not tell the story, simply because they were unaware of their Aboriginal descent.)[20] The factor of greatest importance in this regard was the impact the assimilationist code of racism had upon the children who were removed. Many, perhaps even most, became deeply ambivalent about being Aboriginal or being of Aboriginal descent, and they spurned their 'Aboriginality' and tried to 'pass'. Consequently, their relationship to their own past lives was a vexed one; for most of those separated, their descent or background was scarcely relevant to how they understood and/ or represented themselves—in fact many wanted to deny their origins—and so their memory of separation was marginalised in the life stories they told. This silence was especially pronounced among those who had grown up in an era when government policy and practice distinguished between 'Aborigines' of 'full' and 'mixed' descent and determined their rights and privileges accordingly.[21]

One might further argue that, inasmuch as Aboriginal families or communities might have wanted to tell the story of the removal of their children, they lacked the resources to make their accounts heard beyond the Aboriginal domain. In the postwar era of assimilation, new and old Australians were urged to abandon both their communities and their communal memory—to forget the past and enter into the future—and there were few Australians who wanted to hear their histories. Australian history was a grand narrative of modernity and progress, and had no place for 'a dying race' or 'a primitive culture'.

These various explanations of the nature of postwar remembrance—of remembering and forgetting—are undoubtedly logical but any such consideration can only be satisfactory where there is a recognition of the manner in which the present plays a crucial role in the construction of accounts of the past. This is to acknowledge, in other words, the degree to which any history is the product of both the past and the present or, more precisely, the fruit of a dialogical relationship between the present and the past. We need to remind ourselves that there is always a difference between what happened in the past and what was and is narrated later, that history is not the past but always the past represented and re-presented.[22] As numerous studies of memory and history have shown, historical narratives undergo considerable change over time, shifting as the time of their telling changes. This is so because one of the basic tasks of any history-work, particularly memory-work, is that of making sense of and composing ourselves in the light of present circumstances, and it is invariably framed and shaped by the wider cultural and political discourses of that time.

To be more specific, the most popular explanations for the postwar histories minimise the influence that historians, autobiographers, informants and the discourses of history and memory have had on these stories.[23] As well as obscuring the historicity of the stolen generations narrative—its origins in a particular present—these explanations also confuse the earlier stories with the stolen generations narrative. In emphasising the similarities between the stories that have been told over time, we can overlook the more striking differences. At first glance the stories might seem to be the same but upon closer examination we can see that they only partly resemble the stories that comprise what we today recognise as the stolen generations narrative: the new narrative is *not* simply an old one returned. In the following two parts of this chapter I will consider the articulation and circulation of this narrative and the contemporary discourses that have determined this.

In order for new historical narratives to emerge and become prominent there are at least three prerequisites, it can be argued: authoritative figures who offer conceptual and moral frameworks that interpret the past in new ways, and who are, for whatever reasons, determined to articulate this historical perspective (for example, C.E.W. Bean as the champion of the Anzac legend); either a group of vulnerable or embattled people who suffer a range of confusing problems and who are subsequently attracted by narratives that offer satisfying explanations of and resolutions for their plight and posit a right of entitlement (for example, World War I returned soldiers), or a group of ambitious people who aspire to an unprecedented degree of power and status and who are therefore drawn to narratives that can legitimise their new position (for example, the bourgeoisie in the eighteenth and nineteenth centuries); and, lastly, political and cultural environments that enable, even demand, that particular narratives reach and be accepted by a large number of people.[24]

In this case, Peter Read played a crucial role in defining and naming, and, thereby, creating a historical event—'the removal of children'.[25] As is the case in any (hi)storytelling, he provided definition by rendering the heterogeneous nature of the past homogenous. First of all, the historical event was produced, like any historical fact, by an act of interpretation,[26] in this case by casting many of the ways in which Aboriginal children were separated from their kin as examples of 'child removal'. So, for instance, the apprenticing of adolescent children, which had been regarded by a previous generation of historians as an example of the draconian and harsh controls over Aboriginal people generally and by a still earlier (and, now, later) generation of storytellers as the work of a benevolent state seeking to uplift Aborigines, was now interpreted in this way. Second, it was created by imputing an overriding motive for these policies and practices to the state, that of a genocidal goal of destroying Aboriginality. Third, it was forged by telling a history and gathering a considerable body of historical sources to support it.[27]

At the same time as Read defined the phenomenon, he and his partner Jay Arthur, a lexicographer, provided another important ingredient in the production of a historical event—a name, 'the Stolen Generations'.[28] This term, which was preferred to 'the lost generations' that Read had earlier coined (but which continued to be used),[29] reflected the assumption of intent that lay at the heart of Read's storytelling; it was a departure from the terms that had previously been used by non-Aboriginal and Aboriginal people alike, such as 'adopted' and 'fostered' (or, less often, 'taken').[30]

Read's account gained authority by virtue of the fact that it was based upon and could readily be represented as scholarly research; it formed part of a PhD thesis about the Wiradjuri people of southern New South Wales,[31] which involved not only collecting oral testimony among these Aboriginal communities but also considerable archival work. This historical research was also, however, framed by Read's work for Link-Up, an agency he co-founded in 1981 with the aim of reuniting Aboriginal people who had been removed or had had their children removed.[32]

The historical narrative that Read and co-director Coral Edwards created for Link-Up originally struck a chord among a particular group of people, of whom Edwards herself was one. Born in 1950, and removed from her family when she was five months old, Edwards had spent all her childhood—sixteen years—at Cootamundra Aboriginal Girls Home (where Margaret Tucker had been sent over 30 years earlier);[33] she had grown up 'ashamed of being black', and had tried to pass as non-Aboriginal. (This was not uncommon and is hardly surprising given that staff at homes like this portrayed Aboriginality in such an unfavourable way.)[34] By 1980, however, Edwards wanted to become acquainted with the Aboriginal family and community from which she had been removed, and sought Read's assistance to help her do so. In the wake of her 'return' she suggested to Read that they begin 'a service to get other people home'—what became Link-Up—and shortly afterwards Edwards made a short documentary film, *It's a Long Road Back*, funded by the Australian Institute of Aboriginal Studies, which told of the experiences she and other Aboriginal women had had at Cootamundra. This, it has been claimed, was 'one of the first times that Aboriginal adults who had been removed as children got together and talked about their removal'; whether this is so or not, it is apparent that in this process they, together with Read, forged a common understanding of the past by narrating their removal as a 'collective rather than . . . [an] individual [experience]'.[35]

Through Link-Up Edwards and Read created for those who approached the agency a narrative that was underpinned by a set of assumptions inherently historical in nature. Link-Up asserted that those who had been removed suffered a common plight: they did not know who they were: 'There is one thing you have in common, the dark hole inside that can't be filled without knowing who you are.'

This, Read and Edwards asserted, was caused by the fact that they had no historical relationship to their 'birthplace', that is, they had no histories that could connect an 'Aboriginal' past to their present and so give Aboriginality a presence; Edwards wrote: 'One important loss is their history. I don't mean history in the wide sense, but [in the] sense of knowing who they are . . . They missed out on all the stories . . . That's what I mean by history.' At the same time Link-Up asserted that such people *did* have 'a[n Aboriginal] history and a background' by virtue of their birth or descent: they *were* Aboriginal because that was their origin. This, Link-Up told its people, is 'who [you] really are', and 'an Aboriginal identity can never be said to be lost while people know the simple fact that they are descended from an Aboriginal parent or grandparent'. 'The problem' they had lay in their 'loss' of Aboriginality, and so the answer resided in their 'searching' and 'finding' or, more commonly, 'recapturing', 'recovering' or 'reestablishing' their 'real self' or 'real identity', that of being Aboriginal (though Link-Up also conceded that these people often had no 'shared background' and had 'to start making it'). 'Regain[ing] their Aboriginal identity' was represented by Link-Up as a *return* to their *place*—'If a people should lose something/And turn back, and look carefully for it/They will find it'—or, more specifically, as a return *home*: 'By coming home to your family, you're finally coming home to yourself, to the self that is your birthright. It's a coming home to the realisation of the person you really are, so that you can finally stand up and know inside: this is me.' From the beginning, 'home' was a guiding metaphor in Link-Up's narrative imagination, a place where longing would become belonging. An early publicity pamphlet, written by Read, ended in this way: 'Physically, emotionally and spiritually your Aboriginality as well as your family are holding out their hands to say—WELCOME HOME!'[36]

Link-Up's evangelical approach was embraced by many of the separated children who encountered it. They differed from earlier generations who had been separated from their families and kin. The likes of Tucker and Jimmie Barker, for example, had grown up in a milieu in which official and popular racial discourses attacked Aboriginality and denied that many Aborigines were Aboriginal. And, for the most part, they had understood themselves in terms of a distinct historical experience, one characterised by living on and off reserves and under an overtly discriminatory regime, though often in areas that they regarded as their country, whether through traditional or historical association. They or other Aboriginal people had also fought for equal rights and mostly claimed these rights on the grounds of their being 'part-Aboriginal' or on the basis of being the same as other Australians. Consequently, they had both a strong sense of what it meant to be Aboriginal and an understandable ambivalence about being Aboriginal.

By contrast, the Link-Up people, most but by no means all of whom were born c.1950 or later, had grown up at a time when the program of assimilation, which included the granting of civil rights, had had a considerable impact on many Aboriginal people. They had come of age, moreover, when government and popular discourses had begun to question assimilation and even valorise cultural difference and pluralism, and would soon promote racial policies that sought to solicit rather than suppress Aboriginality. At the same time, Aboriginal spokespersons were increasingly adopting new modes of collective understanding and representation that were in keeping with a new set of demands—for indigenous rather than equal rights, and self-determination rather than integration—and which emphasised cultural difference, most often in terms of 'traditional Aboriginal culture'. This meant that, as they grew up, those like Edwards had had little if any sense of being Aboriginal and its cost, yet as adults they found themselves in contexts where they, on the one hand, realised it was being valued but, on the other, knew they had little personal understanding of it: 'Aboriginality' was a thing they had previously 'lost', but was now an 'identity' they should—and needed to—'regain'.[37] Consequently, these people recognised themselves in the figure of 'lost Aboriginal children' that the organisation formulated, and some came to narrate their life stories in terms of its historical framework and to become Aboriginal either through making their past genealogical connection to Aboriginal families and kin present, and/or by working for Aboriginal community or cultural organisations.[38]

Link-Up's work also consisted of making Aboriginal and non-Aboriginal people 'aware of the issue of separation and its profound effect on many Aboriginals'. Its historical narrative soon won political support. In 1983 Edwards addressed a National Aboriginal Conference meeting in Canberra, an occasion that Read described later as 'a turning point':

You could hear a pin drop. You could see people thinking, 'Do you mean, is *that* why we were taken?' 'Do you mean there was a government policy that was supposed to turn us into whitefellas?

Was that why it happened? But we never knew that'. No one was actually saying these words, but their faces were saying, 'Ah . . . Now things are falling into place. Now we realise'.

The Conference immediately agreed to grant a small amount of funding to the agency and recommended that the Commonwealth's Ministry for Aboriginal Affairs provide full-time funding for its work. In the same year a paper Read had written, 'The Stolen Generations', which was the first extensive history devoted to the subject, was published as a pamphlet by the New South Wales Ministry of Aboriginal Affairs, won attention from the media, and was widely circulated.[39]

In the early 1980s, at the same time as Read and Edwards' narrative began to circulate, a similar historical account was also being articulated by an Aboriginal community that had had strong links with the Wiradjuri, the people at the centre of Read's research. The Yorta Yorta had been a political force since the 1880s[40] and had long publicly told stories of the removal of children—when they occurred first of all in the late 1910s and again in protest during the late 1930s, in Clements' memoir in the 1950s, and, most recently, in 1977 in an autobiography by the activist Tucker (to cite just some examples)—and so they had a tradition to build upon.

This process of narrative repetition and accretion continued when Yorta Yorta participated, first of all, in the making of a four-part television series, *Women of the Sun*. It was co-scripted by Hyllus Maris, a niece of Tucker and herself a child in the late 1930s when the Yorta Yorta once more feared the removal of their children. The series included many members of the community as actors and extras, and drew heavily on their collective memory in portraying a history of colonisation from the invasion to the present. Most importantly, in this context, three of the four episodes featured the removal of Aboriginal children. In the second, set in the 1890s, missionaries threaten to remove a girl from her mother, and it ends with a heart-rending scene of the latter chasing a buggy taking her child away to Cootamundra, which repeated Tucker's account of her mother 'pathetically' watching a car take her and one of her sisters to that training home.[41] The following episode focuses upon an Aboriginal reserve called 'Koomalah'—an amalgam of Cummeragunja and Moonahcullah from which Tucker and other children were taken in the late 1910s—and highlights both the fear of children being removed and, eventually, the 'forcible remov[al]' of a twelve-year-old girl by the police, a scene also based on Tucker's account of being taken. And the final episode was devoted to the subject of the removal of an Aboriginal child, her later discovery of her 'Aboriginality' as a young woman, and her return to her Aboriginal mother, who says of her daughter in one of the closing scenes, 'Her mother is [Aboriginal] . . . And my mother is, and my mother's mother and her mother before that. That makes her Aboriginal right back to the time of the ancestors'; in the climax of the program—and of the series—the girl's grandmother, played by Tucker, greets her with the words, 'So you've come *home*'.[42] The series was broadcast on Channel 0/28 (now SBS, the Special Broadcasting Service, a multicultural television channel funded by the federal government) in 1982, and won several awards.[43]

The following year Tucker's account of her and her sister's removal, and the separation of Aboriginal children more generally, was told once more and so gained further circulation. It was central to a documentary film, *Lousy Little Sixpence*, which was co-produced by Alec Morgan and Aboriginal playwright and poet Gerry Bostock, and drew on Goodall's research (and so mirrored the collaboration between Read and the Wiradjuri—and hence between history and memory—that had helped produce the stolen generations narrative they were formulating). Exploiting the potential of an oral and visual medium, the film more starkly represented the experience of removal than Tucker's autobiographical accounts had. The forceful voice-over commentary, done by longtime Aboriginal activist Chicka Dixon, claimed that 'once removed, [the] children would never be allowed to return home' and that 'by 1930 one-third of Aboriginal children [in NSW] had been sent into apprenticeships'; Tucker testified to 'beltings' at Cootamundra and the cruelty of her employers; another elderly political activist described the children as 'slave labour' and told of sexual abuse (thus echoing the claims of the Australian Aborigines Progressive Association in the 1920s);[44] and Tucker's account of being removed was accompanied by 'documentary footage' of a train, an image commonly associated with the Shoah or the Holocaust.[45] The film won a wide screening in cinemas (unusual for an Australian documentary) and considerable publicity, was greatly applauded by critics, and later screened on ABC television.[46]

Simultaneously a new printing of Tucker's autobiography was done to capitalise on the series and the documentary that featured her story; publicity for the book emphasised her removal:

At the age of thirteen Margaret Tucker—Lilardia— left school. Left school? Was snatched from school, by the police! Taken *forcibly* from her part-Aboriginal parents to be trained as a domestic servant. Lilardia was born in 1904 on an Aboriginal settlement on the New South Wales-Victoria border. Her memories of her early years are the happiest part of her story . . . All this came to an abrupt end when Lilardia was sent to the Cootamundra Domestic Training Home for Aboriginal Girls.

If Everyone Cared was reprinted three times between 1983 and 1984 and became recommended school reading for the study of Australian History.[47]

It seems likely that, as a result of this conjunction of the television series, the documentary film and the autobiography, Tucker's account became the paradigmatic story of forcible removal, just as it, along with the stories told by Read and Edwards, made Cootamundra a central site or place for the history, much in the same way as Gallipoli and Auschwitz have come to symbolise wider events.[48]

Over the following ten years stories of the separation of Aboriginal children, which had previously been told in various ways by some Aboriginal people and largely in local or community settings, increasingly became a more homogeneous 'stolen generations narrative' that was produced and circulated in regional and national forums. As a result, the removal of children came to assume a central place in a broader Aboriginal collective memory and historical consciousness.[49]

Representations of child removal, or texts that could be read in these terms, were increasingly performed in a widening number of cultural forms. A growing number of Aboriginal histories, mostly in the form of autobiographies and family histories, were published, and most told stories of Aboriginal children being separated from their families or their families being broken up; for example, Elsie Roughsey, *An Aboriginal Mother Tells of the Old and the New* (1984), Sally Morgan, *My Place* (1987), Glenys Ward, *Wandering Girl* (1987), Alice Nannup, *When the Pelican Laughed* (1992), and Stuart Rintoul, *The Wailing* (1993). None of these were to have the impact of Morgan's narrative of three generations of her family, all of whose stories *could* be read as accounts of 'stolen children'.[50] This redemptive story of a return to place (which mirrored the Link-Up accounts) was very popular, selling over 330 000 copies in Australia by 1991.[51]

Much less read but important in terms of the authority they bestowed on the narrative were accounts by academic historians: an oral history collection, a monograph and a biography of Charles Perkins by Read (1984, 1988 and 1990), monographs by Anna Haebich, Andrew Markus and Tony Austin (1988, 1990 and 1993), and several chapters in one of the bicentennial histories, *The Australians: A Historical Library* (1987). All of these described either government policies and practices that broke up Aboriginal families, or removal itself.[52] Other books which focused specifically on the separation of children were published as well, such as Edwards and Read's *The Lost Children* (1989), and Barbara Cummings' *Take This Child . . . : From Kahlin Compound to the Retta Dixon Children's Home* (1990).

As well as these literary accounts, there was a documentary film by ethnographic film-maker David MacDougall, *Link-Up Diary* (1985), which told of the work of the agency; recordings of songs by Aboriginal performers, most significantly Bob Randall's 'Brown Skin Baby' in 1983 (first performed c. 1964),[53] Archie Roach's 'Took the Children Away' in 1989 (which won a Human Rights and Equal Opportunity Award the following year), and ongoing performances of it by Roach and his partner Ruby Hunter,[54] and Tiddas' version of Randall's song in 1993; radio series such as *Being Aboriginal* (later published in 1990 as a book by the ABC); and a National Archives of Australia exhibition (that was suggested and advised by Read), *Between Two Worlds: The Commonwealth Government and the Removal of Aboriginal Children of Part Descent in the Northern Territory*, which toured nationally in 1993–94 (and a book of the same name). Most importantly, perhaps, the 1987–91 Royal Commission into Aboriginal Deaths in Custody emphasised the ongoing impact of separation on Aboriginal people's lives, and had considerable political impact.[55]

By the early 1990s, in other words, narrative accrual or coalescence was clearly occurring: stories of removal were being reproduced again and again, and/or were being interpreted in terms of 'the stolen generations'. Furthermore, like any memory and history, the stories were being both prompted and shaped by earlier ones.[56]

This narrative accrual could not have happened had there not been an appropriate cultural and political milieu for it. Any narrative that achieves such prominence depends upon a supportive environment; indeed, often this not only enables particular narratives to be told and heard but also demands that their 'truths' be uttered. As Peter Novick has noted, 'public discourse doesn't just shape private discourse, it is its catalyst; it sends out the message "This is something you should be talking about"'.[57] Contrary to any assumption that Aboriginal historical narratives continue to be suppressed, one can contend that there has been a readiness, indeed an eagerness, for more than two decades now to produce, circulate and consume work by Aboriginal writers, artists, singers and so forth: '"Tell us what you are like", the white institutions seem to be saying, "sing your songs ... and tell your stories"'.[58] There have been, as Stephen Muecke has argued further, a number of 'discursive formations' that have encouraged Aboriginal representations.[59] These include social history; feminism, psychoanalysis and autobiography; family history and genealogy; and identity politics.

Perhaps the most immediate factor in the telling and hearing and reading of the stolen generations narrative was the emergence of new fields of historical study in the 1960s and 1970s. These decades saw the rise of social history and 'history from below', which were concerned to recover those people who had allegedly been 'hidden from history' and which led to new sub-disciplines, such as oral history, women's history and Aboriginal history. As far as the latter was concerned, what the eminent Australian anthropologist W.E.H. Stanner called 'the great Australian silence' ended as academic historians turned their attention to the study of the country's Aboriginal past, publishers were keen to publish scholarly histories, documentary collections and Aboriginal autobiographies, and many Australians were eager to read this new work.[60] Most importantly, there were, by the late 1970s, academic historians who were no longer relying upon the documentary record but were drawing upon oral sources as well; it was in the context of this conjunction between history and memory, which I have emphasised already, that the stolen generations narrative was first produced.

Similarly, feminism has played a major role in the narrative. Most of the stolen generations narrators have been women, which cannot simply be attributed to the fact that more girls than boys were removed,[61] and the best known testimonies regarding removal have been autobiographical works by women, most obviously Tucker and Morgan.[62] Their publication has been assisted by the fact that (auto)biography—and especially such writing by and/or about women—has become increasingly popular in recent decades.[63]

There has also been a strong intersection between feminism, auto-biography and psychoanalysis (defined loosely), especially as far as matters of gender and sexuality have been concerned. Both the work of Link-Up, and the acceptance of the stolen generations narrative that it and others have told, have taken place at a time when accounts of sexual abuse and incest—and trauma more generally—have been widely circulated and have commanded enormous audiences.[64]

Family history and genealogy has also shaped and lent support to the stolen generations narrative. As Graeme Davison has commented, there has been a remarkable upsurge in this popular historical practice in Australia since the mid-1970s, following that of other 'new world' societies,[65] partly because it 'answers a widely felt need to reaffirm the importance of family relationships in a society where mobility, divorce and intergenerational conflict tend to dissolve them'. What he calls the 'redemptive quality of family history'—its potential to release pain and its promise to 'shore up' or recover 'links of kinship'—has appealed to Aboriginal people (as it has to African Americans and other subaltern groups), who have borrowed its techniques 'to repair their ... shattered sense of identity', just as it has touched the hearts of non-Aboriginal readers of their family histories.[66]

The search for 'roots' that has characterised the family history boom of recent decades has coincided with and been encouraged by the rise of identity politics—the formulation of group or communal identity of any kind for political purposes—in which claims for difference have been advanced. Beginning in the early 1970s, governments in Australia adopted the ideals of multiculturalism and self-determination, and began to play a crucial role in both nurturing cultural difference and addressing social disadvantage. In this political context, history- and memory-work have been crucial since historical narratives, more than anything else, have provided the basis for a group's sense of a distinctiveness rooted in 'past' loss and suffering and for its claims to restitution. The stolen generations narrative not only lends itself readily to these tropes but has been especially important in the context of Aboriginal identity politics because 'family' and 'kinship' have increasingly become a crucial way of publicly defining and articulating Aboriginality in settled Australia. It tells, on the one hand, of the destruction of the Aboriginal collectivity, and on the other of its reconstruction—or survival. So, for example, a Wiradjuri woman and family historian,

Iris Clayton, removed and placed in Cootamundra as a child, has simultaneously bemoaned the 'lost family genealogy' and 'the missing links', and claimed these can be recovered and '[our] true identity . . . returned to [us]'.[67]

This is to argue, then, that the stolen generations narrative became (and remains) very important because, as a result of the factors that have been described here, it came to constitute a collective memory and to be a vehicle for the construction of identity. To express this another way, in these years the stolen generations became, in Pierre Nora's terms, a *lieux de mémoire*—a site of memory—a place (in various senses of that word) which, as a result of the convergence or condensation of various histories, embodies a collective memory that has become central to Aboriginal identity in settled Australia.[68]

In the course of the narrative accrual that occurred between the mid-1980s and the early 1990s the stories that comprised the stolen generations narrative increasingly came to assume some common features. This in itself is unremarkable, because it is the nature of narrative accrual. As Elaine Showalter has commented, all stories are characterised by particular conventions and, since narrators consciously and unconsciously appropriate the 'themes, structures, characters, and images' of the most powerful narratives currently in circulation, we tend to tell the same kind of stories.[69]

In the accounts of removal that were told in the 1970s—such as the autobiographies and the testimonies noted earlier—nearly all the narrators recalled the pain of separation and the unhappiness that followed but also remembered pleasant times as well, even telling funny stories about their experience. Furthermore, some expressed love for those who cared for them, or observed that there were non-Aboriginal people who had tried to prevent their removal or later protested, or remarked that some children had been removed because of neglect; a few blamed their mothers for removals; and still others expressed gratitude for being removed.[70] By contrast, the stories that were recounted and reported in the early 1990s, at least in the non-Aboriginal domain, had a greater forthrightness and presented, as Read has noted, 'a harsher and accusing account of separation'.[71]

This shift can be illustrated by reference to the Tucker narrative.[72] Following *Women of the Sun* and *Lousy Little Sixpence*, this story was produced again and again, though it was not Tucker but her youngest sister, Geraldine Briggs, six years old and absent at the time her sisters were removed, who was now doing the telling.[73] Although there are marked similarities between the accounts, there are also some notable differences in perspective. Echoing the starker lines of interpretation presented by *Lousy Little Sixpence*, Briggs remarked: 'Many of our girls didn't come back. Terrible things happened . . . [A] lot of little girls died at Cootamundra. And that was run by the Aborigines Protection Board, you know, *protecting* Aborigines. But they were sending them out to work for sixpence a week. That's what my sisters got, *sixpence a week*.'[74]

Two of Briggs' testimonies that were published in 1991 and 1993 are characterised by a bitter resentment that was absent from Tucker's 1977 autobiography.[75] For instance, she reflects on the removal of her sisters and other such occurrences in this way:

> You know, that is why a lot of our people have never liked white people. It took me a long time before I could get used to the fact that the white man took my sisters away and divided us. We never saw them until they grew up . . . I'm afraid I get very angry when I think of the terrible things that have been done to our people. A lot of things . . . Can you wonder why Aborigines didn't forget? They never forget and they hate the people that did it.[76]

These changes in the Tucker narrative were part of widespread shifts that were taking place in the form in which the stories were being produced and the purported significance of the history the narrative told. Whereas the stolen generations narrative of the early 1980s had been created as the result of collaboration between inform- ants and historians and involved a conjunction of memory- and history-work, now the accounts were more the product of memory and other discursive and textual practices, and they were becoming increasingly symbolic in nature. Prior to the creation of the stolen gen- erations narrative, stories had focused on historically specific instances—on events at a particular, localised place and/or time—and took the form of family or community histories—most importantly of the Wiradjuri and the Yorta Yorta. Beginning in the early 1980s, these stories increasingly referred to particular regions and soon assumed the form of state or territory histories, especially that of New South Wales but later the Northern Territory as well, and by the early 1990s the narrative was taking on the cast of a national history and was drawing on general collections of oral testimony, which, unlike the earlier storytelling, was not supported by historical research.[77] Furthermore, whereas the removal of children had previously been placed in a broad historical context—for example, that of a particular state or territory's Aboriginal or welfare policies and practices—or had been narrated as part of telling a bigger story about the removal and destruction of Aboriginal communities, now it was increasingly treated and told as a singular phenomenon, all on and of its own.[78] This metamorphosis coincided with and contributed to the narrative increasingly becoming a collective memory for Aboriginal people, and these changes would deepen as it was mobilised more and more for cultural and political purposes.

In the early 1990s the stolen generations narrative unequivocally entered the Australian public domain and, soon after, penetrated its political and legal arenas. It began to be pressed into service by the cause of national reconciliation, on the one hand, and the case for reparation, on the other. Reconciliation had been officially inaugurated in 1991 by an act of parliament that established a body to oversee the process. The Council for Aboriginal Reconciliation (CAR) saw historical understanding as fundamental to its goal of reconciling Aboriginal and other Australians.[79] Both it and the Commonwealth Labor government (which initiated the Council) championed the High Court's June 1992 Mabo judgment on native title as a new history, believing that it set the record straight and provided a new foundation for the Australian nation.[80] In December that year, in the course of a speech to mark the forthcoming United Nations Year of Indigenous Peoples, Prime Minister Paul Keating called upon Australia to come to terms with the historical truth of its Aboriginal past, saying:

> [Reconciliation] begins, I think, with that act of recognition. Recognition that it was we who did the dispossessing. We took the traditional lands and smashed the traditional way of life. We brought the diseases. The alcohol. We committed the murders. *We took the children from their mothers.* We practised discrimination and exclusion. It was our ignorance and our prejudice. And our failure to imagine these things being done to us.[81]

By 1994, at the same time as the work of the CAR gathered momentum, human rights lawyers and Aboriginal legal services on the one hand and, on the other, Link-Up and one of its offshoots in the Northern Territory (the Karu Aboriginal Child Care Agency, led by Barbara Cummings), were exploring avenues for gaining restitution for the stolen generations. The lawyers were encouraged by the High Court's Mabo decision and were familiar with international legal rulings on war crimes and compensation; the Aboriginal organisations were hopeful of the prospects the Commonwealth government's 'Social Justice Package' seemed to offer. [82]

These political and legal currents led to the calling of a major conference in Darwin that year, at which over 600 members of the stolen generations, as well as lawyers and political activists, gathered together. Its work was shaped by previous history-making and the conference sought to make more: it frequently invoked the historical narrative that had accumulated by this time;[83] was called the 'Going Home Conference', echoing a chain of signification that Link-Up had begun in the early 1980s; provided a chronology for the policy and practice of removals; and was hailed as a 'historic' occasion. In political terms the conference proceedings were framed by the project of the CAR, one of its sponsors. For example, Cummings, one of the stolen generations narrators, argued that 'the history of the Stolen Generations should be the focus of the debate surrounding Reconciliation', and another speaker told the conference: 'Reconciliation will not be possible unless Australia is prepared to rediscover the true history of this land, and learn from this history. The challenge of this Conference is for the rest of Australia to learn from the history of the stolen generations.' The proceedings were also heavily influenced by legal considerations of reparation. There were assertions that the Commonwealth and State governments bore responsibility for the removal of children and that this amounted to genocide, and there was much discussion of and advice regarding the basis of a legal case. This soon led to the filing of a writ for a High Court challenge, and, later, to a Federal Court case, but most immediately the conference ended with a call for a national investigation into the removal of children, which was immediately endorsed by the federal Minister of Aboriginal Affairs, Robert Tickner (who had been invited to the conference and who had recently learned he was an adopted child),[84] and the President of the Human Rights and Equal Opportunity Commission (HREOC) and Deputy Chairperson of the CAR, Sir Ronald Wilson (who was similarly sympathetic, as he was a devout churchman who had come to the opinion that his church, of which he was a leading layman, had acted wrongly in removing Aboriginal children).[85]

Several months later, the federal Attorney General Michael Lavarch directed the HREOC to undertake a national inquiry.[86]

The Inquiry led to a proliferation of the narrative since the Commission was determined to use it as 'an opportunity to reveal this history and the devastating impact it continues to have on the lives of the stolen generations'. It encouraged Aboriginal people to participate by making written submissions and giving oral evidence to hearings; indeed, within the limits of its relatively small budget, it went to considerable lengths to assist the stolen generations in telling their story. Between December 1995 and October 1996 the Inquiry moved around the country conducting both public and private hearings that were, it claimed, 'as informal as possible'. There were many, the HREOC later reported, who 'wanted to be able to tell their stories', and over 500 individuals and organisations either gave oral evidence or made written submissions.[87] (This emphasis on enabling Aboriginal people to represent their own past was also a feature of the Inquiry's final report.[88])

The Commission's secretariat and the Inquiry's proceedings played a major role in shaping both the stories that were presented to it and its report. For example, in its publicity booklet, *Longing to Return Home* . . ., it answered a rhetorical question 'Why hold a National Inquiry' by claiming that there was 'hardly an Aboriginal family that is not affected in some way'.[89] It also deployed the moving personal testimony of a well-known stolen generations narrator, Archie Roach,[90] as well as evidence uncovered by the historian Anna Haebich. This emphasised not only the experience of Aboriginal people but a particular kind of experience—that of loss and suffering, of trauma.[91] In its other materials and at the hearings themselves, too, the Inquiry encouraged people to 'tell their experience'. Thus, whilst it claimed to offer the opportunity for people to tell their stories 'in their own way', the Inquiry actually called upon them to provide a particular form of testimony, reminiscent of the confessional and the courtroom, that of witnesses who 'tell it how it was' and so bear the truth about history. (This made the hearings extraordinarily powerful psychic and emotional events.) In turn, the Inquiry emphasised this dimension in its 'findings'; it began: 'Grief and loss are the predominant themes of this report.'[92]

The Commission framed the Inquiry in other ways, too. The head of the Inquiry, Ronald Wilson, perhaps influenced by the legal considerations that lay behind the calls for such an investigation, made clear from the outset—indeed, in his earlier support for it—that the removal of children constituted genocide as it was defined by the 1948 International Convention on the Prevention and Punishment of the Crime of Genocide. Subsequently, the Inquiry began its sittings in the place best known for the near-extermination of its indigenous peoples—Tasmania—and there, and at other hearings throughout the country, legal counsel and organisations such as Link-Up made written and oral submissions that represented the removal of children as an act of genocide. More specifically, spokespersons compared the separation of children to the Holocaust and called for compensation on the grounds that Germany had provided financial restitution to its Jewish victims, whilst outside the Inquiry commentator Colin Tatz repeated his claims that the removals constituted genocide.[93]

Like the Going Home Conference that led to it, the Inquiry was also heavily influenced by the ideal of reconciliation. Indeed, it was imagined in similar terms to this political project, which presumes and assumes a particular kind of storytelling and listening—a kind of 'talking cure' whereby the repressed Aboriginal past is released from the national unconscious, its truths uttered, the pain of the dispossessed Aborigines acknowledged, the sins of non-Aboriginal Australians or their forebears confessed, and forgiveness sought. The Inquiry's publicity booklet extracted this passage from Sally Morgan's foreword to Read and Edwards' *The Lost Children*:

> In the telling we assert the validity of our experiences and we call the silence of two hundred years a lie. And it is important for you, the listener, because like it or not we are part of you. We have to find a way of living together in this country, and that will only come about when our hearts, minds and wills are set toward reconciliation. It will only come when thousands of stories have been spoken and listened to with understanding.[94]

For his part, Wilson expressed his hopes that, by 'telling the story . . . and having it listened to', the Inquiry would 'heal, educate and unify' and thus 'enable the nation to go forward as one'.[95] This purpose was also articulated by those who came before the Inquiry. Finally, it called upon the 'whole community [to listen] with an open heart and mind to the stories of what happened in the past and, having listened and understood, [commit] itself to reconciliation'.[96]

The HREOC's report—the title of which, *Bringing Them Home*, so clearly repeated Link-Up's earlier and ongoing signification of the stolen generations narrative—claimed that very large numbers of

Aboriginal children had been 'forcibly removed', as many as one in three between 1910 and 1970; that removal had occurred from the beginning of European colonisation and throughout Australia; and that the main purpose of removal was to prevent the reproduction of Aboriginality, and so amounted to genocide.[97] This historical narrative, it is clear, had been heavily influenced by oral and written submissions that political figures and organisations, especially Link-Up, had presented to the Inquiry, and by claims made outside the inquiry, all of which had been shaped by the narrative accrual that has been described here.[98]

The Inquiry made a lengthy series of recommendations, which included a call for reparation 'in recognition of the history of gross violations of human rights'; recording and preservation of testimonies; annual commemoration of 'the history of forcible removals and its effects' (in the form of a national 'Sorry Day'); and funding for 'family tracing and reunion assistance and referral'. The reparation was to include compensation and an 'acknowledgment and apology': all Australian parliaments should 'officially acknowledge the responsibility of their predecessors for the laws, policies and practices of forcible removal; [and] negotiate . . . a form of words for official apologies to Indigenous individuals, families and communities . . . and make appropriate reparation'.[99]

The report was officially released during the first-ever National Reconciliation Convention in Melbourne in May 1997 and was immediately embraced by that movement, became front-page headline news, and won a large and sympathetic nation-wide audience for its narrative of the stolen generations.[100] As Haydie Gooder and Jane Jacobs have noted, the 'narrative style' of the report—its detailed individual accounts of forced removal—'made a claim on the nation' and shocked it into listening,[101] while the term 'home' had enormous resonance because of its significance in widely circulated (Australian) narratives. The Inquiry's call for an apology from the Commonwealth government quickly became the central symbolic gesture of Reconciliation,[102] it being tailor-made for the CAR's vision of redemption and healing.[103]

If the Inquiry itself (as well as two legal cases that were concurrently being fought) prompted a proliferation of stolen generations stories,[104] the release of the report sparked a veritable explosion of the narrative. It became widely available in the form of the report— a near 700-page tome, *Bringing Them Home* (which sold extraordinarily well and was also available on the Internet)—and a smaller booklet and a video.[105] The stolen generations were debated in the national and state parliaments; featured in major news-stories and editorial comment on radio and television and in newspapers; considered in the letters to the editor columns, and depicted in cartoons; and made the topic of special Websites by the Aboriginal and Torres Strait Islander Commission, Aboriginal organisations, and news services. Later it was the subject of a national 'Sorry Day' (at which the day was compared to 'another great Australian day of remembrance', Anzac Day)[106] and 'Sorry Day' books that over a million Australians signed; extensive commentary (for example, by political scientist and historian Robert Manne, and philosopher Raimond Gaita);[107] further books (such as *The Stolen Children: Their Stories*, 1998); exhibitions (*The Stolen Generations* at the Western Australian Museum, 1999); plays (such as *Stolen*, 1998, and *Box the Pony*, 1999); documentary films (such as *Stolen Generations*, 2000, and *Cry From the Heart*, 2000), and so forth. As a result, the narrative reached a public that had neither previously heard, seen nor read the earlier storytelling and who had been unmoved by the histories of dispossession and discrimination produced in the previous two or more decades.

Consequently, the stolen generations narrative, which had previously become a collective memory for Aboriginal people, now became a symbol of the history of the colonisation of Australia for non-Aboriginal Australians as well, standing for a broader and more complex past. On the one hand it constituted for indigenous people a condensation of their experience of dispossession and displacement, on the other it provided settler Australians a focus for their sense of shame as the descendants of a white Australia responsible for this history.

The popularity of the narrative in turn provoked a major counterattack by conservatives. Since the mid-1980s they have been startled, unsettled and dismayed by a new Australian history whose truths about Australian racism and the dispossession and destruction of Aboriginal people they have been unable or unwilling to accept. Upon coming to office in March 1996 Prime Minister John Howard and his supporters, particularly a small group of aged and disaffected commentators, launched an assault on what they called 'black armband history', which included an increasingly large-scale attack upon the Inquiry's work and its findings.[108] This and 'the history wars' that followed failed, however, to prevent the stolen generations narrative winning more adherents: large numbers of Australians had become very attached to its symbolic historical truth, believing that the removal of Aboriginal children was paradigmatic of the nature of historical relations between non-indigenous and indigenous in Australia, and the Howard government's refusal to follow the states and issue a proper apology to the stolen generations only served to deepen support for it.[109]

This disputation reached a new peak in April 2000, when a government submission to a Senate committee attacked the historical accuracy of *Bringing Them Home*, denied there '[ever] was a "generation" of stolen children' (since 'no more than ten percent' were 'separated'), and claimed the separation of children was 'essentially lawful and benign in intent'.[110] This provoked outrage and condemnation. The federal government was lambasted by spokespersons across the political spectrum. It was repeatedly accused of being in 'a state of denial' about this past, and its approach was compared to those who deny the Holocaust. Many spokespersons and commentators quoted testimonies from *Bringing Them Home* as historical evidence, calling for them to be treated as first-hand and true accounts of history, and nearly all asserted or assumed that Australia had to accept the stolen generations as a 'fact of history' if the nation was to 'move forward'.[111]

The HREOC Inquiry, and several legal cases (*Williams v NSW*, 1994–1999, *Kruger v the Commonwealth*, 1995–97, and *Cubillo and Gunner vs the Commonwealth*, 1996–2000), not only brought the stolen generations to the attention of an incomparably larger number of Australians than it had previously reached, but considerable changes in the narrative—and the nature of its truth claims—had also occurred. As with the narrative accrual that occurred in the late 1980s and early 1990s, but to a much greater degree, the content of the narrative had become more singular, and in this process a good deal of the messy reality of the past being represented had been lost. This was so because these political and legal contexts demanded a simpler narrative than the ones that had framed the narrative at its inception.

The political and legal processes and mechanisms that increasingly shaped the narrative required a story that emphasised the loss and suffering of Aboriginal people on the one hand, and the responsibility of non-Aboriginal Australians for the policy and practice of removal on the other. As a result, experiences and subjectivities—both of the times of the removal and since—that were incongruent with popular understandings of what it means to be oppressed and to be

Aboriginal were marginalised or excluded; and the destruction of Aboriginal families and communities was attributed to one program, that of the removal of children, rather than to a series of complex policies and practices through which families and communities were dispossessed and links between them and their country undermined over time. To put this another way, on the one hand the narrative, especially in the context of the legal cases, sidelined or omitted anything that did not fit with the image of unhappy victims who had always identified as Aboriginal—most importantly, any act of 'passing' by those removed and any complicity in the removal of children on the part of Aboriginal parents or kin. On the other hand, especially in the context of reconciliation and, most of all, the apology, the narrative emphasised the (genocidal) intent—or white agency generally—in order to provide a much-needed focal point for the nebulous sense of shame many white Australians felt about the role their forefathers played in the dispossession of Aboriginal people.

In these circumstances, the various historical sources that comprised the narrative and the ways in which they were used also changed considerably. As noted previously, in the earliest phases of the narrative it had comprised both documentary and biographical sources; that is, it had consisted of both history- and memory-work, of both academic research of contemporary or historical sources, and retrospective autobiographical and oral sources. Moreover, for the most part, the former were deployed as evidence for what actually happened in the past, and the latter were used as evidence for the consequences of removals for the present and the past in between (though these were also used to evidence removal when they could be tested against the historical record). This is to argue that historical research in government and other archives was largely used in telling a story about the reasons for the policy and the extent of its implementation (which included estimates of how many children might have been removed); and the biographical accounts were mostly deployed as examples to illustrate instances of removal and, more especially, to reveal the historical consequences of removal. This narrative, furthermore, initially only made claims about the history of the stolen generations that referred to particular communities or localities.

By contrast, in the political and legal battles that have largely framed the narrative of late, it has increasingly consisted of biographical, literary and political representations rather than historical ones. The HREOC Inquiry undertook little if any original historical research, even though the removal of children had really only been the subject of historical research in two jurisdictions (New South Wales and the Northern Territory), and much of its evidence consists of oral testimony, autobiography and political submissions; and, in the legal cases, historical interpretation and evidence have been called but they have often been either supplanted by testimony or discarded by lawyers and/or judges who have, of course, been pursuing points of law rather than history.[112] Consequently, in the presentation of the narrative some of the important 'grounding' in historical 'sources' that are held to verify what happened in the past and which provide the basis for the discipline of history's truth claims, at least in the eyes of most people (but also for many historians, too), has been lost. Simultaneously, the retrospective biographical accounts have, in effect, been given not only the burden of witnessing the impact of the program of separating Aboriginal children on individuals but also the responsibility of telling the broader, collective history about the past, a forensic task these sources are not traditionally thought capable of doing, at least single-handedly, mainly because it is widely recognised that memory can be notoriously malleable and so unreliable. To compound this problem, the narrative (at least in the political context) has presumed to tell a national history—before the historical research has been completed that might lend it weight—and proposed an estimate of the number of children removed *nationally* that no historical research has supported (or is likely to). These changes in the narrative have seriously undermined the truth claims it has been making at the very same time as the increasingly symbolic nature of the narrative has resulted in a heightening of its claim for the historical significance of the removal of children.[113]

The reformulated narrative has been ruthlessly attacked of late, especially by conservatives who often seem intent on denying the historical realities and/or the historical legacy of the colonisation of Australia.[114] In the light of both these developments, the truths that the stolen generations narrative might tell about the history of Aboriginal people and the history of relations between Aboriginal and non-Aboriginal people are now greatly endangered. What can be done, in this context, to advance historical understanding? In my opinion, two moves are necessary.

On the one hand, it is vital that the weaknesses in the stolen generations narrative, including its earliest forms, be recognised and acknowledged, and the perils of sidestepping contemporary or historical sources in any history-work be noted and conceded. On my reading, the narrative is flawed in two major senses. First, it has mistakenly conflated 'separation' with 'forced removal' and thereby obscured the range of circumstances in which Aboriginal children were taken from their parents or kin. There are undoubtedly grounds for arguing that separation in any form—whether consensual or forcible—had a considerable impact on Aboriginal families and communities (though one might want to distinguish between those who very belatedly or never returned and those who did within a relatively short period of time), but too often separations are seen as being all of a kind in terms of policy, which is a more tendentious claim. In this sense the narrative has worked to reduce the range of reasons for separation of children to one—that of a genocidal plan on the part of government to destroy Aboriginality— and so it obscures the fact that children were removed for a variety of reasons. (In arguing this one should not overlook that some Aboriginal policy-making was governed by what could be called a genocidal logic; indeed, it is very important to recognise this since it tells us much about white Australia.)

Second, the narrative tends to conflate intent with implementation, erroneously asserting or implying that one followed the other. This is so even though historical studies of Aboriginal administration have shown that government agencies seldom had the resources to implement fully the policies they wanted to execute; that they were often foiled by non-Aboriginal and Aboriginal opponents of those plans; and that they adapted and even abandoned policies as circumstances changed. As a result, the narrative has exaggerated the number of children removed. The historical research that we require to establish an estimate of the number of children removed has yet to be conducted and perhaps never will because of the absence and/or loss of data. However, the work done so far suggests that many fewer children were separated in the nineteenth century and that the number separated in the twentieth century varied greatly according to time and place. An informed historical guess would be that removal occurred at a higher rate than one in ten in some areas, much less in others, and none in still others.[115]

As well as addressing these weaknesses in the stolen generations narrative, historical research can also do more to recover the broader history of which the removal of children is simply but importantly one part. Especially of late, the narrative has lost sight of the myriad ways in which Aboriginal communities have been undermined by ongoing dispossession and destruction. This is still a story that has not been adequately told or heard in Australia. Indeed, one of the costs of the foregrounding of the stolen generations is that settler Australians are allowed to overlook—or are prevented from seeing—this bigger picture.

All this is work of a kind that history has conventionally done and can readily do more of. It is crucial that it do so given the privileged status it, unlike memory, has in the context of legal and political regimes, due to their common empiricist procedures of storytelling and story-testing. Once this work is done, many of the truths of the stolen generations will probably remain standing and will stand stronger. However, another move is also required of the discipline, one that runs contrary to many of its traditional procedures.[116] This needs to be made with reference to the way history interprets or reads memory. Conventionally, historians have tended to reject such a 'subjective' source, noting, as conservative critics of the stolen generations narrative have done, the ways in which its retrospectivity can make it unreliable, and have opted for the 'objectivity' of contemporary or historical sources.[117] This approach makes much sense, and should not be abandoned unless we want to regard history as merely another kind of fiction. However, if we merely adopt this tack, we deny ourselves the opportunity of deepening our understanding of both the past and relationships between the past and the present, both traditional objects of historical study.

More recent historical approaches to memory proceed in two different directions. The first begins by accepting, in the words of one practitioner, that 'the importance of [autobiographical and] oral testimony may often lie not in its adherence to facts but rather . . . [at the points] where imagination, symbolism, [and] desire' are evident, and by seeking to work with these 'errors' on the basis that they can 'sometimes reveal more than factually correct accounts'.[118] Quite obviously, this requires a methodology that does not naively regard texts such as the narratives of the stolen generations as simple sources that provide a transparent window onto the past, but which considers them instead as murky texts that require sophisticated techniques of reading before they can be said to reveal a past reality or yield insights into it. Recent advances in the historical understanding of traumatic events such as the Holocaust have rested upon this kind of interrogation of testimony.[119]

The second point of departure proceeds from a recognition that memory is collective and presentist, and so subject to external influences and change, and that as a result it is uniquely valuable for the insights it can provide into the ways communities, including nations, remember the past. As such it can shed light on the relationships between past and present, and present and past, and, more specifically, reveal how history as narrative can shape a people over several generations. By adopting both these approaches, we can explore the complex meanings that histories like the stolen generations narrative have to tell.

Endnotes

We wish to thank Heather Goodall, Alan Ward and Bridget Williams for their helpful comments on drafts of this introduction.

1. These are the forms of storytelling or history-making that are considered in this volume, and they consist almost entirely of written and oral mediums. Other forms include, for example, painting, photography, dance, theatre and museums.

2. For discussion of some aspects of this phenomenon, see Nicholas Thomas, *Possessions: Indigenous Art/Colonial Culture*, London, 1999, especially chapters 3–8.

3. For a discussion of this, see Graeme Davison, 'The Great Voyage: National Celebration in Three New Lands', in his *The Use and Abuse of Australian History*, Sydney, 2000, pp. 56–79.

4. Jeremy Beckett, 'Walter Newton's History of the World—or Australia', *American Ethnologist*, vol. 20, no. 4, 1993, p. 675.

5. Louis Mink, *On Historical Understanding*, Ithaca, 1987, p. 185–6; Jerome Bruner, 'The Narrative Construction of Reality', *Critical Inquiry*, vol. 18, no. 1, 1991, p. 16.

6. See Heather Goodall, '"The Whole Truth and Nothing But . . .": Some Interactions of Western Law, Aboriginal History and Community Memory', in Bain Attwood and John Arnold (eds), *Power, Knowledge and Aborigines*, Melbourne, 1992, especially pp. 114–18.

7. Bruner, 'The Narrative Construction', p. 4.

8. For a discussion of the role that history and historians have played in the work of the Waitangi Tribunal, see M.P.K. Sorrenson, 'Towards a Radical Interpretation of New Zealand History: The Role of the Waitangi Tribunal', in I.H. Kawharu (ed.), *Waitangi: Maori and Pakeha Perspectives of the Treaty of Waitangi*, Auckland, 1989, pp. 158–78; Alan Ward, 'Historical Method and Waitangi Tribunal Claims', in Miles Fairburn and W.H. Oliver (eds), *The Certainty of Doubt: Tributes to Peter Munz*, Wellington, 1996, pp. 140-56; Paul McHugh, 'Law, History and the Treaty of Waitangi', *New Zealand Journal of History*, vol. 31, no. 1, 1997, pp. 38–57. For a consideration of the role that anthropology and anthropologists have played in land rights and native title claims in Australia, see, for example, Kenneth Maddock, *Anthropology, Law and the Definition of Australian Aboriginal Rights to Land*, Amsterdam, 1980; Mary Edmunds (ed.), *Claims to Knowledge, Claims to Country: Native Title, Native Title Claims, and the Role of the Anthropologist*,

Canberra, 1994; Julie Finlayson and Diane Smith (eds), *Native Title: Emerging Issues for Research, Policy and Practice*, Canberra, 1995; Julie Finlayson and Ann Jackson-Nakano (eds), *Heritage and Native Title: Anthropological and Legal Perspectives*, Canberra, 1996; Deborah Bird Rose, 'Histories and Rituals: Land Claims in the Territory', in Bain Attwood (ed.), *In the Age of Mabo: History, Aborigines and Australia*, Sydney, 1996, pp. 35–53.

9.   Feminist scholars have argued that this is not only peculiarly bourgeois but masculinist as well. See, for example, Sidonie Smith, *A Poetics of Women's Autobiography*, Bloomington, Ind., 1987.

10.   See, for example, Working Party of Aboriginal Historians, 'Preparing Black History', *Identity*, vol. 4, no. 5, 1981, pp. 7–8; Judith Binney, 'Maori Oral Narratives, Pakeha Written Texts: Two Forms of Telling History', *New Zealand Journal of History*, vol. 21, no. 1, 1987, pp. 16–28; Te Ahukaramu Charles Royal, *Te Haurapa: An Introduction to Researching Tribal Histories and Traditions*, Wellington, 1992; Tipene O'Regan, 'Old Myths and New Politics: Some Contemporary Uses of Traditional History', *New Zealand Journal of History*, vol. 26, no. 1, 1992, pp. 5–27; Jeremy Beckett, 'Aboriginal Histories, Aboriginal Myths: An Introduction', *Oceania*, vol. 65, no. 2, 1994, pp. 97–115; Te Maire Tau, 'Matauranga Maori as an Epistemology', *Te Pouhere Korero*, vol. 1, no. 1, 1999, pp. 10–23; Danny Keenan, 'Predicting the Past: Some Directions in Recent Maori Historiography', *ibid.*, pp. 24–35; Michael Reilly, 'Imagining Our Pasts: Writing Our Histories', in Bronwyn Dalley and Bronwyn Labrum (eds), *Fragments: New Zealand Social & Cultural History*, Auckland, 2000, pp. 14–37.

11.   See Judith Binney, 'Myth and Tradition in Ringatu Tradition', *Journal of the Polynesian Society*, vol. 93, no. 4, 1984, pp. 345–98; Erich Kolig, 'Captain Cook in the Western Kimberleys', in R.M. and C.H. Berndt (eds), *Aborigines of the West: Their Past and Their Present*, Nedlands, 1979, pp. 274–82; Kenneth Maddock, 'Myth, History and a Sense of Oneself', in Jeremy Beckett (ed.), *Past and Present: The Construction of Aboriginality*, Canberra, 1988, pp. 11–30; Chris Healy, *From the Ruins of Colonialism: History as Social Memory*, Melbourne, 1997, chapters 1, 2.

12.   See Michael King, *Being Pakeha Now: Reflections and Recollections of a White Native*, Auckland, 1999, chapter 8; Bain Attwood, 'Introduction', in Attwood and Arnold (eds), *Power, Knowledge and Aborigines*, pp. xii–xvi, and 'Introduction', in Attwood (ed.), *In the Age of Mabo*, p. xxii.

13.   It might be noted that we solicited essays from several indigenous scholars for this volume but unfortunately only one was able to contribute.

14.   For a recent consideration of such histories, see Klaus Neumann *et al.* (eds), *Quicksands: Foundational Histories in Australia & Aotearoa New Zealand*, Sydney, 1999.

CHAPTER 1: INDIGENOUS AUSTRALIAN LIFE WRITING

1. See, for example, David Unaipon, *My Life Story*, Adelaide, [1951]; Douglas Lockwood [and Phillip Roberts Waipuldanya], *I, the Aboriginal*, Adelaide, 1962; Lazarus Lamilami, *Lamilami Speaks*, Sydney, 1974. A comprehensive list of relevant texts to 1995 is provided in Anne Brewster, *Literary Formations*, Melbourne, 1995.
2. Michel de Certeau, *The Practice of Everyday Life*, Berkeley, 1984, p. 37.
3. *ibid.*, p. xix.
4. *ibid.*, pp. 34–9.
5. The seminal theoretical texts on this topic are Roland Barthes, 'The Death of the Author' (1977), in his *Image, Music, Text*, Stephen Heath (trans.), New York, 1991, pp. 142–8; Michel Foucault, 'What is an Author?' (1969), in Donald Bouchard and Sherry Simon (eds), *Language, Counter-Memory, Practice*, Ithaca, 1977, pp. 113–38; Mikhail Bakhtin, 'Discourse in the Novel', in *The Dialogic Imagination*, Michael Holquist (ed.), Austin, 1981, pp. 259–422.
6. De Certeau, *The Practice of Everyday Life*, p. 40.
7. Sydney, 1999.
8. Nan Kivell Collection (NK 4048), National Library of Australia.
9. 'Aboriginal Texts and Narratives', in Elizabeth Webby (ed.), *Cambridge Companion to Australian Literature*, Cambridge, 2000, p. 22.
10. Arnold Krupat, *For Those Who Come After*, Berkeley, 1985, p. xi.
11. The news that Bennelong lives and eats with the Governor, and that his wife has been stolen away, may also be read as a mode of social positioning—Bennelong's way of telling Mr and Mrs Phillips and Lord Sydney that he is now an unmarried man living under the care of their associate, the Governor.
12. See Alison Ravenscroft's discussion of Rita Huggins' relations with her readers in 'Strange and Sanguine Relations: Aboriginal Writing and Western Book Culture', *Meridian*, vol. 16, no. 2, 1997, pp. 261–9.
13. Mudrooroo Narogin, *Doin Wildcat*, Melbourne, 1988, p. 113.
14. 'Prospectus', 10 September 1836, in Michael Rose (ed.), *For the Record: 160 Years of Aboriginal Print Journalism*, Sydney, 1996, p. 3.
15. *ibid.*, p. 18.
16. *ibid.*, p. 17.
17. *ibid.*, p. 208, note 2.
18. Petition to Her Majesty Queen Victoria, 17 February 1846, in Bain Attwood and Andrew Markus, *The Struggle for Aboriginal Rights: A Documentary History*, Sydney, 1999, pp. 38–9.
19. Barbara Harlow, *Resistance Literature*, New York, 1987; Caren Kaplan, 'Resisting Autobiography: Out-Law Genres and Transnational Feminist Subjects', in Sidonie Smith and Julia Watson (eds), *De/colonising the Subject: The Politics of Gender in Women's Autobiography*, Minneapolis, 1992, pp. 115–38.

20. *Domination and the Arts of Resistance*, Newhaven, 1990, p. 24.
21. Walter George Arthur to Colonial Secretary, 15 July 1846, in Attwood and Markus, *The Struggle for Aboriginal Rights*, p. 40.
22. Henry Reynolds, *Fate of a Free People*, Melbourne, 1995, p. 12.
23. Attwood and Markus, *The Struggle for Aboriginal Rights*, p. 31.
24. Reynolds, *Fate of a Free People*, p. 7.
25. *ibid.*, p. 15.
26. State Records Office of Western Australia, AN 1/2, Aborigines' Department, Acc. 255, 1898/118, *Crown v Pompey alias Nipper*, emphasis in original, marked by underlining.
27. Evidence of Benjamin, *Report of the Committee to Inquire into Treatment of Aboriginal Native Prisoners of the Crown in the Colony*, Legislative Council, Perth, 1884, Paper 32, p. 13.
28. *ibid.*
29. Public Records Office of Victoria, VPRS 1226, Box 4, *Minutes of Evidence Taken Before the Board Appointed to Enquire into the Condition of the Aboriginal Station at Coranderrk*, p. 67.
30. For a more detailed account of the sociology of nineteenth-century Aboriginal writing on Coranderrk and Lake Condah Reserves, see my 'Authors, Scribes and Owners', *Continuum*, vol. 13, no. 3, 1999, pp. 333–43.
31. Stephen Muecke, *Textual Spaces: Aboriginality and Cultural Studies*, Sydney, 1992, p. 137; Penny van Toorn, 'Discourse/Patron Discourse: How Minority Texts Command the Attention of Majority Audiences', *SPAN*, no. 30, 1990, pp. 102–15.
32. For further discussion of consumption of indigenous life writings, see my 'Stories to Live In: Discursive Regimes and Indigenous Canadian and Australian Historiography', *Canadian Literature*, no. 158, 1998, pp. 42–63; 'Tactical History Business: The Ambivalent Politics of Commodifying the Stolen Generations Stories', *Southerly*, vol. 59, nos 3 & 4, 1999, pp. 252–66.
33. See, for example, *Milli Milli Wangka: The Indigenous Literature of Australia*, Melbourne, 1997, pp. 184–5.
34. For example, Sally Morgan told the story of her grandfather ('through Aboriginal kinship') Jack McPhee in *Wanamurraganya*, Fremantle, 1989; Rosemary van den Berg presented the life story of her father, Thomas Corbett, in *No Options, No Choice!*, Broome, 1994; Wayne King devotes almost a quarter of his autobiography, *Black Hours*, Sydney, 1996, to his mother's experience of life as a stolen child; and Jeannie Bell tells Celia Smith's story in *Talking About Celia*, St Lucia, 1997.
35. Canberra, 1994; Alison Ravenscroft has written illuminatingly about her work with Rita Huggins and her daughter Jackie Huggins ('Strange and Sanguine Relations').
36. Ruby had worked with poet Susan Hampton when writing her auto-biography, *Don't Take Your Love to Town*, Melbourne, 1988, but

the nature of their collaboration was different to that between Ruby and myself.

37. The editor's integration into the Aboriginal author's family structure is discussed in Ravenscroft, 'Strange and Sanguine Relations', and in Jennifer Isaacs (ed.), *Wandjuk Marika: Life Story*, St Lucia, 1995, pp. 5–6.

38. Langford Ginibi, *Haunted by the Past*, p. 58.

39. The more usual spelling is 'eh'.

40. See Ian Henderson's discussion of Ruby's use of 'aye' in his 'The Getting of Wisdom', *Southerly*, vol. 60, no. 1, 2000, p. 229.

CHAPTER 2: STORIES FOR LAND

1. After a preliminary experiment under an Act of 1862, the Native Land Court (today the Maori Land Court) was constituted in its lasting form by the Native Lands Act 1865, and this became the foundation of many laws relating to Maori land passed over subsequent decades. In 1865 the Crown was confiscating lands in regions of the central North Island where Maori who had fought to protect their lands and autonomy were deemed to be 'rebels'; the Land Court was designed to process lands outside the confiscation areas. For a recent study of laws and Crown policies concerning the operation of the Native Land Court, analysed in the light of current understandings of Treaty of Waitangi jurisprudence, see D.V. Williams, *'Te Kooti Tango Whenua': The Native Land Court 1864–1909*, Wellington, 1999.

2. Here the conventional translations of these Maori terms for categories of descent groups are given. In recent years much debate has taken place in various contexts as to understandings of social groups to which these terms may be applied.

3. Judge W.G. Mair, prominent in various court hearings in the King Country, stated at the outset that Rohepotae was 'perhaps one of the most important cases ever brought before any Court' (Judge W.G. Mair, 28 July 1886, Maori Land Court (MLC) Minute Books, Otorohanga Book 1, p. 36). Mair stated that the Rohepotae block was estimated to contain 1 636 000 acres (20 October 1886, MLC Otorohanga Book 2, p. 55). The hearing of the Pirongia East and West subdivision (also referred to in the minute books as Kopua-Pirongia-Kawhia) occupied 44 days in the first half of 1888.

4. Technically the claimant was required to establish a prima facie case; if successful the counter-claimant was 'in the position of a plaintiff' and proceeded with his case, followed by the claimant's case 'in defence'. The claimant thus had the final right of reply after the counter-claimant addressed the court. See Rules under the 'Native Lands Act, 1865', made by the Chief Judge, *New Zealand Gazette*, 5 April 1867.

5. See, for instance, minutes of 3, 6, 7 April 1888, MLC Otorohanga Book 3, pp. 34, 42, 46.

6. The judge, interpreter and clerk may have been the only Pakeha always present in court, though it is clear there were others on occasion.

7. Those giving evidence spoke their own language—the judges in this period generally had a good knowledge of Maori—but the evidence was translated by interpreters into English and recorded in English in the official minute books. This process means that the traditions and statements of Maori as they were given in te reo Māori (the Maori language) have been largely lost, a matter greatly regretted today. It means, of course, that today, in reading the official books, we are already at one remove from the narratives of the old people in the court. It is interesting to compare the text in the judges' personal minute books (sometimes in two languages) and, occasionally, the Maori text as transcribed in official books or in private family books.

8. Te Maire Tau, 'Matauranga Maori as an Epistemology', *Te Pouhere Korero*, vol. 1, no. 1, 1999, p. 11.

9. The court consisted of the Chief Judge and other appointed judges, most of whom, up to 1903, were civil servants or soldiers; judges were assisted by the advice of a 'Native' Assessor, from an area outside that being adjudicated. In any given hearing in this period, at least one judge and one assessor had to be present. The Pirongia case, like the first Rohepotae case, was heard by Judge W.G. Mair, with Paratene Ngata as the Assessor; both were respected. Maori could seek a rehearing of any case, but the Chief Judge had sole power to allow or to dismiss such applications.

10. Minutes of 19 April 1888, MLC Otorohanga Book 3, p. 96.

11. I am grateful to Tui Adams QSO, Kingitanga Kaumatua and Emeritus Professor James Ritchie ONZM for discussions on this passage. On Tawhiao's tongi, see p. 40 below.

12. The five were Ngati Maniapoto; Ngati Hikairo; Ngati Whakatere and Ngati Takihiku (described by the judge as sections of Ngati Raukawa, and counted together); Ngati Tuwharetoa; and Ngati Rangatahi of Wanganui. Wahanui Te Huatare was widely known by the name Wahanui.

13. See, for instance, minutes of 9, 10, 11 and 13 September 1886, MLC Otorohanga Book 1, pp. 261, 269–71, and 12 October 1886, Otorohanga Book 2, p. 44.

14. Hone Te One of Ngati Hikairo also set his own parameters, starting with a direct, and unwarranted, disclaimer: 'I wish to inform the Court that I know nothing about genealogy neither do I know anything about ancient history' (13 June 1888, MLC Otorohanga Book 4, p. 41).

15. A parallel may be found in Waitangi Tribunal and Court hearings in recent years, which claimant groups may feel place unwarranted pressure on those who should most be protected from it.

16. Women might also have been placed in a difficult position if they had been asked to give whakapapa (genealogies), which they might be familiar with but whose formal transmission (in this tribal area) was generally reserved for men. I am grateful to Tom Moke and Helen Crown of Pirongia for discussions on this point (14 July 1999, 22 May 2000).

17. Tom Moke, in discussion, 14 July 1999.

18. In the Rohepotae Judgment delivered on 20 October 1886 the court made orders in favour of some counter-claimants—notably those of Waikato at Kawhia—and of the five claimant tribes for all the balance of the block (MLC Otorohanga Book 2, pp. 67–9).

19. In fact the counter-claims were recorded by the court in the names of individuals on behalf of their hapu; as noted below, many hapu were encompassed in each of the claims to Pirongia; the names given here are simply the main hapu names for some of the main counter-claims. Some counter-claimants amalgamated their claims for the purpose of the hearing.

20. See minutes of 9 April 1888, MLC Otorohanga Book 3, pp. 47–9, and 10 and 11 April, *ibid.*, pp. 49–59.

21. The use of the term 'occupation' raises interesting questions. As has often been noted, Maori 'saw themselves as users of the land rather than its owners', but in the sense that 'they saw themselves not as owning the land but as being owned by it . . . for the land was Papatūānuku, the mother earth who conceived the ancestors of the Maori people' (*Muriwhenua Land Report*, Waitangi Tribunal Report 1997, p. 23). To the British, however, whose world view was rather different, the legal term 'occupation' had long been useful for 'reading down' Maori land rights. The Maori text of the Treaty of Waitangi, by contrast, guarantees 'tino rangatiratanga' ('the unqualified exercise of their chieftainship') over their lands.

22. Evidence of Wahanui, 2 August 1886, MLC Otorohanga Book 1, p. 47. In Judge Mair's minute book he has translated Wahanui's statement as: 'I claim also through my kaha [strength] in holding the land' (Judge Mair's Notebook, 2 August 1886. Land Court: hearings of various Court cases, 1886–91, microfilm 1532, reel 2, University of Auckland, p. 216). Hone Kaora defined atete on one occasion as 'the power to prevent the land being occupied by those who have no right to it & to warn them off, & even to forcibly eject them' (Hone Kaora, cross-examined by (henceforth Xd)) Haimona Patara, 27 September 1886, MLC Otorohanga Book 1, p. 369). William Hughes, of Ngati Makahori, challenged in the Pirongia hearing to prove this take, cited his ancestors 'being able to hold the land against the Kāwhia people' (Xd John Ormsby, 30 April 1888, MLC Otorohanga Book 3, p. 171).

23. Ormsby, for instance, might have claimed through Maniapoto, as he explained in Court, but because of tensions in his relationship with Ngati Maniapoto he decided on a claim through Hikairo and Paiariki

instead. At least one counter-claimant disputed his right because of this decision, but would have admitted it if Ormsby had claimed through Punga, Tipi or Tukitaua (Evidence of Te Anga Toheroa, 17 April 1888, MLC Otorohanga Book 3, p. 89).

24. Te Oro Te Koko, Xd Assessor, 16 May 1888, *ibid.*, p. 288.

25. The court, which was empowered to admit 'such evidence as it shall think fit', established among its principles that 'modern occupation' was inadmissible, unless it [had] for its foundation or authority either conquest or descent from previous owners' (Chief Judge Fenton's Oakura judgment, 1866, cited in B.G. Gilling, 'By Whose Custom?: The Operation of the Native Land Court in the Chatham Islands', *Victoria University of Wellington Law Review,* vol. 23, no. 3, 1993, p. 48). Since evidence in the Pirongia hearings on post-1840 'occupation' was given by those claiming by ancestral take, Judge Mair seems to have had no trouble admitting it.

26. Pei Te Hurinui Jones (comp.) and Bruce Biggs (ed.), *Nga Iwi o Tainui: The Traditional History of the Tainui People*, Auckland, 1995, p. 7.

27. See, for instance, the account of the death of Te Putu (*ibid.,* pp. 294–301); the context is the encroachment of Ngati Raukawa on the lands of Waikato, but the story—well known in Tainui oral traditions—is about the death of the aged chief Te Putu at the hand of Nga Tokowaru of Ngati Raukawa who had been captured. Nga Tokowaru stabbed Te Putu, and smeared himself with Te Putu's blood in order to save himself from being eaten; in the aftermath of this disturbing event a peace was eventually sealed by a very significant chiefly marriage.

28. Moke, in discussion, 14 July 1999.

29. Te Oro Te Koko, 14 May 1888, MLC Otorohanga Book 3, p. 255.

30. According to Te Oro Te Koko, Kahu was a great-grandchild of Raka who married Uenga, a great-grandson of Hoturoa (Xd Ormsby, 17 May 1888, *ibid.*, p. 278).

31. Te Oro Te Koko, 14 May 1888, *ibid.*, pp. 255–6. In *Nga Iwi o Tainui* a similar account of Kahupeka's journey is sourced to Te Oro Te Koko. Translations of the names into English are taken from a similar version of the tradition, published in *He Korero Purakau mo nga Taunahanahatanga a nga Tupuna: Place Names of the Ancestors: A Maori Oral History Atlas*, Wellington, 1990, pp. 25–9, and based on unpublished manuscript sources written by E.H. Reweti and Huirama, held by Te Aue Davis. In court, of course, Te Oro Te Koko merely gave the names in Maori. The reader may find different interpretations of them in other sources.

32. *He Korero Purakau,* p. xiii.

33. Te Oro Te Koko, 14 May 1888, MLC Otorohanga Book 3, pp. 255, 256.

34. Evidence of Rihari Tauwhare, 24 May 1888, *ibid.*, p. 326. Ngati Hikairo today consider that Tauwhare, an acknowledged expert,

made an error, perhaps deliberately, in attributing the journey to Rakataura and Kahukeke. His account placed more emphasis on the connection of Rakataura with the land (Moke, in discussion, 23 August 1999).

35. Te Mapu Tahuna, 21 May 1888, *ibid.*, pp. 296–7.
36. Motai was a son of Onetapu, a younger brother of Turongo, hence Motai was teina to Turongo. Upokotaua was the great-great-grandson of Motai (16 May 1888, *ibid.*, p. 276).
37. Te Mapu Tahuna, Xd Ormsby, *ibid.*, p. 299. He added that there had been a second gift, made by Hie, a descendant of Paiariki and Kuo, to Ngawaero.
38. Te Oro Te Koko, 16 May 1888, *ibid.*, p. 276.
39. This sort of distinction, between mana tangata (in this context, jurisdiction over and responsibility for people) and mana whenua (variously interpreted as authority over, or power from, the land), was made not infrequently in the court. Te Oro Te Koko stated elsewhere that mana whenua was given to Motai, and mana (tu)tangata to Turongo (Xd Assessor, 17 May 1888, *ibid.*, p. 286). I am grateful to Te Rita Papesch of Ngati Apakura, Tumuaki, Department of Maori, University of Canterbury, for advice and interpretation into English of these and other phrases in this essay.
40. Evidence of Te Rauroha Te Ngare, 20 April 1888, *ibid.*, p. 98.
41. *ibid.*
42. Evidence of Rihari Tauwhare, 24 May 1888, *ibid.*, p. 330.
43. Moke, in discussion, 14 July 1999.
44. Evidence of Te Wi Papara, 1 June 1888, MLC Otorohanga Book 3, p. 375.
45. Evidence of Te Oro Te Koko, 15 May 1888, *ibid.*, pp. 265–6.
46. There were other traditions of the naming of Paewhenua, and of the great bird; in Rihari Tauwhare's narrative the bird was not only seen but called up by the first overland expedition of Raka's people who left the Tainui waka at Manukau, sent south to the mountains because 'they were skilled in causing birds to appear' (Evidence of Rihari Tauwhare, 24 May 1888, *ibid.*, pp. 323–4).
47. Evidence of Te Wi Papara, 1 June 1888, *ibid.*, p. 373.
48. Papara had referred to this gift of the mokai (servant) the day before, made to Wetere Te Kauae (*ibid.*, p. 369).
49. *ibid.*, pp. 373–4. It is interesting that Judge Mair records only a brief summary of this history in his own notebook; clearly it was not as interesting to him as it was to the kaumatua who gave it (Judge Mair's Notebook, 1 June 1888. Land Court: hearings of various Court cases, 1886–91, microfilm 1533, reel 3, University of Auckland, p. 338).
50. Evidence of Waretini Tukorehu, 14 April 1888, MLC Otorohanga Book 3, p. 70. He may first have seen books in the late 1830s or early 1840s.

51. Evidence of Te Anga, 17 April 1888, *ibid.*, p. 86. There was a North Island measles epidemic in 1854, and Ormsby stated that he heard the mill was built about 1855 (Evidence of Ormsby, 7 June 1888, MLC Otorohanga Book 4, p. 9).

52. Evidence of Hone Te One, 13 June 1888, *ibid.*, p. 42.

53. Evidence of Te Rauroha Te Ngare, 20 and 21 April 1888, and evidence of Hauauru, 23 April 1888, MLC Otorohanga Book 3, pp. 99–100, 111, 121–2, 128.

54. Evidence of Hauauru, 24 April 1888, *ibid.*, pp. 124–5. The court clerk's problems with distinguishing Ngati Makahori and Ngati Matakore persist in this passage.

55. The fact that the Wesleyans embarked on a purchase in 1840 does not necessarily mean that Ngati Maniapoto interpreted the transaction as a property conveyance; the Waitangi Tribunal has found that in the Muriwhenua (far northern) region pre-Treaty transactions were interpreted by Maori as a 'social contract' involving an allocation of land to incorporate outsiders into the community (*Muriwhenua Land Report*, p. 73).

56. Ngati Ngawaero histories explained why it was that other chiefs were able to enter into such a transaction in the absence of Te Meera (18 May 1888, MLC Otorohanga Book 3, pp. 288–9).

57. Evidence of Te Wi Papara, 1 June 1888, *ibid.*, p. 380. See also p. 397. The Maori text of the final phrase, as recorded in a family book kindly made available by Tom Moke, reads: 'ko te tangata tērā nōna te whenua.'

58. *ibid.*, p. 381. And see whakapapa, *ibid.*, facing p. 365.

59. Evidence of John Ormsby, 7 June 1888, MLC Otorohanga Book 4, p. 10. The name 'Te Mera' does in fact appear on the 1847 deed, but this cannot stand as a contradiction of the oral history; it is possible either that his name, with a mark beside it, was inserted in his absence as an act of courtesy, or that it was added later, after he returned.

60. Evidence of Thomas Hughes, 26 April 1888, MLC Otorohanga Book 3, pp. 145–6. The Ngati Makahori history did not explain why Pakeha readily capitulated to the leasing payments, though Ngati Hikairo's did! According to John Ormsby, Te Toenga decided the charge should be two shillings and sixpence per head of cattle, and when Ormsby's father resisted payment 'he missed one of his beasts and Tāwhia's slave pointed out to him the horns & skins . . . and my father found that the bullock did not come to a natural death & was satisfied that it was killed because he wouldn't pay grazing fees' (Evidence of John Ormsby, 7 June 1888, MLC Otorohanga Book 4, p. 11). Ormsby stated that this was in the time of Rev. G. Buttle, the second missionary, and that disputes about the land started in 1851. Buddle left Te Kopua at the end of 1844.

61. Evidence of Te Rauroha Te Ngare, 20 April 1888, MLC Otorohanga

Book 3, p. 100. Te Mapu Tahuna of Ngati Ngawaero, who had been Mr Reid's shepherd, stated that 100 sheep were given in rent (i.e. ten per cent), which were divided four ways (Ngati Ngaupaka also shared in them) (22 May 1888, *ibid.*, pp. 308–9).

62. Evidence of Thomas Hughes, 26 April 1888, *ibid.*, p. 146.
63. Evidence of Te Anga, 17 April 1888, *ibid.*, p. 87. Thomas Hughes stated: 'Te Anga wanted to make it into a canoe, my brother and I cut it up, so ended this dispute' (26 April 1888, *ibid.*, p. 147).
64. Evidence of Te Anga, 17 April 1888, *ibid.*, p. 90.
65. In a confrontation over the construction of an eel weir, for instance, those who opposed it might try to set fire to it while its owners battled the flames, continually dousing them with water.
66. Evidence of John Ormsby, 8 June 1888, MLC Otorohanga Book 4, p. 15.
67. *ibid.*
68. Moke, in discussion, 19 August 1999.
69 R.T. Mahuta, 'Tawhiao's Vision', unpublished lecture, 1990, p. 5.
70. Judith Binney, 'Maori Oral Narratives, Pakeha Written Texts: Two Forms of Telling History', *New Zealand Journal of History*, vol. 21, no. 2, 1987, p. 26.

CHAPTER 3: CRYING TO REMEMBER

I would like to thank, in particular, Deborah Bird Rose, those at the Australian National University's Research School of Asian and Pacific Studies seminar, and my fellow editor whose insightful comments and suggestions have been critical to the development of this essay. The Yolngu orthography used here is found across northeast Arnhem Land. In particular, /rr/ is trilled, and /r/ is a continuant; on the first syllable of words three long vowels occur, /e/, /o/ and /ä/; and Yolngu languages distinguish six places of articulation for stops and nasal consonants, including the postalveolar retroflexes [t], [d] and [r], the lamino-dentals [th], [dh] and [nh] and the lamino-alveolars [tj], [dj] and [ny].

1. Songs (manikay) are used for all ritual occasions and are referred to as madayin, indicating that they comprise part of the sacra of Yolngu religious life (which also includes paintings, dances, stories, sand sculptures and ritual objects). Some of the ritual knowledge embodied in the sacra is confined to secret and restricted realms of knowledge formally accessible to men only. Yolngu make distinctions between degrees of restricted knowledge insofar as songs and dances are said to be either secret (dhuyu), inside (djinaga), open (garma), and outside (warranggul). Although manikay are used for a variety of occasions such as initiation, fertility and memorial rituals, I am only concerned here with bäpurru manikay (men's funeral songs) and ngäthi manikay (women's crying-songs).

2. I use the term 'ritual' to refer to the body of traditional song knowledge that is based on the Ancestral Law and is most commonly heard performed for ritual events. As northeast Arnhem Land has been a focus of considerable missionary activity since the 1920s, and, more recently, has become a centre for an increasing number of popular music bands, ritual songs are also to be distinguished from Christian hymns and choruses as well as from popular musical forms. As some ritual song genres have been adapted for Christian worship, men have occasionally employed the women's crying-song style for this type of song text. The reasons for this innovation are complex and have been discussed elsewhere (see my 'The Joy of Mourning: Resacralising "the Sacred" Music of Yolngu Christianity and Aboriginal Theology', *Anthropological Forum*, vol. 9, no. 1, 1999, pp. 11–36.

3. Earlier, Wilson had adopted me as his sister and, in doing so, had bestowed upon me the honorary status of a relatively senior D̲atiwuy woman and member of the shark clan, but had sought to ensure I learned Yolngu songs in an appropriate manner.

4. Yolngu is the name that the people of the northeast Arnhem Land region use to refer to themselves.

5. As all Yolngu are related, they refer to one another by kin terms, actual and classificatory. The remark came from a dhuway who was a potential husband from the Gumatj clan.

6. Murukun's desire to perform for a research context was remarkable given that the collection of personal memories through song could often be painful. However, she was particularly concerned that younger women should be able to hear her voice and the song words in the future via her song recordings.

7. Alfred Schutz and Thomas Luckmann, *The Structures of the Lifeworld*, Richard Zaner and H. Tristran Englehardt Jr (trans.), Evanston, 1973.

8. Ritual songs have associated ancestral stories that are told as glosses to the lists of names recited in each song. Several song subjects combine to create a song series. The stories explain the travels and actions of the ancestors at each of the places named in the songs. Consequently, storytelling is intimately related to singing and will be dealt with as a continuum in this analysis.

9. For a broad and detailed coverage of mapping processes in Aboriginal societies, see Peter Sutton, 'Icons of Country: Topographic Representations in Classical Aboriginal Traditions', in David Woodward and G. Malcolm Lewis (eds), *The History of Cartography: Volume Two, Book Three, Cartography in the Traditional African, American, Arctic, Australian and Pacific Societies*. Chicago, 1998, pp. 353–416.

10. See Mikhail Bakhtin, *The Dialogic Imagination: Four Essays*, Michael Holquist (ed.), Caryl Emers and Michael Holquist (trans.),

Austin, 1981; Alan Duranti and David Brenneis, 'The Audience as Co-author', *Text*, vol. 6, no. 3, 1986, pp. 239–347.

11. This concept parallels what Kenneth Olwig refers to as 'poetic synergy' in his 'Sexual Cosmology: Nation and Landscape at the Conceptual Interstices of Nature and Culture; or, What Does Landscape Really Mean?', in Barbara Bender (ed.), *Landscape: Politics and Perspectives*, Oxford, 1983, p. 308.

12. Deborah Bird Rose, 'To Dance with Time: A Victoria River Aboriginal Study', *Australian Journal of Anthropology*, vol. 12, no. 3, 2000, pp. 287–96; In this argument about the temporal dimensions of dance, Rose elegantly outlines the interwoven relationship between sound, movement, ecosystems and Aboriginal cosmology.

13. The Morning Star ceremony is used by Dhuwa clans only (see endnote 26), and its mythology and ritual significance is too extensive for discussion here. (However, see John Rudder, 'Yolngu Cosmology', PhD, Australian National University, 1993; A. Bonfield, 'A Dhanbul Ritual', PhD, Manchester University, 1998; and Ian Keen, 'Morning Star: Exchange and the World of the Dead in Northeast Arnhem Land', paper prepared for the Musical Visions Conference, Adelaide, July 1998.

14. I use the term 'projected' rather than 'collective' since it can be argued that collective experience is only reckoned as a projection of the personal; in other words, collective experience is always and necessarily the other made through the experiences of the self.

15. Paul Ricoeur, *Time and Narrative*, Chicago, 1983, p. 47.

16. Jerome Bruner, *Actual Minds, Possible Worlds*, Cambridge, Mass., 1986, p. 30.

17. Deborah Bird Rose, 'Remembrance', *Aboriginal History*, vol. 13, no. 2, 1989, p. 144.

18. In the post-contact situation, there are necessarily two ways of moving along the path: by following strings of Yolngu connectedness and the European way. Here I am concerned primarily with the Yolngu dhukarr of ancestral knowledge. These two paths may run parallel to one another, or diverge significantly.

19. Ian Keen, *Knowledge and Secrecy in an Aboriginal Religion*, Oxford, 1994, p. 384.

20. Young men are allowed to sing with their fathers in a group, but they will not lead the singing until they are much older. The percentage of texts known by younger women varies depending on their interest in ritual, and their ability to recall the details of people and places associated with the myths.

21. The word 'milkarri' literally means 'tears' and it may be used interchangeably with 'ngäthi' ('crying') when referring to women's songs.

22. During mortuary rituals in Arnhem Land, women may only cry at specific times of the day, when natural elements appear that are metaphors for relatives—for example, the blood of deceased kin in

the red clouds at sunset, and memories of loved ones in the morning star at sunrise. In this way, the natural world is anthrogeomorphically connected to living and deceased relatives, who share the same ritual names as elements of the natural world.

23. The non-strophic crying-song structure allows women a certain freedom to adapt specific knowledge about people in their own clan and their personal interests as they do not have to incorporate words in time with the rhythmic accompaniment of clapstick and didjeridu as in men's composition. In addition, the same singer performing the same song consecutively will alter the word order, insert additional lines, or change the order of the song images.

24. *Landscape and Memory*, London, 1996, p. 25.

25. This is important when deciding which clans should take charge of a body at a funeral site and in what order clans ought to sing. For example, if the deceased were an important clan leader, relatives would increase their status by holding the funeral on their clan land.

26. The entire universe (including humans, animals and the natural elements) is divided into two halves or moieties that are referred to as Dhuwa and Yirritja. Everything in the world is permanently located in one or other half. Several clusters of individual mythological subjects are combined to create an entire song series.

27. The onus is on skilful female singers to help lead others who are not as competent. Younger women are 'gora' ('ashamed' to sing). Although they may be gifted singers they realise that they are not yet old enough to demonstrate the full extent of their knowledge and musical potential.

28. This can be sad if a close family relative such as an uncle has died without seeing the child.

29. Ritual knowledge of the land created by the shark was handed down to Murukun's father by her mari'mu (paternal grandfather). She shares the ability to cry this song with other elderly Djambarrpuyngu women such as Rärrkminy Dhamarrandji of the Gundangur Djambarrpuyngu subgroup, as well as with Murukun's eldest classificatory sister of the Datiwuy clan, Gunmukul, as the shark travels from Djambarrpuyngu clan land on Galiwin'ku to Datiwuy clan land at Rorruwuy, forming creeks until it is speared and finally dies in the freshwater at Ngaymil clan land. Men and women sing of the arrival and actions of the shark at their land as well as its actions at other homelands. For example, Wilson Manydjarri would sing the Datiwuy shark song at Rorruwuy, where it gouged out the creek named Bulurrumu, the bundurr name of the Datiwuy clan and the shark ancestor. Similarly Murukun will sing of the shark at the Djambarrpuyngu land at Garrata. Murukun also has the right to songs of her own clan, her mother's mother's (brother's) clan, Golumala, her sister's clan, Gälpu, her sister's son's clan, Wangurri, and her two mothers' clans, Warramiri and Lamamirri.

30. The fin is also the name for the ritual spear of the Djambarrpuyngu clan that is used to depict the fin of the shark in ritual dances. See my 'Yolngu Dance, Arnhem Land', in Adrienne Kaeppler and J. Wainwright Love (eds), *Australia and the Pacific Islands: The Garland Encyclopaedia of World Music*, vol. 9, 1998, pp. 457–60.

31. I had the opportunity to hear Murukun perform the shark song on ten occasions, four times at funerals and six times in our informal teaching sessions; and in order to establish the variability between other clan versions I also recorded this shark song with two other senior women of the Djambarrpuyngu and Datiwuy clans (Rärrkminy and Gunmukul).

32. This interweaving of animal and topographical surfaces compares with the spiritual associations noted by Suzanne Küchler with regard to Malangan houses and gardens in New Ireland: 'House sites as place of womb become garden sites as place of the skin, where the inside and outside become merged so that the surface or landscape testifies as much to what lies buried beneath the forest to what is imagined and remembered as to what is visible and known' ('Landscape as Memory: The Mapping of Process and its Representation in a Melanesian Society', in Bender (ed.), *Landscape: Politics and Perspectives*, pp. 96–7).

33. Yolngu construct ritual shades from eucalyptus trees and canvas. The body is placed under this tarpaulin on a canvas ground sheet. The funeral shade is the central focus of the ritual with the singing and dancing taking place around it.

34. The shark is shared by Djambarrpuyngu, Datiwuy, Ngaymil and Djapu clans. These groups have the right to perform the shark song in any ritual context.

35. Deborah Bird Rose, 'Indigenous Ecologies and Environmental Ethics', paper prepared for the International Conference on Environmental Justice, Melbourne, October 1997, p. 10.

36. Bruce Kapferer, *Celebration of Demons: Exorcism and the Aesthetics of Healing in Sri Lanka*, 2nd edn, Washington, 1991, p. 278.

37. For an analysis of these aspects of personhood and experience see Martin Heidegger, *Being and Time*, John Macquarie and Edward Robinson (trans.), New York, 1962, p. 106.

38. Suzanne Küchler notes a similar phenomenon among Malangan where the 'skin' of painting and the carving on which it is made are inseparable, seen as both container and envelope merging the transition from deceased person to ancestor through the surface designs of objects ('Making Skins: Malangan and the Idiom of Kinship in Northern New Ireland', in Jeremy Coote and Anthony Shelton (eds), *Anthropology, Art and Aesthetics*, Oxford, 1992, p. 102).

39. Elinor Ochs and Lisa Capps, 'Narrating the Self', *Annual Review of Anthropology*, vol. 25, 1996, pp. 19–43.

CHAPTER 4: THE SAGA OF CAPTAIN COOK

This chapter is a newly edited version of an earlier article, 'The Saga of Captain Cook: Morality in Aboriginal and European Law', *Australian Aboriginal Studies*, no. 2, 1984, pp. 24–39.

1. Kim Benterrak, Stephen Muecke and Paddy Roe, *Reading the Country: Introduction to Nomadology*, Fremantle, 1984, p. 173.

2. The research was funded by the Australian Institute of Aboriginal Studies and the National Science Foundation (USA).

3. The oral traditions that I taped on these and other field trips form the basis of a subsequent book: *Hidden Histories: Black Stories from Victoria River Downs, Humbert River, and Wave Hill Stations, North Australia*, Canberra, 1991. For more works on the history of the region, see: Ronald and Catherine Berndt, *End of an Era: Aboriginal Labour in the Northern Territory*, Canberra, 1987; J. Doolan, 'Walk-off (and Later Return) of Various Aboriginal Groups from Cattle Stations, Victoria River District, Northern Territory', in Ronald Berndt (ed.), *Aborigines and Change: Australia in the 70's*, Canberra, 1977, pp. 106–13; Frank Hardy, *The Unlucky Australians*, Melbourne, 1968; Darrell Lewis, *A Shared History: Aborigines and White Australians in the Victoria River District, Northern Territory*, Darwin, 1997; Frances Merlan, '"Making People Quiet" in the Pastoral North: Reminiscences of Elsey Station', *Aboriginal History*, vol. 2, no. 1, 1978, pp. 70–106; Peter Read and Jay Read, *Long Time, Olden Time: Aboriginal Accounts of Northern Territory History*, Alice Springs, 1991.

4. See Erich Kolig, 'Captain Cook in the Western Kimberley', in Ronald and Catherine Berndt (eds), *Aborigines of the West, their Past and their Present*, Perth, 1981, pp. 274–82; Chips Mackinolty and Paddy Wainburranga, 'Too Many Captain Cooks', in Tony Swain and Deborah Bird Rose (eds), *Aboriginal Australians and Christian Missions*, Adelaide, 1988, pp. 355–60.

5. For an alternative approach to Aboriginal morality, see Ronald Berndt, 'Traditional Morality as Expressed through the Medium of an Australian Aboriginal Religion', in Ronald Berndt (ed.), *Australian Aboriginal Anthropology*, Canberra, 1970, pp. 216–47.

6. I discuss these issues in greater detail, and use the extended case method to show how moral principles are applied in social life, in *Dingo Makes Us Human; Life and Land in an Australian Aboriginal Culture*, Cambridge, 1992.

7. John O'Neill, 'Critique and Remembrance', in his *On Critical Theory*, New York, 1976, pp. 1–11.

CHAPTER 5: ENCOUNTERS ACROSS TIME

1. Judith Binney, Gillian Chaplin and Craig Wallace, *Mihaia: The Prophet Rua Kenana and his Community at Maungapohatu*, Auckland, 1979; Judith Binney and Gillian Chaplin, *Ngā Mōrehu: The Survivors*, Auckland, 1986; Judith Binney, *Redemption Songs: A Life of Te Kooti Arikirangi Te Turuki*, Auckland, 1995.
2. An earlier talk about the biography of Te Kooti, given in London in 1996, was subsequently published as 'The Making of a Biography of Te Kooti Arikirangi Te Turuki', *Journal of Pacific Studies*, vol. 20, 1996, pp. 113–22. Some passages from this article have been adapted for the present essay.
3. Melbourne University Press, 1997; University of Hawai'i, 1997.
4. See my 'Maori Oral Narratives, Pakeha Written Texts: Two Forms of Telling History', *New Zealand Journal of History*, vol. 21, no. 1, 1987, pp. 16–28. I would also like to acknowledge particularly Jeffrey Sissons' work. I refer not only to his book, *Te Waimana: The Spring of Mana. Tuhoe History and the Colonial Encounter*, Dunedin, 1991, but also to his review of *Mihaia* in the *Journal of the Polynesian Society*, vol. 89, no. 4, 1980, pp. 385–8, in which he posed crucial questions about using oral sources and writing Maori history, which directly influenced the construction of *Ngā Mōrehu*.
5. *New Zealand Herald*, 28 October 1998.
6. Oral source (OS): 17 May 1978, Tataiahape; also quoted in Judith Binney and Gillian Chaplin, 'Taking the Photographs Home: The Recovery of a Maori History', *Visual Anthropology*, vol. 4, 1991, p. 432.
7. OS: Te Akakura Rua, 24 November 1979, Auckland.
8. OS: 26 November 1983, Manutuke, quoted in Binney and Chaplin, *Ngā Mōrehu*, pp. 93–4.
9. Joanne Rappaport, *The Politics of Memory: Native Historical Interpretation in the Colombian Andes*, Cambridge, 1990, pp. 140–2.
10. See my 'Myth and Explanation in the Ringatu Tradition', *Journal of the Polynesian Society*, vol. 93, no. 4, 1984, pp. 356–7.
11. OS: 19 May 1978, Matahi, quoted in Binney, *Redemption Songs*, p. 506.
12. OS: 14 February 1982, Mangatu, quoted in *ibid*.
13. OS: 16 May 1982, Muriwai, Poverty Bay.
14. The text, with a translation, is to be found in Binney, *Redemption Songs*, pp. 378–80.
15. OS: 15 December 1981, Opotiki, quoted in *ibid*., p. 449.
16. Keith Sinclair, *The Origins of the Maori Wars*, Auckland, 1957 (and reprinted several times); Alan Ward, *A Show of Justice*, Auckland, 1973 (and reprinted several times); James Belich, *The New Zealand Wars and the Victorian Interpretation of Racial Conflict*, Auckland, 1986 (and reprinted several times).

17. OS: 16 May 1982, Muriwai, quoted in Binney, *Redemption Songs*, pp. 508–9.
18. See Mircea Eliade, 'The Terror of History', in David Carrasco and Jane Marie Law (eds), *Waiting for the Dawn: Mircea Eliade in Perspective*, rev. edn, Colorado, 1991, pp. 70–86.
19. 'The canoe for you to paddle after me is the Law. Only the Law will pound the Law' ('Ko te waka hei hoehoenga mo koutou i muri i ahau, ko te Ture, ma te Ture ano te Ture e aki'), April 1893: quoted in Binney, *Redemption Songs*, p. 490.
20. A phrase of John Pocock's when commenting on *Redemption Songs* in a paper given at the conference 'The Politics of History', Tulane University, New Orleans, 22–24 March 1996. This paper was subsequently published as 'The Historian as Political Actor in Polity, Society and Academy', *Journal of Pacific Studies*, vol. 20, 1996, pp. 89–112.
21. This decision was in fulfilment of a prophecy of Te Kooti to turn the Seventy ('Te Whitu Tekau') into the Eighty. Te Whitu Tekau was the chosen name for the collective unity of the Urewera hapu (tribes); it was also traditionally considered the appropriate number for a fighting force (ten times seven). 'Eighty', Te Kooti's predicted number for the completion of unity, was probably an intentional statement of peaceful union. For a discussion of his prediction, see my *Redemption Songs*, p. 478.
22. *A Grammar and Vocabulary of the Language of New Zealand*, London, 1820; Judith Binney, *The Legacy of Guilt: A Life of Thomas Kendall*, Auckland, 1968.
23. See Ian Wedde and Harvey McQueen (eds), *The Penguin Book of New Zealand Verse*, Auckland, 1985, pp. 267–70.
24. *Islands and Beaches: Discourse on a Silent Land, Marquesas, 1774–1880*, Melbourne, 1980.
25. Kendall to Rev. John Eyre, 27 December 1822, Mss 71/40, Hocken Library, Dunedin.

CHAPTER 6: IN THE ABSENCE OF VITA AS GENRE

1. W.E.H. Stanner, 'Durmugam, a Nangiomeri', in Joseph Cassagrande (ed.), *In the Company of Man*, New York, 1960, p. 76.
2. There is also 'career' to consider, a forward projection that also (as Max Weber would tell us) has origins in religious perceptions; career derives from a Protestant preoccupation with one's calling.
3. This is argument from fact of absence; there is also argument from theory that would posit the incongruence of life story with other aspects of Aboriginal culture and ideology, with especial reference to both Aboriginal constructs of temporality and Aboriginal conceptions of the self.
4. Richard Baker constructs a history of the Yanyuwa people that does some justice to its ethnohistorical sources, presenting a parade of

collectively recognised 'times': wild times, police times, war time, welfare times, cattle times, land rights [Gough Whitlam] times, tourist times (*Land is Life: From Bush to Town, the Story of the Yanyuwa People*, Sydney, 1999, p. viii.) 'Times' belong to local speech communities; thus Grace Koch and Harold Koch record how Katie Ampetyane of Barrow Creek in Central Australia 'describes the period of time known to her as "naked time"' (*Kaytetye Country: An Aboriginal History of the Barrow Creek Area*, Alice Springs, 1993, p. 73).

5. Colin Meissner, 'Recovery and Revelation: On the Experience of Self-Exposure in James's Autobiography', *Genre*, vol. 29, no. 4, 1996, p. 485.

6. 'Introduction', in his *Native American Autobiography: An Anthology*, Wisconsin, 1994, p. 4.

7. See Ira Bruce Nadel, *Biography: Fiction, Fact and Form*, New York, 1984.

8. Richard Hoggart, *The Uses of Literacy: Aspects of Working Class Life, with Special Reference to Publications and Entertainments*, Harmondsworth, 1958; Walter Ong, *Orality and Literacy: The Technology of the Word*, London, 1982.

9. 'Mediation in Contemporary Native American Writing', *Genre*, vol. 25, no. 4, 1992, pp. 321–7.

10. *Earthdivers: Tribal Narratives on Mixed Descent*, Minneapolis, 1981, p. xvii.

11. On the other hand, Aboriginal playwrights such as Jack Davis and Jimmy Chi have plays that rely throughout on dualities of cultural mediation.

12. Fremantle, 1987.

13. See Bain Attwood, 'Portrait of an Aboriginal as an Artist: Sally Morgan and the Construction of Aboriginality', *Australian Historical Studies*, vol. 25, no. 99, 1992, pp. 302–18.

14. 'Introduction', in his *In the Company of Man*, p. xiii.

15. *ibid.*, p. xiv.

16. *African Voices, African Lives: Personal Narratives from a Swahili Village*, London, 1997, p. 16.

17. Paddy Roe, *Gularabulu: Stories from the West Kimberley*, Stephen Muecke (ed.), Fremantle, 1983. Also Krim Benterrak, Stephen Muecke and Paddy Roe, *Reading the Country: Introduction to Nomadology*, Fremantle, 1984.

18. Stephen Muecke, *Textual Spaces: Aboriginality and Cultural Studies*, Sydney, 1992, p. 41. Muecke neatly defines a dilemma: 'as long as one emphasises performance one will miss out on factual detail and interpretation; as long as one does ethnography, one will miss out on the linguistic aspects of performance style' (p. 42). The problem is made acute because he wants to make authentic text broadly available to readers who are not specialist scholars with a taste for footnotes.

19. Caplan, *African Voices*, p. 22.

20. Canberra, 1980.

21. Under provisions of the Aboriginal Land Rights (Northern Territory) Act of the Commonwealth of Australia (1976), 42.3 per cent of the lands of the Territory (573 000 square kilometres) have been ceded to Aboriginal Lands Trusts. See Graeme Neate, 'Review of the Northern Territory Land Rights Act', *Indigenous Law Bulletin*, vol. 4, no. 15, 1998, p. 7.

22. Aborigines in Northern Australia identify themselves by using European first names and surnames. Furthermore, the surnames are treated as family names, children taking them from one or other parent. European names are 'whitefella names' in contradistinction to 'blackfella names' which are enunciated in an Aboriginal language and are given to people in infancy in honour of the particular Dreaming Power which has caused them to be conceived (their 'personal totem'). While 'whitefella names' (including additional nicknames like 'Tarpot' or 'Lefty') are public, Dreaming names are reserved names known to those who have business to know them. They are used sparingly and with due care. To voice a Dreaming name may be either to designate its human bearer or to call that person to attention. But, at the same time, the voicing of such a name invokes the Power of which it is itself an aspect. Voicing the names of Powers brings one into communion with the sacred. In contrast, 'whitefella names' have no sacred content.

23. The structure and production of humbug (the tale of cock and bull) is discussed at length in my *Wallaby Cross*, chapters 7 and 9.

24. Used in this way, 'Daddy' is a term of address with no regular reciprocal (unlike the priestly title 'Father', which makes all lay Christians the 'children' of the priest). For preference, Roy would call those who called him 'Daddy' by their 'whitefella names' rather than by any kinship term which might often contradict 'Daddy', making the addressee a person who did not by real kinship fall within the prohibited degrees but was, rather, defined as a potential spouse or sexual partner.

25. Individuals who either beget a child, or bear a child and then neglect that child, are not credited as proper parents but instead become 'father for nothing' or 'notta mother really'. It is those who truly 'rear up/grow up' children who are counted as the people who, in their declining years, can expect attention and care from the children they brought up. (On relations between parents and children, see Basil Sansom and Patricia Baines, 'Aboriginal Child Placement in the Urban Context', in Bradford W. Morse and Gordon R. Woodman (eds), *Indigenous Law and the State*, Dordrecht, 1988, pp. 347–66.)

26. Ellipses (. . .) in all texts transcribed from tapes stand for pauses; they do not indicate the editing of statements. A second convention is that capitalised words or passages are BIG WORDS as the speakers would call them.

27. The period 1942–45 was indeed a time of upheaval and transfers of population in the Top End. The first bombing attack on Darwin was mounted by the Japanese in December 1941. Air raids continued until November 1943 and a general evacuation of European women and children from Darwin was approved on 12 February 1942 (see Alan Powell, *A Far Country: A Short History of the Northern Territory*, Melbourne, 1982, p. 197). Aborigines were rounded up and interned in especially established camps run by the Australian Army (Baker, *Land is Life*, pp. 91–3). The time of internment is often given by Aboriginal speakers as 'Army Time'.

28. In this, more than precision is lost. One's conversation begins to move out of intimacy and into a less confidential and public realm in which 'outside' rather than 'inside' accounts are given.

29. Brazen eye contact defies everyday Aboriginal conventions of politeness.

30. David Kunzle, 'World Upside Down: The Iconography of a European Broadsheet Type', in Barbara Babcock (ed.), *The Reversible World*, Ithaca, 1978, p. 52.

31. 'Durmugam on Kinship and Subsections', *Canberra Anthropology*, vol. 2, no. 2, 1979, p. 49.

32. Like the concept of vita, the notion of 'death due to natural causes' is foreign to Roy Kelly and his countrymen. For them, nearly all deaths are compassed deaths, caused by the malevolence of a jealous or vengeful person who either personally works sorcery against the chosen victim or, if not well-versed in sorcery, employs an accomplished sorcerer to do the work.

33. The word 'clear' is, perhaps, more frequently used; 'clear' has retrospective time valence, 'free' points to futures still to be realised.

34. One could say that the ex-spouse was already dead to you. There is, of course, a social dimension to not going to a ceremony; the act is called 'throwing (ceremony) away'. One spurns those among the living who mourn the dead. But, also, one may not wish to face the possibility of fractious encounter with the subsequent partner(s) of one's ex-spouse.

35. Roy's return to 'life story thing', the pattern of recounted episode that subserves verity, is documented in my account of 'Divorce Painting' in 'The Wrong the Rough and the Fancy: About Immortality and an Aboriginal Aesthetic of the Singular', *Anthropological Forum*, vol. 7, no. 2, 1995, pp. 294–7.

36. Kingsley Palmer's preface to the co-authored biography of McKenna (Kingsley Palmer and Clancy McKenna, *Somewhere Between Black and White: The Story of an Aboriginal Australian*, Melbourne, 1978). Ruppert remarks that seeing writers and subjects as being 'between two cultures' is 'a romantic and victimist' perspective for it denies their capacity to act as 'participants in two rich cultural traditions' ('Mediation in Contemporary Native American Writing', p. 321).

37. Powell, *A Far Country*, p. 232.

38. Alfred Schutz, *The Phenomenology of the Social World*, Evanston, 1967; Michael Polyani, *Personal Knowledge: Towards a Post-Critical Philosophy*, London, 1962.
39. Mark Lester (trans.), New York, 1990, p. 148.
40. *ibid.*, p. 150.

CHAPTER 7: AUTOBIOGRAPHY AND TESTIMONIAL DISCOURSE IN MYLES LALOR'S 'ORAL HISTORY'

Earlier drafts of this paper were given to the Anthropology seminars at the Universities of Lund, Tromsø, Stockholm and Sydney. My thanks to colleagues for their comments and suggestions.

1. The book has now been published: *Wherever I Go: Myles Lalor's 'Oral History'*, Melbourne, 2000.
2. John Beverley makes this point in connection with debates over the autobiography of Rigoberta Menchú ('The Real Thing', in Georg M. Gugelberger (ed.), *The Real Thing: Testimonial Discourse and Latin America*, Durham NC, 1996, pp. 272–3).
3. Arnold Krupat, *The Voice in the Margin: Native American Literature and the Canon*, Berkeley, 1989, and *Ethnocriticism: Ethnography, History, Literature*, Berkeley and Los Angeles, 1992; Brian Swann and Arnold Krupat (eds), *I Tell You Now: Autobiographical Essays by Native American Writers*, Lincoln, 1987; Hertha Dawn Wong, *Sending My Heart Back Across the Years: Tradition and Innovation in Native American Autobiography*, New York, 1992.
4. *Ethnocriticism*, p. 196.
5. *ibid.*, p. 133.
6. Gugelberger (ed.), *The Real Thing* (this is a collection of articles published elsewhere between 1989 and 1995). See also Georg M. Gugelberger and Michael Kearney, 'Voices of the Voiceless: Testimonial Literature and Latin America', *Latin American Perspectives*, vol. 19, no. 3, 1992, pp. 3–14.
7. Miguel Barnet (ed.), *Esteban Montejo: The Autobiography of a Runaway Slave*, New York, 1973.
8. The Spanish original is *Me llamo Rigoberta Menchú y así me nació la conciencia*.
9. Elisabeth Burgos-Debray (ed.), *I, Rigoberta Menchú: An Indian Woman in Guatemala*, London, 1984.
10. 'Testimonio and Postmodernism', *Latin American Perspectives*, vol. 18, no. 3, 1991, pp. 42, 44, 46.
11. 'The Hyperreal Indian', *Critique of Anthropology*, vol. 14, no. 2, 1994, pp. 153–71.
12. 'Narrating Cultural Resurgence: Genre and Self-Representation for Pan-Maya Writers', in Deborah E. Reed-Danahay (ed.), *Auto/Ethnography: Rewriting the Self and the Social*, Oxford, 1997, pp. 21–46.

13. See, for example, Bertrand de la Grange and Maite Rico, *Marcos la Genial Impostura*, Mexico DF, 1997.
14. 'Testimonio and Postmodernism', p. 43.
15. *Ethnocriticism*, p. 210.
16. 'What's Wrong with Representation?', in Gugelberger (ed.), *The Real Thing*, p. 166.
17. Frederic Jameson, 'On Literary and Cultural Import-Substitution in the Third World: The Case of the Testimonio', in Gugelberger (ed.), *The Real Thing*, pp. 180–1.
18. 'The Constitution of Human Life in Time', in J. Bender and D. Welbery (eds), *Chronotypes: The Construction of Time*, Stanford, 1991, p. 161, his emphasis.
19. 'The Writer: Commitment and Alignment', *Marxism Today*, vol. 24, no. 6, 1980, p. 25.
20. See Elzbieta Sklodovska, 'Spanish American Testimonial Novel: Some Afterthoughts', in Gugelberger (ed.), *The Real Thing*, p. 88.
21. 'What's Wrong with Representation?', p. 170.
22. *ibid.*
23. 'The Real Thing', p. 278.
24. 'What's Wrong with Representation?', p. 170.
25. 'Narrating Cultural Resurgence', p. 22.
26. Burgos-Debray, *I, Rigoberta Menchú*, p. 1.
27. *Rigoberta Menchú and the Story of All Poor Guatemalans*, Westview, 1999.
28. 'Sacred Text', *London Review of Books*, vol. 21, no. 11, 1999, pp. 17–19.
29. *Writing From the Fringe: A Study of Modern Aboriginal Literature*, Melbourne, 1990, p. 153.
30. Fremantle, 1987.
31. See particularly Bain Attwood, 'Portrait of an Aboriginal as an Artist: Sally Morgan and the Construction of Aboriginality', *Australian Historical Studies*, vol. 25, no. 99, 1992, pp. 302–18. See also the replies to Attwood: Tony Birch, 'Half-Caste'; Jackie Huggins, 'Always Was, Always Will Be'; Tim Rowse, 'Sally Morgan's Caftan'; Isabel Tarrago, 'Response to Sally Morgan and the Construction of Aboriginality', *Australian Historical Studies*, vol. 25, no. 100, 1993, pp. 458–68. See also Eric Michaels, 'Para-Ethnography', in his *Bad Aboriginal Art*, Sydney, 1994, pp. 165–76.
32. Attwood, 'Portrait of an Aboriginal', p. 305; Michaels, 'Para-Ethnography', p. 167; Mudrooroo, *Writing From the Fringe*, p. 149.
33. Michaels, 'Para-Ethnography', p. 173.
34. See particularly Huggins, 'Always Was, Always Will Be'.
35. 'Para-Ethnography', p. 174.
36. 'The Constitution of Human Life', p. 164, his emphasis.
37. Jeremy Beckett, 'George Dutton's Country: Portrait of an Aboriginal Drover', *Aboriginal History*, vol. 2, no. 1, 1978, pp. 2–31.

38. Myles heard the recording of our first session in the presence of my wife, whom he had not previously met; he expressed some embarrassment at the amount of 'swearing', though he did not reduce it once he got into the swing of the next recording.

39. This corresponds to the Bakhtinian concept of 'chronotope' which Pam Morris glosses as 'the spatio-temporal matrix which shapes any narrative text' (*The Bakhtin Reader: Selected Writings of Bakhtin, Medvedev, Voloshinov*, Pam Morris (ed.), London, 1994, p. 246).

40. 'On Literary and Cultural Import-Substitution', pp. 185–6.

CHAPTER 8: TAHA MAORI IN THE *DNZB*

I am grateful to Claudia Orange and Angela Ballara for their helpful comments and equally helpful criticisms on this chapter.

1. 'Why Be Bicultural?', in Margaret Wilson and Anna Yeatman (eds), *Justice and Identity: Antipodean Practices*, Wellington, 1995, pp. 122–5. The supremely bicultural and bilingual William Parker, who helped the *DNZB* immensely in its earlier years, once told a story about a Maori who 'confessed' to a Maori group that he did not know the language except in a rudimentary way. 'I stood up to address him', he said, 'and told him never to speak like that again, and that whether he had good Maori or not did not affect the work he had done and would do for Maori people'. I suspect that the story was told for the benefit of those of us with little or no Maori.

2. See *Why Weren't We Told?: A Personal Search for the Truth About Our History*, Melbourne, 1999. Perhaps a New Zealand equivalent would be entitled 'Why was what we were told quite wrong?', though such a title would invite arguments as to the possibility of making 'truth-claims'.

3. Anecdotal evidence suggests that this memory may be much less present among those who grew up after 'social studies' displaced history in schools in the mid-century. However, if this is the case, there is still a rough element of 'ethnic' equality since the memory of Pakeha heroes and feats will have suffered a similar fate, that of death by abstraction. But even if the historical memory has been dulled in this manner, awareness of the Maori presence and of the Maori past had, by the 1980s, been sharpened by the prominence of Maori 'causes' since the 1970s.

4. There is a sizeable literature on this topic. See Peter Gibbons, 'Non-fiction', in Terry Sturm (ed.), *The Oxford History of New Zealand Literature in English*, 2nd edn, Auckland, 1998, pp. 31–118. Much more is to be found in Gibbons' unpublished '"Going Native": A Case Study of Cultural Appropriation in a Settler Society, With Particular Reference to the Activities of Johannes Andersen in New Zealand During the First Half of the 20th Century', DPhil, University of Waikato, 1992.

5. G.H. Scholefield (ed.), *The Dictionary of New Zealand Biography*, 2 vols, Wellington, 1940. And for Ngata see M.P.K. Sorrenson (ed.), *Na To Hoa Aroha: From Your Dear Friend: The Correspondence Between Sir Apirana Ngata and Sir Peter Buck 1925–50*, 3 vols, Auckland, 1986–88.

6. Soon after the project was launched in 1983, the present writer, it was reported, caused offence to the Prime Minister, Robert Muldoon, by referring to the 'British annexation' of 1840. His objection was apparently based upon the belief that the British did not do that sort of thing—that was what, at that very time, Russians had done in places like Afghanistan. Muldoon, thanks to the advocacy of the noted New Zealand historian Keith Sinclair at a dinner party, had at the outset supported the venture, but (so it was rumoured) his enthusiasm waned when he was told that only the dead would be selected. (He has, however, found a prominent place in vol. V.)

7. When I outlined the *DNZB* objectives and strategies to some of the staff of the *DCB* in Toronto, the then General Editor, Frances Halpenny, responded by describing the problems, chiefly linguistic, which would have inhibited such an effort in Canada. The member of staff nearest to me whispered in my ear: 'Didn't actually try.'

8. Report to the Policy Committee (PC), 9 November 1984, *DNZB* files. It was recognised that it would be difficult to find such a person but it was hoped that secondments, say from the Departments of Maori Affairs and Education, and the appointment of consultants, would constitute an effective package. In the event, this did not prove to be the case.

9. Literally, 'the hundred peak people'. When this title was proposed to the Policy Committee one of its Maori members looked at the other and asked 'What does that mean?' 'I'm dashed if I know', was the reply. It seems likely that some intra-Maori point, perhaps relating to the use of high-flown language rather than everyday speech, was being scored.

10. The interpenetration of the two histories was recognised by the Maori Advisory Committee when it sought representation on the Commissioning Sub-committee (solely concerned with finding authors for Pakeha subjects) to keep a watch on the authorship of essays on Pakeha who had been significant in Maori history. Ranginui Walker and Miriama Evans were appointed (Maori Advisory Committee minutes, 16 October 1985, PC minutes, 6 November 1986, *DNZB* files).

11. Report to the Policy Committee by Claudia Orange, 25 May 1984, *DNZB* files. The notion of partnership was beginning to gain currency around this time, through the Waitangi Tribunal, and later the 1987 judgments of the Court of Appeal. Orange's influential book, *The Treaty of Waitangi*, Wellington, 1987, reinforced the trend.

12. Miria Simpson, Report to the Policy Committee, 6 November 1986, *DNZB* files.

13. The history of this episode is obscure. Methuen were the prospective publishers, and the project may well have originated with them. Bruce Biggs, Professor of Maori at the University of Auckland, chaired the only meeting of which there appears to be a record and urged writers to go ahead with or without full tribal approval, advice he was to repeat to the *DNZB*—'Just do it', he said to the present writer who seemed, to Biggs' mind, to be fussing needlessly about Maori participation. The prospective editor of the projected history, Michael King, later claimed that 'This project came to grief in 1980 because two tribal groups out of 12 declined to be involved' (*New Zealand Listener*, 13 April 1985).

14. See Tipene O'Regan, 'Old Myths and New Politics: Some Contemporary Uses of Traditional History', *New Zealand Journal of History*, vol. 26, no. 1, 1992, pp. 5–27. Elsewhere O'Regan, reflecting upon the effect of the government's award of a major share of fishing resources to Maori in general, leaving the job of allocation to Maori, coined the splendid aphorism, 'Add water, instant iwi'.

15. Report to the Policy Committee, 23 May 1984, and a report on a meeting with Ruka Broughton on 16 April 1984, *DNZB* files.

16. It need not be assumed that such a publication would be a simple replication of the stories told on the marae and in the wharenui (meeting house). A notable Maori intellectual, interviewed in connection with a Maori historical project (not the *DNZB*), was asked whether he would produce a book of a 'western' or a 'tribal' kind. He replied: 'Which do you want? I do both.'

17. It also intended to be in a position to supplement essays as received to ensure coverage, balance and accuracy; if there is one consensus among biographical dictionary professionals it is that authors must be both treasured and distrusted.

18. Claudia Orange, Maori listings and research paper, [29 September 1987], *DNZB* files.

19. A meeting with three Ngati Porou leaders may serve as an example of this process. The *DNZB* provided a list of some 18 names as a basis for discussion. By the end of a long afternoon, six had been agreed upon.

20. Janet Davidson, 'The Polynesian Foundation', in G.W. Rice (ed.), *The Oxford History of New Zealand*, 2nd edn, Auckland, 1992, p. 11. Davidson concludes that 'a figure of around 100,000 seems probable'.

21. Policy Committee minutes, 5 November 1985, *DNZB* files. It seems likely that Sinclair was taking the mickey.

22. In 1985 Ballara, who, even as a part-time staff member, made a major contribution to the preparation of this volume, drew up a regional allocation of Maori based upon the Fenton estimation of 1858 and the census of 1874. It is not recorded whether or not this was used as a guide.

23. In 1985 a number of specialists were consulted about the desirable characteristics of Maori biography. One replied in terms which exemplify the kind of conventions which were not followed and (so it is argued here) could not be followed except in a wholly different kind of book: 'I have been musing . . . on entries which cite the person's whakapapa, mihi to him/her and descendants, then have a kaupapa on his/her life—character, events of note etc which includes e.g. a whakataukī he/she created or which refers to him/her, individually or as a descendant of someone, and concludes with a waiata composed on his/her death and poroporoaki' (Paper prepared for Maori Advisory Committee meeting, 16 October 1985, *DNZB* files).

24. Material in these two paragraphs is drawn from the minutes of the Maori Advisory Committee meeting of 16 October 1985, a draft paper and a final paper prepared for its meeting of 27 January 1987 by Orange, and the minutes of that meeting (*DNZB* files).

25. Material in this paragraph is drawn from Maori Working Party minutes, 29 June 1987, 10 March 1987, 28 May 1987; a commissioning list drawn up probably in late 1987; and the Policy Committee minutes, 17 June 1988, DNZB files.

26. Orange, report to the Policy Committee, 9 March 1990, *DNZB* files. The information in the following paragraph is drawn from this report.

27. In only seven instances had Maori writers been able to submit their essays in both languages.

28. The irony is that the *form* of these traditional place names was determined by the National Geographic Board earlier in the twentieth century, largely under the influence of that busy Pakeha assimilator of 'Maoriness' into the New Zealand self-image, Johannes Andersen. The board had a fixed antipathy to the use of hyphens in place names.

29. These problems were discussed in a paper prepared for the Maori Working Party by Ballara (*DNZB* files).

30. The English texts of the first two volumes were published as separate collections. The equivalent figures for these two publications are: *The People of Many Peaks*, Wellington, 1991, printed 3182, sold 2517; *The Turbulent Years*, 1994, printed 2500, sold 1402 (*DNZB* summary report to 31 December 1999, *DNZB* files).

31. This can be translated as 'in the shadow of eternity'; in other words, 'in the really long term'.

CHAPTER 9: MAORI LAND LAW AND THE TREATY CLAIMS PROCESS

1. As Angela Ballara has shown, however, it is possible, if one reads the evidence exhaustively and critically, to get behind the manifold

expressions of particular interests, apply the historian's usual tests for consistency, corroboration and coherence, and see the wider picture emerge, albeit incompletely (see her *Iwi: The Dynamics of Maori Tribal Organisation from c.1769 to c.1945*, Wellington, 1998; and, for a recent discussion of these and other related matters, her '"I riro i te hoko": Problems in Cross-Cultural Historical Scholarship', *New Zealand Journal of History*, vol. 34, no. 1, 2000, pp. 20–33).

2. The New Zealand Law Commission and the Law Faculty of the University of Waikato have played some role in this research on Maori customary law, but progress has been slow.

3. On 25 November 1999 Heads of Agreement were signed between the Crown and leaders of the Rangitane tribe of Manawatu district (centred on modern Palmerston North and Fielding) for a settlement amounting to about $8 million. But the district is historically one of intersection between several large tribes, and has not been the subject of a Tribunal Case Book or hearing. The Heads of Agreement are conditional on the resolution of overlapping claims with other tribes, so that it is currently of very limited effect.

4. In *The Puriri Trees are Laughing: A Political History of Nga Puhi in the Inland Bay of Islands*, Auckland, 1987, Pat Hohepa, anthropologist and linguist, and Jeffrey Sissons, anthropologist and historian, examined the oral traditions of one of Hohepa's elders, Wiremu Wi Hongi, in relation to the documentary record left by missionaries of the same period. They showed that Nga Puhi, one of the great iwi of the Northland peninsula and of modern New Zealand history, had only in the 1820s and 1830s attained the particular territorial and human dimensions it assumed at the time of the Treaty.

5. Salmond, *Two Worlds: First Meetings Between Maori and Europeans 1642–1772*, Auckland, 1991, and *Between Worlds: Early Exchanges Between Maori and Europeans 1773–1815*, Auckland, 1997; Binney, *Redemption Songs: A Life of Te Kooti Arikirangi Te Turuki*, Auckland, 1995; Ballara, *Iwi*.

6. A significant exception (in addition to the works cited above) is Lyndsay Head, 'Land, Citizenship and the Mana Motuhake Movements Among Ngati Kahungunu: A Study of Maori Language Documents in Ngati Kahungunu History, 1840–1865', June 1999, Doc W 11 in claim Wai 201. This work is largely based on the extensive correspondence of Maori leaders to McLean and other British officials of the time.

7. Native Land Court Minutes Books, Whanganui Book 1F, p. 237.

8. This complex history and evidence is summarised in Alan Ward, 'Maori Customary Interests in the Port Nicholson District, 1820s to 1840s: An Overview', a report commissioned by the Waitangi Tribunal, October 1998, Document M1 in claim Wai 145.

CHAPTER 10: 'LEARNING ABOUT THE TRUTH'

I am indebted to several people who have either generously provided comments on one or more drafts of this chapter and/or have patiently discussed the matters raised in it with me: Graeme Davison, Esther Faye, Heather Goodall, Paula Hamilton, Jane Jacobs, Paul James, Marilyn Lake, Amanda Macdonald, Robert Manne, Andrew Markus, Mark Peel, Peter Read and Liz Reed, and my fellow editor, Fiona Magowan. I also wish to acknowledge the Institute of Postcolonial Studies in Melbourne, which gave me the opportunity to present a draft of this chapter as a seminar paper, and where John Cash, Michelle Grossman, Chris Healy, Marcia Langton and Lynette Russell offered helpful suggestions. I alone, though, am responsible for the interpretation advanced here.

1.   This is how an Aboriginal man, Peter Costello, described the work of the 1996–97 Human Rights and Equal Opportunity Commission Inquiry into the separation of Aboriginal and Torres Strait Islander children (HREOC, *Bringing Them Home* (video), Sydney, 1997). In Aboriginal English, 'learning' refers to both the telling and hearing of stories. It is the argument of this essay that the truths presented by the stolen generations narrative are more complex than is generally recognised.

2.   The first term is Jerome Bruner's: 'The Narrative Construction of Reality', *Critical Inquiry*, vol. 18, no. 1, 1991, p. 18; the second is Paul A. Cohen's: *History in Three Keys: The Boxers as Event, Experience and Myth*, New York, 1997, p. 65.

3.   I am assuming that, while there are presently many different stories about the removal of children, these share certain similarities, hence the term 'stolen generations *narrative*'. Furthermore, I am making a fundamental distinction between the earlier *stories* regarding removals and the later *narrative*.

4.   'Half-Caste Aborigine' [Margaret Tucker], 'Conditions at Cummeroogunga', *Workers' Voice*, 1 March 1939, reproduced in Bain Attwood and Andrew Markus, *The Struggle for Aboriginal Rights: A Documentary History*, Sydney, 1999, pp. 160–1; see also an account by Tucker reported by *Shepparton News*, 27 February 1939. At this time, William Morley, the secretary of the Association for the Protection of Native Races, noted that this event had 'remain[ed] in the memory of the natives' of Cummeragunja and that they now feared it was '1919 over again' (Morley to New South Wales Chief Secretary, 15 March 1939, and enclosure B.N. Dow to Herbert and Florence Nicholls, 19 May 1919, Association for the Protection of Native Races Papers, Series 7, University of Sydney Archives; the latter documents what occurred in 1919). For other Aboriginal historical accounts of removal of children in the inter-war period, see Attwood and Markus, *The Struggle for Aboriginal Rights*, pp. 71–3, 92–4, 109–11, 121–3, 126–30.

5. *From Old Maloga: The Memoirs of an Aboriginal Woman*, Melbourne, [195?], pp. 2, 6. (Maloga was an Aboriginal mission, the predecessor of Cummeragunja, where Clements mostly grew up.)

6. Mollie Dyer, in Alick Jackomos and Derek Fowell, *Living Aboriginal History of Victoria: Stories in the Oral Tradition*, Melbourne, 1991, p. 134.

7. There are problems of historical evidence here, of the kind that commonly beset the study of the Aboriginal past; in the absence of Aboriginal contemporary historical records of what gets narrated inside Aboriginal communities, we cannot be sure whether and to what degree stories of removal were told however much 'common sense' has it that they would have been told—and told often.

8. Ronald Morgan, *Reminiscences of the Aboriginal Station at Cummeragunga and its Aboriginal People*, [Melbourne, 1952]. Recently, Peter Read has noted that in the early 1970s, '[t]here was scarcely a mention of child removals . . . among Aboriginal leaders, nor among the stolen generations themselves' ('The Return of the Stolen Generation [sic]', *Journal of Australian Studies*, no. 59, 1998, p. 8; 'Generation' should read 'Generations', but the journal made a mistake).

9. *A Rape of the Soul So Profound: The Return of the Stolen Generations*, Sydney, 1999, pp. x, 70, 71, 167, 169. Read actually states that they 'regained' this understanding. This contention, like the subtitle of his book, reflects Read's approach, which, like that of most historians, is teleological: he attempts to explain the presence of the stolen generations narrative today by providing an account for its previous 'absence'. In doing so, he naturalises it.

10. Tucker in Alec Morgan (dir.), *Lousy Little Sixpence*, Sydney, 1983; see also Margaret Tucker, *If Everyone Cared* (1977), 2nd edn, Melbourne, 1983, p. 95.

11. It could be argued that Read is also making this point when he argues that Aboriginal people have '*regained* an understanding' (see endnote 9, my emphasis).

12. Fred Maynard, President, L. Lacey, Secretary, Australian Aborigines Progressive Association, to J.T. Lang, Premier of NSW, 28 May 1927, A.E. McKenzie-Hatton, Secretary, and Maynard to the Royal Commission on the Constitution, 22 February 1928, reproduced in Attwood and Markus, *The Struggle for Aboriginal Rights*, pp. 66–7, 71–3, and see other documents here, pp. 65–6, 70–1. For a discussion of AAPA protest, see Heather Goodall, *Invasion to Embassy: Land in Aboriginal Politics in New South Wales, 1770–1972*, Sydney, 1996, pp. 149–56, 165–6.

13. I am indebted to Paula Hamilton and Esther Faye for suggesting both these arguments.

14. Read, *A Rape of the Soul*, pp. 171–2. Feminist historians Marilyn Lake and Fiona Paisley have drawn our attention to several white

women campaigners in the 1920s and 1930s who attacked the removal of Aboriginal children; see, for example, Lake, 'Childbearers as Rights-Bearers: Feminist Discourse on the Rights of Aboriginal and non-Aboriginal Mothers in Australia, 1920–50', *Women's History Review*, vol. 8, no. 2, 1999, pp. 347–63; Paisley, *Loving Protection?: Australian Feminism and Aboriginal Women's Rights 1919–1939*, Melbourne, 2000, chapter 4.

15. This is even true, as Read has noted, of the well-known autobiographical accounts produced in the same decade—Charles Perkins' *A Bastard Like Me* (Sydney, 1975), Tucker's *If Everyone Cared*, and Jimmie Barker's *The Two Worlds of Jimmie Barker, as told to Janet Matthews* (Canberra, 1977)—in which the authors represent their experience as children who were separated from their parents as a serious matter but do not dwell upon this, treating it as 'just something that happened to them' and a part of 'a complex life history' (Read, in Jackie Huggins and Peter Read, 'Speaking Up for the Stolen Generations', manuscript, p. 6. I am indebted to Huggins and Read for permission to cite this unpublished paper; Read, 'The Return', p. 13). For example, in the opening chapters of his autobiography, Perkins gives considerable prominence to the removal of children in Central Australia in the 1930s and 1940s, condemning their forced separation and describing the impact of removal upon Aboriginal families and children like himself, but his life story is not framed in terms of this experience. This can be compared to the way he later came to tell his story (see Read's discussion of this shift in *A Rape of the Soul*, chapter 6). The fact that the accounts of Perkins, Tucker and Barker *do* give prominence to their removal might partly be attributed to the role that non-Aboriginal authors and editors played in the production of their 'autobiographies' (for a brief discussion of the role of non-Aborigines in the production of such texts, see R.H.W. Reece, 'The Aborigines in Australian Historiography', in John A. Moses (ed.), *Historical Disciplines and Culture in Australasia*, St Lucia, 1979, p. 273).

16. 'Aboriginal History and the Politics of Information Control', *Oral History Association of Australia Journal*, no. 9, 1987, pp. 18, 28; see also Barry Morris, 'Making Histories/Living History', *Social Analysis*, no. 27, 1990, p. 90.

17. Goodall, 'Aboriginal History and the Politics', pp. 28–9. The playing down of oppression might have been more pronounced in the accounts that Aboriginal narrators presented to non-Aboriginal people; when speaking to such an audience, Goodall has argued, Aboriginal people often chose 'another body of stories and another approach to story telling' to the ones they used when they talked in their own families or communities. There might have been, therefore, considerable differences between, say, narratives of removal that were being told in an informal Aboriginal setting and those recounted

formally to a non-Aboriginal audience, where many might have been 'reluctant to offend ... non-Aboriginal [people] by recounting the crimes of other non-Aborigines' (*ibid.*, p. 29; Heather Goodall, 'Aboriginal History, Narration and New Media', paper delivered at the Association for History and Computing Conference, Glasgow, July 1997, http://www.transforming.cultures.uts.edu.au/Heather/hg-Aboriginal.html; Karen Flick and Heather Goodall, 'Angledool Stories: Aboriginal History in Hypermedia', in Robert Perks and Alistair Thomson (eds), *The Oral History Reader*, London, 1998, pp. 428–30). Closely related to this matter of 'modes of address' is that of linguistic codes; anthropologist Barry Morris has observed that when Aboriginal people told him stories of their oppression they tended to do so in the form of similes, metaphors and metonyms; for example, they often drew analogies between the way they were treated and the way animals are 'rounded up' or 'herded', in order to convey a sense that they were treated as less than human (see also Tucker's account quoted above) (Morris, 'Making Histories', p. 90). Audiences who are not alert to these ways of telling can readily overlook the significance storytellers are bestowing upon the events they are recounting. In the case of accounts like Barker's, for instance, non-Aboriginal 'outsiders' can misinterpret the meaning of his laconic and ironic narration, and, as Goodall notes, be 'puzzled by an apparent lack of anger and judgemental comment' (whereas for Aboriginal 'insiders' such accounts lay even *greater* emphasis on the oppression he and other contemporaries suffered, than do more overt ones) ('Aboriginal History, Narration and New Media', and Goodall to author, 30 August 2000).

18. *A Rape of the Soul*, pp. vii, xi, 101–2, 172.
19. *Living Black: Blacks Talk to Kevin Gilbert*, Melbourne, 1978, p. 1.
20. See, for example, the story about 'a full-blood boy' who seems to have thought he was Dutch (Molly Dyer, in Gilbert, *Living Black*, p. 225).
21. Their dilemma is expressed very clearly in the following testimony by an Aboriginal woman:

> It wasn't [sic] that people wouldn't identify as Aboriginal. It was that ordinance [The Northern Territory Ordinance 1957]. A lot of our people, when they'd been known as part-Aboriginal had a horror of being called Aboriginals again because it meant the same as second-grade citizens ... they had no citizenship. And many of them didn't want to be known as Aboriginals because they were completely institutionalised and the fact that you were half-white meant that you weren't completely on the bottom. It was drummed into them in the institutions that they'd been given this opportunity ... (angrily and sarcastically) they must be a little bit clever because they were half-white, after all. Because the tribal people, look at them, they're so dirty and illiterate, stupid

and nasty, smelly . . . all this indoctrination. The divisions form unconsciously within the institutionalised person (Vi Stanton, in *ibid.*, p. 11, ellipses in the original).

22. This disjunction between history as occurrence and history as story, it has been argued, can be especially marked in cases of trauma. This subject has been discussed at considerable length with reference to the Holocaust (see, for example, Saul Friedlander (ed.), *Probing the Limits of Representation: Nazism and the 'Final Solution'*, Cambridge, Mass., 1992).

23. My argument here differs most obviously from the accounts of the stolen generations narrative that have been provided by Read and Goodall. Read, the historian primarily responsible for producing this history, has contended that he reached his 'finding' that large numbers of Aboriginal children were removed by government not through hearing the testimonies of the Wiradjuri people, whose history he researched in the late 1970s, but by reading the documentary records of the New South Wales Aborigines Protection Board in that state's archives office: 'In the 1970s', he has stated, 'I interviewed a number of Aboriginal people who had been separated, but I listened to them as individuals . . . [and saw their stories] as individual tragedies'; it took 'a long time for the penny to drop', and 'the turning point' was the research he undertook 'in the files of the old Aborigines Welfare Board', in particular the register of Aboriginal wards of the state for the period 1916–28: 'When at length I reached the end of those 700 files, I at last understood that the red herrings of missionary zeal, malnutrition, parental neglect, the best interest of the child and the standards of the day, concealed a violent attack not only on Aboriginal family structure but on the very basis of Aboriginality.' As a consequence of reading these sources, Read argues, the stories he had previously interpreted as 'individual tragedies' were now 'recognisable' as part of a broader history; what he had been unable to see previously now seemed 'so obvious' (*A Rape of the Soul*, pp. 2, 46, 47, 71, 101–2, 124–5; Read, in Huggins and Read, 'Speaking Up for the Stolen Generations', p. 6). By contrast, Goodall, who was also working on a history of Aboriginal communities in New South Wales at this time, has claimed that it was 'Aboriginal insistence' that 'children had been taken away systematically and in high numbers . . . [and] that this was a major impact of Protection Board policy [which] led [her] to reassess Board records', and that it 'has been Aboriginal accounts which [have] revealed the full, tragic impact on communities with active family ties' ('Aboriginal History and the Politics', p. 18). In my opinion, both Read and Goodall overlook the conjunction between the Aboriginal memory and non-Aboriginal historical research—the fact that they both heard Aboriginal oral testimonies *and* read official documents regarding the removal of children—and ignore the kind of transference between present and past that occurs in any history-work (see

Dominick LaCapra, *History & Criticism*, Ithaca, 1985, pp. 11, 139).

24. I am drawing upon Elaine Showalter's work on what she calls hystories (*Hystories: Hysterical Epidemics and Modern Culture*, New York, 1997, especially p. 17). For interesting accounts of notable Australian historical narratives of the kind I am describing here, see Peter Cochrane, *Simpson and the Donkey: The Making of a Legend*, Melbourne, 1992, and Alistair Thomson, *Anzac Memories: Living With the Legend*, Melbourne, 1994.

25. Some of the personal reasons for Read's role in this are suggested, perhaps, by the themes of his later work, in particular, his *Returning to Nothing: The Meaning of Lost Places* (Melbourne, 1996), and *Belonging: Australians, Place and Aboriginal Ownership* (Melbourne, 2000).

26. Carl L. Becker, *Everyman His Own Historian: Essays on History and Politics*, New York, 1935, pp. 246–55.

27. Here, I am following Jerome Bruner's argument that narratives are constructed by acts of interpretation and that they rely upon what he calls a 'part-whole textual interdependence'; he observes: 'The accounts of protagonists and events that constitute a narrative are selected and shaped in terms of a putative story or plot that then "contains" them. At the same time, the "whole" ... is dependent for its formation on a supply of possible constituent parts. In this sense ... parts and wholes rely on each other for their viability ... [A] story can only be "realised" when its parts and wholes can, as it were, be made to live together' ('The Narrative Construction', p. 8).

28. For another discussion of the role and importance that naming has in historical signification, see Peter Novick, *The Holocaust in American Life*, Boston, 1999. He notes that 'during [World War II], and for some time thereafter, there was no agreed-upon word for the murder of Europe's Jews ... [I]nsofar as the word "holocaust" (lowercase) was employed during the war ... it was almost always applied to the totality of the destruction wrought by the Axis ... [T]he "Holocaust", as we speak of it today, was largely a retrospective construction' (see pp. 19–20, 29, 133–4, 144–5).

29. This point might alert us to the fact that the term had another meaning beyond the singular one it currently seems to have. As far as I can see, the term 'stolen' is now taken to refer to the stealing of children, and so places emphasis on the role of the state (and in that sense, it might be argued, the narrative becomes more of a non-Aboriginal one); restored to its earlier context, it had another meaning as well, that of having one's life or birthright stolen away (and in that sense, I would contend, it was more clearly an Aboriginal narrative). In his PhD thesis Read suggests another meaning when he concludes a long chapter on the removal of children in this fashion: 'The ultimate legacy of the policy of child dispersal was not the disassociation of individuals from a culture or race, but from their fellow human beings'

(A History of the Wiradjuri People of New South Wales, PhD, Australian National University, 1983, p. 354), to which, we might add, from themselves as well.

30. Read, *A Rape of the Soul*, p. 49; see, for example, Dyer, in Gilbert, *Living Black*, pp. 224–6.

31. On my reading, Read's treatment of the removal of children in his thesis differs in important ways to his Link-Up work, which can be said to include his influential pamphlet, *The Stolen Generations* (see below). First, the separation of children is treated as part of a broader policy of the 'dispersal' of Aboriginal communities. Second, although the estimate of the proportion of children removed is the same as that suggested in *The Stolen Generations*, the impact of the policy is characterised as 'localised'. Third, while the impact of the practice is regarded as considerable, it is noted that the Wiradjuri moved around to prevent their children being taken, and that some of the children removed later returned to their families. Last, the diverse reasons for their removal, including neglect, are noted, and the term 'stolen generations' is not used (see A History of the Wiradjuri People, especially chapters 4, 8).

32. In the same year, a New South Wales government agency, which wanted historical background so it could understand present-day practices of separating Aboriginal children from their families and communities, commissioned Read to prepare a historical report. This resulted in a paper, 'The Stolen Generations: The Removal of Aboriginal Children in New South Wales 1883 to 1969' (Read, *A Rape of the Soul*, pp. 49, 219, endnote 1).

33. For a discussion of the significance of this point, see below, p. 195.

34. Read, A History of the Wiradjuri People, pp. 327–9.

35. Coral Edwards (dir.), *It's a Long Road Back* (video), Canberra, 1981 (the video case calls it a 'film about identity' —'the struggle of one woman to regain her aboriginality'); *Link-Up*, [Canberra, 1983], p. 1; Edwards, 'Is the Ward Clean?', in Bill Gammage and Andrew Markus (eds), *All That Dirt: Aborigines 1938*, Canberra, 1982, p. 4; Edwards, in *Being Aboriginal: Comments, Observations and Stories from Aboriginal Australians*, compiled by Ros Bowden and Bill Bunbury, Sydney, 1990, p. 5; Read, *A Rape of the Soul*, p. 70; Read, in Read and Huggins, 'Speaking Up', p. 7; Link-Up (NSW) Aboriginal Corporation and Tikka Jan Wilson, *In the Best Interest of the Child?: Stolen Children: Aboriginal Pain/White Shame*, Canberra, 1997, pp. 2–3; Read, 'The Return', p. 13.

36. *Link-Up*, back cover; *Link-Up*, reproduced in Read, *A Rape of the Soul*, pp. 70, 73–4, 89, 93–4, 98, 100; Coral Edwards and Peter Read (eds), *The Lost Children*, Sydney, 1989, pp. ix, xv–xvii, xxi–xxv; *Being Aboriginal*, pp. 5, 12. See also Pauline McLeod's poem, 'The Yearning of My Soul', which was featured in a Link-Up poster, cited Read, 'The Return', p. 18. More recently, in a submission to the

1996–97 Human Rights and Equal Opportunity Inquiry into the Separation of Aboriginal and Torres Strait Islander Children from their Families, Link-Up explained:

> Home and journey home are used throughout [this submission]. Home means the place where you belong and the place where you feel totally yourself. Home may be a physical place, similar to belonging to place . . . Home may also be a space inside a person—we are at home with ourselves and with our identity . . . It is a process of discovery and recovery . . . The journey home is a journey to find out where we came from, so that we can find out who we are and where we are going (Link-Up and Wilson, *In the Best Interest of the Child?*, pp. xiii, 2, 5, 28, 185).

37. See the testimonies in Edwards and Read (eds), *The Lost Children*, pp. xvi, and *passim*; publicity leaflet for *It's a Long Road Back*, AIATSIS library catalogue entry for this film. 'Aboriginality' here can be read as a signifier of something that is felt to be lost, which reminds us, as Natalie Zemon Davis and Randolph Starn have noted, that '[m]emory is of course a substitute, surrogate or consolation for something that is missing', a marker of 'rupture and loss' ('Introduction' to a special issue of *Representations* on Memory and Counter-Memory: no. 26, 1989, p. 3).

38. See Edwards and Read (eds), *The Lost Children*, pp. 72, 76 and *passim*. In this regard there are marked similarities between these people and author and painter Sally Morgan; see my 'Portrait of an Aboriginal as an Artist: Sally Morgan and the Construction of Aboriginality', *Australian Historical Studies*, vol. 25, no. 99, 1992, pp. 302–18. See also Peter Sutton's discussion of this process ('Myth as History, History as Myth', in Ian Keen (ed.), *Being Black: Aboriginal Cultures in 'Settled' Australia*, Canberra, 1988, especially pp. 257–60).

39. Read, *A Rape of the Soul*, pp. 71–2, 219, endnote 1; Read, in Read and Huggins, 'Speaking Up', p. 8; Link-Up and Wilson, *In the Best Interest of the Child?*, pp. 3–4.

40. See Attwood and Markus, *The Struggle for Aboriginal Rights*, pp. 51–4.

41. Tucker, *If Everyone Cared*, pp. 93–4.

42. Hyllus Maris and Sonia Borg, *Women of the Sun*, Sydney, 1983, pp. xii, 93–4, 111–13, 117, 132–3, 138, 143–5, 160, 228, 233 (my emphasis).

43. Julie Andrews, 'Introduction', The Annual Hyllus Maris Memorial Lecture, La Trobe University, 5 September 2000.

44. See endnote 12 above.

45. Morgan (dir.), *Lousy Little Sixpence*.

46. See, for example, *Herald* (Melbourne), 6 October 1983; *Age*, 7, 8 October 1983; *Australian Financial Review*, 14 October 1983; *Australian*, 28 October, 23 November 1983; *Sydney Morning*

Herald, 28 October, 5 November 1983; *National Times*, 4 November 1983; *Sun* (Sydney), 3, 6 November 1983; *Daily Mirror*, 3 November 1983; as well as other reviews quoted by a film kit prepared by Ronin Films (File for *Lousy Little Sixpence*, Australian Film Institute Library, Melbourne).

47. *If Everyone Cared*, dust jacket of a 1984 printing, my emphasis.

48. It is always difficult to establish the influence of any text, but Read notes the impact of *Lousy Little Sixpence* on one Aboriginal person (*A Rape of the Soul*, p. 83) and reviews of the film testify to its impact on critics at least. The publicity for the film and many reviews drew attention to 'over one third of Aboriginal children in New South Wales [being] removed' (see endnote 46 above).

49. It is important to note here that the term memory should not be taken literally. Pierre Nora and other historians who have undertaken historical studies of memory have a broad conception of memory. Lawrence Kritzman, for instance, describes memory 'as the variety of forms through which cultural communities imagine themselves in diverse representational modes' ('In Remembrance of Things French', Foreword to Pierre Nora (ed.), *Realms of Memory: Rethinking the French Past, Vol. 1, Conflicts and Divisions*, New York, 1996, p. ix), while Nora notes that little exists today of 'true memory', it consisting only of phenomena like 'gestures and habits . . . ingrained reminiscences, and spontaneous reflexes' ('General Introduction: Between Memory and History', in Nora (ed.), *Realms of Memory*, p. 8).

50. Generally speaking, *My Place* does not seem to have been interpreted in this way when it was first published, though it has undoubtedly come to be in more recent years. Certainly, major newspaper reviewers did not describe Morgan's forbears as 'stolen children'; in fact they offered little commentary on this dimension of the narrative (see the reviews and articles reproduced in Derryn Hammond *et al.* (eds), *Autobiography: The Writer's Story*, Fremantle, 1988, pp. 17–19; Veronica Brady, 'Something that Was Shameful', *The Age Monthly Review*, vol. 7, no. 6, 1987, pp. 3–5). This might strike us as odd today but it is evidence for my argument about the nature and effects of narrative accrual. Those who already knew the stolen generations narrative *did* read it as such a story; Read and Edwards, for example, asked Morgan to write the foreword to their book, *The Lost Children*, which appeared two years later.

51. General Manager, Fremantle Arts Centre Press, to author, 6 June 1991. It has now sold over 500 000 copies (General Manager, Fremantle Arts Centre Press, to author, 13 July 2000).

52. Read, *Down There With Me on the Cowra Mission*, Sydney, 1984; Read, *A Hundred Years War: The Wiradjuri People and the State*, Sydney, 1988; Read, *Charles Perkins: A Biography*, Sydney, 1990; Haebich, *For Their Own Good: Aborigines and Government in the Southwest of Western Australia, 1900–1940*, Fremantle, 1988;

Markus, *Governing Savages*, Sydney, 1990; Austin, *I Can See the Old Home So Clearly: The Commonwealth and 'Half-Caste' Youth in the Northern Territory 1911–1939*, Canberra, 1993; Bill Gammage and Peter Spearritt (eds), *Australians 1938*, Sydney, 1987, Part II.

53.   Clinton Walker, *Buried Country: The Story of Aboriginal Country Music*, Sydney, 2000, pp. 215–19, 304. Walker notes that the ABC screened a documentary, *My Brown Skin Baby, They Take 'Im Away*, in 1970, and a sequel, *Mixed-Up Man*, which told of Randall's removal as a child and his current search for his family. It is note-worthy that they seem to have had little impact.

54.   Both separated from their families as children, Roach and Hunter have come to have iconic status, perhaps because they are often por-trayed as a stolen generations couple, thereby powerfully symbolising the sense of (re)union that 'returning home' evokes (see, for example, 'The Two of Us: Ruby Hunter & Archie Roach', *The Age Good Weekend Magazine*, 14 November 1998).

55.   Of the 99 deaths the Royal Commission investigated, it found that 43 of the people had been separated as children (Royal Commission into Aboriginal Deaths in Custody, *National Report*, Canberra, 1991, vol. 1, p. 44, vol. 2, pp. 72–8).

56.   See, for example, Barbara Cummings, *Take This Child . . .: From Kahlin Compound to the Retta Dixon Children's Home*, Canberra, 1990, pp. xii–xiii; Stuart Rintoul, *The Wailing: A National Black Oral History*, Melbourne, 1993, p. 397, endnote 2. In this, there seems little reason to believe that Aboriginal people are not influ-enced by non-Aboriginal ways of thinking, particularly given their dominance in Australia; as one Aboriginal man noted in the late 1970s: 'Most of our knowledge comes from books, or from the screen, or from what people tell us. Not [from] our own people' (Read, *Down There With Me*, p. 16). For other examples of this phenomenon, see Cochrane and Thomson's respective work on the Simpson and Anzac legends (see endnote 24 above).

57.   *The Holocaust*, p. 107.

58.   Stephen Muecke, 'Aboriginal Literature and the Repressive Hypothesis', *Southerly*, vol. 48, no. 4, 1988, pp. 411, 413.

59.   *ibid.*, pp. 416–17.

60.   For an account of this, see Reece, 'The Aborigines in Australian Historiography', pp. 266–7.

61.   For example, eight of the thirteen testimonies that appear in *The Lost Children* are by women. For a discussion of the role of sexuality and gender in the removal of children, see Heather Goodall, '"Saving the Children": Gender and the Colonisation of Aboriginal Children in New South Wales, 1788 to 1990', *Aboriginal Law Bulletin*, vol. 2, no. 44, 1990, pp. 6–9; Suzanne Parry, 'Identifying the Process: The Removal of "Half-Caste" Children from Aboriginal Mothers', *Aboriginal History*, vol. 19, pt 2, 1995, pp. 141–53.

62. See also Cummings, *Take This Child*; Connie Nungulla McDonald, *When You Grow Up*, Broome, 1996; and Rosalie Fraser, *Shadow Child*, Sydney, 1998.

63. So popular has this genre become that one writer passed himself off as an Aboriginal woman writer; writing anonymously under the name of Wanda Koolmatrie a white man, Leon Carmen, authored *My Own Sweet Time*, purportedly the true story of an Aboriginal woman who grows up in a non-Aboriginal foster family, which was published in 1994 by the Western Australian Aboriginal publishing house Magabala Books, won the 1995 Dobbie Award for a first published book by a woman writer and was shortlisted for the 1995 NSW Premier's Awards before being exposed (*Australian*, 13, 14, 15–16 March 1997).

64. Link-Up and Wilson, *In the Best Interest of the Child?*, pp. vi, 6, 185, 200; Cummings, *Take This Child*, pp. xi, xiii. See Showalter, *Hystories*, *passim*.

65. See John R. Gillis, 'Introduction', in Gillis (ed.), *Commemorations: The Politics of National Identity*, Princeton, NJ, 1994, p. 17.

66. Graeme Davison, *The Use and Abuse of Australian History*, Sydney, 2000, pp. 80, 82, 100. See, for example, Brady's review of Morgan's *My Place*, 'Something that Was Shameful', *passim*.

67. Iris Clayton, 'Foreword', in Diane Smith and Boronia Halstead, *Lookin For Your Mob: A Guide to Tracing Aboriginal Family Trees*, Canberra, 1990, p. vii; Read, A History of the Wiradjuri People, p. 331. More recently, in the video that accompanied the Human Rights and Equal Opportunity Commission inquiry into the separation of Aboriginal children, Aboriginal singer Nerida George emphasised: 'We're family people; everything that we do concerns family, and when there's a split in the family, that's when it's broken, that's when you hear the cry of our heart, because that's where we are. We're family people. Everything revolves around family, everything we do concerns family—close family, extended family. That's it, you know . . . We're family people' (HREOC, *Bringing Them Home*).

68. Pierre Nora, 'Between Memory and History: *Les Lieux de Mémoire*', *Representations*, no. 26, 1989, pp. 7, 19, and 'From *Lieux de Mémoire* to *Realms of Memory*', in Nora (ed.), *Realms of Memory*, p. xv. Nora suggests that a *lieux de mémoire* can be defined as 'any significant entity, whether material or non-material in nature, which by dint of human will or the work of time has become a symbolic element of the memorial heritage of any community' ('From *Lieux de Mémoire*', p. xvii). It is both interesting to note—and helpful given the controversy over the term 'stolen *generations*'—that Nora suggests that a historical generation is one example of a *lieux de mémoire*. He also points out that memory—what I am calling here collective memory—has three aspects that co-exist: the material, the functional and the symbolic. Of a historical generation, he writes: 'A

generation is material in a demographic sense; functional by hypothesis, since memories are crystallised in generations and passed from one to another; and symbolic by definition, since the term "generation" implies that the experience of a small number of people can be used to characterise a much larger number of people who did not participate in [or experience] its central event or events' ('General Introduction: Between Memory and History', p. 14, 'Between Memory and History', p. 19).

69. Showalter, *Hystories*, p. 6; see also Bruner, 'The Narrative Construction of Reality', pp. 18–20.

70. See, for example, Tucker, *If Everyone Cared*, pp. 81, 90–5; Edwards (dir.), *It's a Long Road Back*; Read (ed.), *Down There With Me*, pp. 91–2, 100–1, 103–4. I am indebted to Goodall for a discussion regarding these matters (Goodall to author, 30 August 2000).

71. Read, *A Rape of the Soul*, p. 172; 'The Return', pp. 12–13. Goodall notes that in the context of Aboriginal families and communities (rather than when they make interventions in a contested public and political sphere), Aboriginal narrators continued (and continue) to tell of their experience of removal in a manner that reveals its complexities and their ambivalence ('Aboriginal History, Narration and the New Media'; Flick and Goodall, 'Angledool Stories', pp. 428–30; Goodall to author, 3 October 2000).

72. Contrary to the assumptions and assertions of both stolen generations narrators and the detractors of their histories, we should recognise that accounts of the removal of children have changed over several decades and that there is nothing remarkable about this. In Tucker's case, her account of her removal had altered in its tellings as changes occurred in her life and the wider world. Most obviously, whereas her perspective in the late 1930s was shaped by the Communist Party of Australia circle in which she was moving, and this enabled her to articulate 'a lot of what [she] was feeling' and put '[her] people's plight in the eyes of the world', by the late 1970s her outlook had long been influenced by the message of Moral Rearmament, and so she had sought to quell her anger, 'put aside . . . grievances', and 'forgive past mistakes'. As a result, the manner in which she framed the removal of children changed considerably: 'Wholesale kidnapping' became their being 'separated' and 'taken' (Tucker, in *Lousy Little Sixpence*; Tucker, *If Everyone Cared*, pp. 61, 82, 95, 199–202).

73. *Return to Cummeragunja: Hyllus Maris and . . . Geraldine Briggs Speak* (video), Melbourne, 1985; Briggs, 'It was Just Getting Dark', in Jackomos and Fowell, *Living Aboriginal History*, pp. 160–5; Briggs, in Rintoul, *The Wailing*, pp. 64–6; *Age*, 14 July 1995. There is a sense here, perhaps, in which this parallels second-generation Holocaust testimony (see Helen Epstein, *Children of the Holocaust: Conversations with Sons and Daughters of Survivors*, New York, 1979). This is true for some of the members of Link-Up who tell their

stories in *The Lost Children*, though this phenomenon has become much more marked in recent times (see, for example, *Age*, 5 April 2000).

74. Briggs, 'It was Just Getting Dark', p. 162, her emphasis.

75. This sense has been heightened by the transcription of Briggs' oral testimony. In the case of the one used for *Living Aboriginal History* there are two occasions where she refers to two matrons—at the hospital and Cootamundra—as being 'very nice' and 'very kind' but both have been omitted from the published transcript (tape of the interview, Koori Oral History Programme, Koorie Heritage Trust, master tape no. 146; I am indebted to Lois Peeler for permission to listen to this). Rintoul's transcription is more cavalier; he drew upon a segment of the interview which Jackomos and Fowell conducted with Briggs (which he acknowledged) but did not indicate this in the text of her testimony, and he inserted a passage in her description of the aftermath of her sisters' removal (cited below) from another interview (which he presumably conducted with Briggs)—'They came into the hospital to take me too, but the matron had told my aunty to take me home. *That was the kind of animals they were. That's the kind of things Aborigines had to put up with. They treated us just like animals*'—so that he has her condemning the matron of the hospital even though she described this woman in her interview for Jackomos and Fowell as being 'a very nice person' and there is an implication that the matron might have released her from hospital so that she was *not* seized by the police and so removed from her mother (Rintoul, *The Wailing*, pp. 62, 395, my emphasis). This implication is clarified, it seems, by a later journalist's account: he stated, after interviewing Briggs, that she 'was saved after a matron had tipped off an aunty to discharge her' (*Age*, 14 July 1995).

76. This is a composite quote: Briggs, 'It was Just Getting Dark', pp. 160, 164; and Briggs, in Rintoul, *The Wailing*, p. 65.

77. Something of the latter changes can be illustrated by a comparison between Read's 1984 oral history collection and Rintoul's 1993 one. The earlier book was a scholarly collection of historical sources with a sombre-sounding title, *Down There With Me on the Cowra Mission: An Oral History of Erambie Aboriginal Reserve, Cowra, New South Wales*, which was first published by an Australian university press and later by an international academic publishing house; it largely told of the experiences of the Wiradjuri 'under the Act' in the first half of the twentieth century; and in a chapter near the end of the book, which was dispassionately entitled 'Wards of the State', it included accounts of removed children in which they expressed their ambivalence about that experience.

Rintoul's book was a popular anthology of Aboriginal voices with a dramatic and historically resonant title, *The Wailing: A National Black Oral History*, which was published by a popular press; it consisted of oral testimonies that were drawn from all over Australia and which were placed alongside one another irrespective of their historical context; in a chapter called 'Broken Dreaming', devoted to the removal of children, their separation was treated as unambiguously bad; and it highlighted the phenomenon from the beginning, for example the opening chapter was subtitled 'I Don't Want to Forget' and was prefaced by this passage: 'I seen my cousins were running, like scared rabbits. They'd go in the house and they went under the bed and into the cupboards, and the police went in behind them and hauled them out and put them in the car there screaming for their mother' (Read (ed.), *Down There With Me*; Rintoul, *The Wailing*, especially p. 15.) These slippages in Rintoul's text, it might be argued, were of a kind anticipated by Read's pamphlet, *The Stolen Generations*. In other words, it might be regarded as a simpler or less subtle account of the same interpretation, taken to its extremes. (Rintoul has an honours degree in English and History, and is one of a number of journalists in Australia today who seek to take on the mantle of historian.)

78. This, Novick argues, is similar to what has happened to the Holocaust: 'By the 1970s and 1980s the Holocaust had become a shocking, massive and distinctive *thing*: clearly marked off, qualitatively and quantitatively, from other Nazi atrocities and from previous Jewish persecutions, singular in its scope, its symbolism, and its world-historical significance' (*The Holocaust*, p. 19, his emphasis).

79. Council for Aboriginal Reconciliation, *Australians for Reconciliation: Study Circle Kit*, Canberra, 1993, Part 2, Session 3.

80. See my 'Introduction: The Past as Future: Aborigines, Australia and the (Dis)Course of History', in Bain Attwood (ed.), *In the Age of Mabo: History, Aborigines and Australia*, Sydney, 1996, pp. xxi–xxxvi.

81. This speech, known as Keating's 'Redfern Speech', named after the inner-city Sydney suburb where there is a large Aboriginal community and where Keating gave the speech, was crafted by his principal speech writer, the historian Don Watson ('Australian Launch of the International Year of the World's Indigenous Peoples', in *Paul Keating, Prime Minister: Major Speeches of the First Year*, Canberra, [1993], p. 210, my emphasis). The crowd greeted Keating's acknowledgment of child removal by cheering loudly (video recording of the speech, in Council for Aboriginal Reconciliation, *3 in 1: Walking Together, Talkin' Business, and Making Things Right*, Canberra, n.d.).

82. *Sydney Morning Herald*, 6 March 1995; *The Long Road Home ... The Going Home Conference, 3–6 October 1994*, Darwin, [1995], pp. 1, 3.

83. The works of Read, Roach, Cummings, Randall, Keating/Watson, Morgan and the Royal Commission into Aboriginal Deaths in Custody were featured (*The Long Road Home*, pp. 2, 4, 7, 8, 10, 16).

84. Robert Tickner, *Taking a Stand: Land Rights to Reconciliation*, Sydney, 2001, p. 55.
85. *Australian*, 10 June 1997.
86. *Australian*, 8–9 October 1994; *Sydney Morning Herald*, 11 October 1994; *The Long Road Home*, pp. 1–9, 12–15, 21–2, 28–31; HREOC, *Bringing Them Home: Report of the National Inquiry into the Separation of Aboriginal and Torres Strait Islander Children From Their Families*, Sydney, 1997, p. 18. In the same year, a Truth and Reconciliation Commission was established in South Africa, which points to the fact that there was also, of course, an international context that was influencing what was happening in Australia. See Timothy Garton Ash, 'True Confessions', *New York Review of Books*, 17 July 1997, pp. 33–8, for a discussion of the work of such bodies.
87. HREOC, Information Paper on the National Inquiry into the Separation of Aboriginal and Torres Strait Islander Children from Their Families, p. 1, cited in Link-Up and Wilson, *In the Best Interest of the Child?*, p. 9; HREOC, *Longing to Return Home ...: Information For People Giving Submissions to the National Inquiry into the Separation of Aboriginal and Torres Strait Islander Children from Their Families*, Sydney, 1996, pp. 6, 7; HREOC, *Bringing Them Home*, pp. 18, 667–70; www. hreoc.gov.au/social_justice/stolen_children.
88. See John Frow, 'The Politics of Stolen Time', *Meanjin*, vol. 57, no. 3, 1998, pp. 351–67, especially p. 354.
89. HREOC, *Longing to Return Home*, p. 4. This echoed a self-consciously historical claim made by an Aboriginal leader at the Going Home Conference:

> There is not a single Aboriginal family in all of Australia that has not had at least one of their relations stolen. There is not a single family which has not been scarred and damaged by those church and state policies. There is not a single family which does not live under the shadow of this dreadful history of the Stolen Generations (*The Long Road Home*, p. 17).

This was repeated during the year or so the Inquiry was held, both inside and outside of it. In February 1996 one of the organisers of the Going Home Conference, Jacqui Katona, was reported by the *Sydney Morning Herald* as making more or less the same statement as that made at the Going Home Conference: 'There is not a single Aboriginal family in all of Australia that has not had at least one of their relations stolen. There is not a single family which does not live under the shadow of its appalling legacy' (15 February 1996). In July, Mick Dodson, the HREOC Aboriginal and Torres Strait Islander Justice Commissioner and one of the Inquiry commissioners, was reported as saying: 'Every indigenous family in Australia is in some way affected by this' (*Sydney Morning Herald*, 2 July 1996). These latter statements, if not the former one, anticipate the claim by the HREOC in its report: 'In that time [1910–1970] not one Indigenous family has escaped the effects of forcible removal . . . Most families have been affected, in one or more generations, by the forcible removal of one or more children' (HREOC, *Bringing Them Home*, p. 37). This claim is somewhat similar to one Read made in his pamphlet *The Stolen Generations*: 'Perhaps one in six or seven Aboriginal children have been taken from their families during this century . . . To put it another way, there is not an Aboriginal person in New South Wales who does not know, or is not related to, one or more of his/her countrymen who were institutionalised by the whites' (p. 18; I am indebted to Read for drawing this passage to my attention).

Also repeated during this period was an estimate that 100 000 Aboriginal children had been removed. Again, the provenance of this claim is interesting. In his introduction to *The Lost Children*, Read wrote: 'If Europeans one hundred years ago had accepted the right of Aboriginal parents to raise their children as they wished . . . another one hundred thousand people would be identifying as Aboriginal citizens of Australia' (p. xviii). In a feature article in the *Age* shortly before the Inquiry began its sittings, a journalist misinterpreted this, claiming that 'the historian Dr Peter Read has estimated that as many as 100 000 Aborigines may have been affected by this program [of removal]' (2 December 1995); a few days later Aboriginal leader Michael Mansell made the same claim at the first of the Inquiry's hearings (*Age*, 9 December 1995); and it was repeated later in the year by a journalist (*Sydney Morning Herald*, 10 October 1996), and on later occasions (for example, *Australian*, 26 September 2000). In 1998 Read suggested that 'the number of children removed between 1788 and 1988 would [not] be much less than 50 000', but then repeated the claim referred to earlier in this endnote: 'It is probably fair to say that except for the remotest regions of the nation, there was not a single Aboriginal family which has not been touched by the policy of removal. Everybody had lost somebody' ('The Return', p. 9).

90. In turn, his song 'Took the Children Away' was sung or played at a number of the Inquiry's hearings (*Age*, 30 January 1996; *Sydney Morning Herald*, 2 July 1996).

91. HREOC, *Longing to Return Home*, pp. 4, [12]. References to trauma seem to have been common; see, for example, *Age*, 2, 9 December 1995; *Sydney Morning Herald*, 1, 3 July, 4 October 1996; *Age*, 18 October 1996.

92. HREOC, Information Paper on the National Inquiry into the Separation of Aboriginal and Torres Strait Islander Children from Their Families, p. 1, cited in Link-Up and Wilson, *In the Best Interest*

of the Child?, p. 9; HREOC, *Longing to Return Home*, p. 6; HREOC, *Bringing Them Home*, pp. 1, 18; www.hreoc.gov.au/social_justice/stolen_children; *Bringing Them Home* (video).

93. Wilson, press release, cited *The Long Road Home*, pp. 21–2; *Sydney Morning Herald*, 16 May 1995, 17 October 1996; *Age Good Weekend Magazine*, 11 May 1996; Age, 5, 7, 9 December 1995, 2, 15 November 1996; Aboriginal Legal Service of Western Australia, *Telling Our Story: A Report . . . on the Removal of Aboriginal Children from their Families in Western Australia*, [Perth], 1995, chapter 6; Link-Up and Wilson, *In the Best Interest of the Child?*, pp. 32, 36, 67, 69, 86, 87; Colin Tatz, 'The Evil Face of Humanity', *Sydney Morning Herald*, 20 December 1993, 'Stolen Generations Must Get Justice Whatever the Crime is Called', *Sydney Morning Herald*, 21 October 1996; Gillian Cowlishaw, 'Who Took the Children?', *Sydney Morning Herald*, 7 November 1996. *Longing to Return Home* included a photograph of Aboriginal people, most of them children, seemingly imprisoned by a barbed wire fence, which was reminiscent of famous images of German concentration camps (p. 5). This was not the first instance of such imagery being used, as noted above (see p. 194); in *Link-Up Diary* trains and train lines (reminiscent of those which carried Holocaust victims to their deaths) were shown in a scene where the removal of children was being discussed, and the footage used in *Lousy Little Sixpence* was included again in the HREOC video that was released with its report. More recently, a scriptwriter for a projected telemovie on the stolen generations, insisting on a comparison between these two 'examples of genocide', claimed that 'Aboriginal children were put on trains taking them away from their families' (*Age*, 18 March 2000).

94. *Longing to Return Home*, p. 10.

95. *Sydney Morning Herald*, 16 May, 5 December 1995; *Age*, 30 January 1996.

96. See, for example, *Age*, 7 December 1995; *Bringing Them Home*, p. 3.

97. HREOC, *Bringing Them Home*, pp. 27, 31, 37.

98. Link-Up, *In the Best Interests*, pp. 29, 32, 49, 67–8; see endnote 89 above.

99. HREOC, *Bringing Them Home*, pp. 651–5.

100. See, for example, *Australian*, 21 May 1997. In this the cause was assisted enormously by a speech Prime Minister John Howard made at the convention, during which he banged the podium and shouted at his audience, some of whom stood and turned their backs upon him when he announced that the Commonwealth government would not issue an apology (Transcript of Opening Address to the Australian Reconciliation Convention, 26 May 1997; *Age*, 27 May 1997).

101. ' "On the Border of the Unsayable": The Apology in Postcolonising Australia', *Interventions*, vol. 2, no. 2, 2000, p. 238.

102. *ibid.*, p. 232.

103. It can be argued that Reconciliation—and especially the apology—has had considerable resonance because, for all its secularism, mainstream Australian culture continues to be influenced by Christian tradition.

104. See, for example, *Sydney Morning Herald*, 3, 16 May, 8 July 1995, 15 February, 1, 2, 3 July, 10, 22, 30 October, 7 November 1996; *Age*, 14 July, 10 August, 22 October, 2, 5, 7, 9 December 1995, 30 January, 2, 12, 13, 14, 16 February, 25 May 1996; 'Telling His Story', *Four Corners*, ABC television, 15 July 1996.

105. 12 000 copies had been sold by 2000. The Commonwealth decided early that year to withdraw copies from sale in its Info Shops and not to reprint, ostensibly on the grounds of cost and because it was available on the internet. HREOC decided to print further copies (*Australian*, 24 July 2000).

106. See, for example, *Australian*, 27 May 1998.

107. See, for example, Manne, 'No Soothing Versions of Our Racist Past Here', *Australian*, 26 May 1997, and 'Death By Assimilation', *Australian Magazine*, 26–27 July 1997; and Gaita, 'Weighing Up the Facts on Genocide Claims', *Age*, 19 July 1997.

108. See, for example, *Australian*, 5–6, 7 October 1996; *Age*, 17 October 1996; Ron Brunton, 'Foster or Fester?', *Australian*, 12–13 October 1996; P.P. McGuinness, 'Reconciling the Theory and Practice of Apologies', *Age*, 28 May 1997; Frank Devine, 'Yes, Cry for the Children', *Australian*, 2 June 1997; John Stone, 'Convention is No Way to Reconcile the Past', *Australian Financial Review*, 5 June 1997; Geoffrey Partington, 'Whose Home Truths?', *Bulletin*, 10 June 1997; Brunton, 'Genocide: Truth Stolen', *Age*, 5 March 1998; Devine, 'Bringing the Truth Back Home', and 'Sorry No Way to Say Thank You', *Australian*, 5 March, 28 May 1998; Brunton, 'Black and White', *Institute of Public Affairs Review*, vol. 50, no. 4, 1998, pp. 23–4; Peter Howson, 'Rescued From the Rabbit Hole: Understanding the "Stolen Generation"', *Quadrant*, vol. XLIII, no. 357, 1999, pp. 10–14; McGuinness, 'Poor Fella My "Stolen Generation"', *Quadrant*, vol. XLIII, no. 361, 1999, pp. 2–4. The term 'black armband history' was first coined by the gadfly conservative historian Geoffrey Blainey, 'Drawing Up a Balance Sheet of Our History', *Quadrant*, vol. 37, nos 7–8, 1993, pp. 10–15. The Institute of Public Affairs, a right-wing 'think tank', and, after 1998, *Quadrant*, a right-wing magazine, provided much of the impetus for this counterattack. For a discussion of the conservative reaction to the new Australian history, see my 'Mabo, Australia and the End of History', in Attwood (ed.), *In the Age of Mabo*, pp. 100–16; Andrew Markus, 'John Howard and the Re-Naturalisation of Bigotry', in Geoffrey Gray and Christine Winter (eds), *The Resurgence of Racism: Howard, Hanson and the Race Debate*, Melbourne, 1997, pp. 79–86; Ann Curthoys, 'Entangled Histories: Conflict and Ambivalence in non-Aboriginal Australia', in *ibid.*, pp. 117–27.

109. Gooder and Jacobs, '"On the Border of the Unsayable"', p. 232.

110. *Commonwealth Parliamentary Debates, House of Representatives*, 4 April 2000, http://search.aph.gov.au/search/ParlInfo...000/Autumn/; Federal Government Submission to Senate Legal and Constitutional References Committee, 'Inquiry into the Stolen Generation', March 2000, pp. ii, 4–5. In attacking the narrative the government claimed that, even were a particular estimate for New South Wales to be accepted, 'the proportion of removed children would *only* be 19 percent'! (p. 15, my emphasis).

111. See *Commonwealth Parliamentary Debates, Senate*, 3, 4 April 2000, http://search.aph.gov.au/search/ParlInfor. . .000/Autumn/; *Age*, 3, 4 April 2000; *Australian*, 3, 4, 5 April 2000; AAP, 3 April 2000; 'PM', ABC Radio National, 4 April 2000.

112. For example, in the recent federal court case *Cubillo and Gunner v the Commonwealth*, the claimants commissioned historical research (Peter Read, *Lorna Cubillo and Peter Gunner v the Commonwealth of Australia: Historical Report*, ms, 1999; Read kindly provided me with a copy of this report) but it was not used in court (Read to author, 22 September 2000).

113. This is to argue that the story of the stolen generations, like other sagas, legends or myths such as Gallipoli, has come to be invested with an importance well beyond its historical reality as an *event*.

114. Recently, conservatives have sought to use a *legal* decision—Justice O'Loughlin's ruling in *Cubillo and Gunner v the Commonwealth* (Federal Court of Australia, FCA 1084, 11 August 2000)—to once more dismiss the truth claims of the narrative (see, for example, a Quadrant seminar, reported *Australian*, 11 September 2000; Peter Howson, 'There is No Stolen Generation', *Age*, 24 August 2000; Frank Devine, 'Innocent Demonised in Search for Truth', *Australian*, 14 September 2000; P.P. McGuinness, 'Truth, Sentiment and Genocide as a Fashion Statement', *Sydney Morning Herald*, 14 September 2000. This ignores the fact that whilst the judge at various points in his judgment purports to tell a history, he is only discussing a relatively brief period in one particular jurisdiction, that his findings are open to historical (and for that matter legal) disputation, and that he has ignored the weight of historical scholarship on the nature of racial policy and practice at this time.

115. Having stated this, it needs to be said that a preoccupation with either assessing the various reasons for separating Aboriginal children, attributing responsibility for the policy, or calculating the rate at which this occurred, carries the risk that we miss or misunderstand the *effect* that the practices of separating Aboriginal children—and especially forced removal—had upon Aboriginal families and communities. Let us return to the case of Margaret Tucker, a key stolen generations narrator. As far as we know, she, her sister and other children were removed in the late 1910s at a time when a number of

other children were taken from two closely linked reserves, but, due to Aboriginal and non-Aboriginal protest, and other factors, no other children were removed from these communities over the following twenty or more years. And yet, even if this is so, the traumatic effect of those few forced and seemingly arbitrary and callous removals upon these children, families and communities, and the rupturing of their relations with settler Australians, cannot be gainsaid.

116. There are historians who consider this forensic approach sufficient, and regard the second of the two moves I am describing as either unnecessary and/or dangerous (in the sense that it might be used to discredit the role that historical work can perform in contemporary debate). See, for example, reportage of statements by Henry Reynolds at a conference on Australian historical narratives at the National Library of Australia, *Australian*, 19 April 2000.

117. Davis and Starn, in the course of questioning the differences between memory and history, have written: 'Against memory's delight in similarity, appeal to emotions, and arbitrary selectivity, history would stand for critical distance and documented explanation. In the logic of these oppositions the sceptic about the reliability of memory becomes the true believer in the objectivity of history' ('Introduction', pp. 4–5; see also Nora, 'General Introduction', p. 3).

118. Alessandro Portelli, 'The Peculiarities of Oral History', *History Workshop Journal*, no. 12, 1981, p. 100.

119. See, for example, Lawrence Langer, *Holocaust Testimony: The Ruins of Memory*, New Haven, 1991.

Index